The 784th Tank Battalion
in World War II

ALSO BY JOE WILSON, JR.

The 761st "Black Panther" Tank Battalion in World War II: An Illustrated History of the First African American Armored Unit to See Combat (McFarland, 1999; paperback 2006)

The 784th Tank Battalion in World War II

History of an African American Armored Unit in Europe

JOE WILSON, JR.

Foreword by Bill Smith

*Afterword by First Sergeant
Joseph E. Wilson, Sr., USA (Ret.)*

McFarland & Company, Inc., Publishers
Jefferson, North Carolina

The present work is a reprint of the illustrated case bound edition of The 784th Tank Battalion in World War II: History of an African American Armored Unit in Europe, *first published in 2007 by McFarland.*

LIBRARY OF CONGRESS CATALOGUING-IN-PUBLICATION DATA

Wilson, Joe, 1955–
The 784th Tank Battalion in World War II :
history of an African American armored unit in Europe /
Joe Wilson, Jr. ; foreword by Bill Smith ;
afterword by First Sergeant Joseph E. Wilson, Sr., USA (Ret.)
    p.   cm.
Includes bibliographical references and index.

ISBN 978-1-4766-6272-5 (softcover : acid free paper) ∞
ISBN 978-1-4766-1177-8 (ebook)

1. United States. Army. Tank Battalion, 784th. 2. World War, 1939–1945 — Participation, African American. 3. United States. Army — African American troops. 4. African American soldiers — History — 20th century. 5. World War, 1939–1945 — Campaigns — Western Front. 6. World War, 1939–1945 — Tank warfare. I. Title.

D769.306784th.W55   2015   940.54'1273 — dc22   2006029579

BRITISH LIBRARY CATALOGUING DATA ARE AVAILABLE

© 2007 Joe Wilson, Jr. All rights reserved

No part of this book may be reproduced or transmitted in any form or by any means, electronic or mechanical, including photocopying or recording, or by any information storage and retrieval system, without permission in writing from the publisher.

On the cover: photographs from Sgt. Jesse Roberts,
784th Tank Battalion, along the Elbe River in April 1945
(courtesy James Baldwin)

Printed in the United States of America

*McFarland & Company, Inc., Publishers
Box 611, Jefferson, North Carolina 28640
www.mcfarlandpub.com*

To the memory of
Franklin S. Garrido
(1923–2005)

Acknowledgments

This book would not have been possible without the cooperation and efforts of many dedicated people who have shared their hard-earned knowledge, precious photographs, and rare documents. Many have departed this world leaving their stories and photographs behind. To those who contributed to this effort, I wish to express my sincere gratitude and acknowledge with honor and respect their endowment to future generations.

I make no apologies for any seeming inaccuracies in the combat stories. They are as the eyewitnesses told them, and in the confusion and danger of battle — the "fog of war" — things happen for which there is no obvious explanation. I also realize that the archival accounts such as the Reports After Action and journals are not always entirely accurate, either. The clerks away from the combat recording the events may have come away with, and recorded, different views of reality.

As I reflect with pride on the research, planning and actual writing of this book, my gratitude goes out all who so willingly provided encouragement and inspiration, making this book what it is. This will be a memory I'll forever cherish, and I extend a personal thanks to you all. Please always know that your kindness is etched in my heart and mind forever. Thank you.

Contents

Acknowledgments vii
Foreword by Bill Smith 1
Prologue 3

1. The Double "V" Campaign 5
2. Camp Claiborne 19
3. Camp Hood 25
4. Destination ETO 35
5. Baptism of Fire 41
6. The Raging Roer River 53
7. Task Force Byrne 62
8. Eighty-eight Alley 87
9. Crossing the Rhine 102
10. The Ruhr Pocket 114
11. Eyewitness to Genocide 132
12. Elbe River 140
13. Occupation 146

14. Whatever Happened to the 758th Tank Battalion ... 154
15. Whatever Happened to the 761st Tank Battalion 159
16. Deactivation 167

*Afterword by First Sergeant
Joseph E. Wilson, Sr., USA (Ret.)* 187
Chapter Notes 191
Bibliography 197
Index 201

Foreword
by Bill Smith

African American soldiers returned from Europe after World War II with experience and knowledge that would shape world history. Regional separation before the war produced experiences characterized by degrees of racism: recruits from the South were already too familiar with Jim Crow, while recruits from the North and West were accustomed to less pernicious discrimination. During training and then in Europe, African American soldiers from every region of the United States worked, played, fought and suffered together in segregated units — contributing their own personal wisdom to the common effort of fighting the Axis enemy and the racism of their own countrymen. By the end of the war, these soldiers had seen how England and European countries were less prejudiced, indeed often showing genuine affection for their liberators. They beheld the horror of war first hand, found personal strength to deal with mortal fear, and gained a better perspective on the ignorance that is the foundation of racism. Those experiences helped shape the civil rights movement of later decades. Advances gained from that movement would change the United States and the world.

After a white middle class upbringing, I found myself part of the world of American youth in the turbulent '60s that was indeed revolutionary, with the civil rights movement being the dignified center of the times. I lived in black neighborhoods while working in places, such as the Legal Aid Society, where the revolution continued after the '60s. However, first-hand experience with the Civil Rights revolution never provided insight to the influence of black soldiers returning from World War II. Several years ago an article in the *New York Times*, about the increasingly difficult efforts of aging African American veterans to continue their annual reunions, led to my offer to help make a website for those veterans. The result was an opportunity to get to know Joe Wilson. Joe's father was a veteran of World War II, and Joe's effort to chronicle the history of the first African Americans to serve in armored units brought us together in the design and content of a website about the 761st Tank Battalion.

In this book, Joe relates the World War II history of the 784th Tank Battalion, a lesser-known brother of the 761st Tank Battalion. These tankers came into the war facing difficulties and bearing burdens unknown to their white comrades. Like the Japanese Americans, Native Americans, Filipinos and other non-Caucasian participants in the effort to defeat fascism, the men of the 784th Tank Battalion had to be better to stay even. Prejudice against them resulted in demeaning treatment, diminished glory and crediting of their accomplishments to white units. While in combat, they showed great competence and pride.

My limited interaction with the dignified and gracious veterans of the 761st Tank Battalion during the past few years has resulted in great appreciation for their role in making the world better for everyone through their perseverance and suffering. This story of the 784th Tank Battalion tells of lives led from origins in the very depths of post-slavery racism that emerged into a movement establishing legal equality as more of a reality than a mere rhetoric of 18th-century philosophers. Those lives helped instigate that transition based on the strengths and insights that were gained from the hell of war in Europe. Although much remains to be done to ameliorate racism in the world, the American Civil Rights movement set in motion the formal, modern effort to do so, and also set a standard of non-violence and civil disobedience that represents the highest attainment of civilized people in dealing with conflict. Veterans returning from Europe's war hell brought with them vision that allowed the Civil Rights movement to flourish.

Many African American World War II veterans went through the decades after the war as a large extended family, staying in touch, providing support, remembering their brethren whose lives ended in combat, and encouraging one another with their endless sense of camaraderie. As age has taken its toll, those ranks have decreased in number. In time, the last African American World War II veteran will pass on, and then only history will provide the information needed to appreciate their contributions. They contributed to the defeat of fascism by fighting the war in Europe. They continued the fight against brutal racism in America. They inspired their children to live the higher ideal and allowed the world to see and attain the beauty of that vision.

Bill Smith is a semi-retired freelance provider of research and writing services, a Vietnam era vet living in a Hawai'i rain forest, and webmaster of the 761st Tank Battalion. Meeting Dr. Martin Luther King during a Civil Rights demonstration in 1966 marked the start of his participation in the effort to advance human rights.

Prologue

Winter 1944: Somewhere between Aachen and Eschweiler, Germany, Dog Company, 784th Tank Battalion, pulled over for emergency maintenance. They had endured a tedious 6-day road march across the treacherous and icy roads of France and Belgium and through the tip of Holland at Maastricht. Their M5 Stuart Light Tanks, outdated mini battlewagons, had been pushed to their limits. The weary outfit found shelter in an abandoned factory complex that shielded them and their vehicles from the harsh winter elements.

It was New Year's Eve, 1944! Bottles of champagne given to them in France were fully aged and ready for this special occasion. At exactly one minute past midnight, the men heard a loud bang. The 104th Infantry Division celebrated by simultaneously firing one high explosive round by each serviceable artillery piece. They had sent deadly greetings across the river to the enemy. It was now time to celebrate what would obviously be the last New Year's celebration for many. The bottles popped and the spirits fizzed out into aluminum canteen cups. Axis Sally made the men feel somewhat at home with her radio broadcasts playing familiar tunes, like "Don't Get Around Much Any More," between her propaganda tirades. After feeble attempts by the officers to quell this celebration, they decided to go off on their own for an officers-only party. After all, no one knew if they would survive to celebrate again.

On New Year's Day the men dutifully woke up early and performed first echelon maintenance on their vehicles and equipment. All was quiet. The sunlight reflected off the snow-covered factory complex, making a picturesque setting. Then from out of nowhere, a faint sound, like a drone of bees, started growing louder and louder. As the men looked up they saw a formation of U.S. heavy bombers, B-17s and B-24s, flying directly overhead. There were so many that they almost blotted out the light from the sun as the sound of their engines shook the earth.

Soon the din faded into silence and this great armada was out of sight. The men continued their maintenance. Soon something else caught their attention. There came a rumbling louder than thunder, and it was apparent that the massive air fleet that had flown past minutes ago had released their bombs on enemy targets. The men felt somewhat easier, knowing that no army could survive such punishment. Minutes later that same old sound, a drone of bees, could be heard. The sound increased until the formation was overhead again, but this time there was a difference. There were gaps in the formation. Smoke emanated from the damaged planes and it was clear that some American fliers would not be returning. Soon another wave of heavy bombers appeared. This went on throughout the day.

Later that day someone looked up and yelled: "TAKE COVER AND CLOSE YOUR HATCH! THEY ARE DROPPING BOMBS ON US!" The unthinkable was now inevitable. The men looked up in horror, watching in terror as the bombs fell from the sky. Panic set in. The men ran into each other in their frantic attempt to get out of the way. Some dove into their light tanks and prayed that they would not receive a direct hit. Others scrambled into the lower levels of the factory, seeking even lower levels. Some exited their light tanks and headed for the factory basements. The officers and NCOs threw the textbook to the winds and took cover wherever they could, aware that this was not a textbook situation. Nothing in their training could ever prepare them for this situation. It was every man for himself!

The bombs fell in perceived slow motion with a hellish screech and finally landed. All hell broke loose! These missed target bombs or "shorts" (bombs that fell on American-held areas) became a common problem known as friendly fire. As the men dove for cover, the blast added impetus to their leaps as the concussion lifted some several feet off the ground. As dust and debris covered the area, the men still on deck scrambled for their lives — crawling, praying, anything to survive. Ammunition, including machine guns on the vehicles, went off, and anyone in that vicinity was either blown apart or riddled with bullets.

When the smoke and dust cleared, the survivors, some in a state of shock, had to be attended to by medical personnel. Soon the turmoil passed and they started back on their mission to link up with the 104th Cavalry Reconnaissance Troop. To add insult to injury, the event officially never happened. No one was recorded as killed, even though witnesses saw two bodies carried away. The company clerk was forced not to make any entries in the daily journals. The men felt heavy-hearted because they wanted a memorial service or just simple acknowledgement for their fallen comrades.

They had just undergone their baptism of fire by none other than the U.S. Army *Luftwaffe*.

1

The Double "V" Campaign

Only by confronting the viciousness of World War II at home and abroad can we truly begin to balance our understanding of it. What you've started to read can be disturbing and shocking to some. This is World War II the way the African American soldier experienced it — full of disorder, panic, death, courage, and humiliation. The accounts and images ahead will allow you to go through a small portion of what these brave African American soldiers experienced on the home front and on the field of battle.

December 1941: The worst was just beginning. Hitler had conquered and held control of more than 330 million people from the Mediterranean to the outskirts of Moscow. The Nazis had murdered Jews routinely since 1933, but in July 1941 *Reichsmarschall* Hermann Göring called for the *Endlosung* (final solution). Special units called *Einsatzgruppen* began rounding up Jews for extermination. In September, some 34,000 died in the ghastly pits of Babi Yar (Old Woman's Ravine) near Kiev, Ukraine. In December, Jews in Latvia were taken into the Rumbuli Forest, stripped naked, and shot. Many were only wounded and buried alive. Some dug themselves from their graves only to be shot again. Approximately 36,000 died in less than two weeks. This marked the beginning. Millions of people that the Nazis deemed politically and socially undesirable would die under Hitler's crushing rule.

In North Africa, forces under Italian Fascist dictator Benito Mussolini invaded Ethiopia and indiscriminately used poison gas. Ethiopian Emperor Haile Selassie called the attack a "refinement of barbarism." In Libya, an army of British, Australian, and Indian soldiers defeated the Italians and took more than 40,000 prisoners. Several months later the desert winds shifted as Germany's *Afrika Korps*, commanded by Field Marshall Erwin Rommel (the "Desert Fox"), came to Mussolini's aid.

In the North Atlantic Ocean, packs of German U-boats prowled the depths in an attempt to cut England's vital supply artery with North America. In May 1941, President Franklin D. Roosevelt (FDR) declared an "unlimited national emergency" and thereafter waged an undeclared war against German submarines. Destroyers from the U.S. Navy joined the British Royal Navy's convoy network in September. In October, the USS *Reuben James* became the first American warship sunk. By the end of 1941, nearly 200 Allied ships had been torpedoed and sent to the bottom of the ocean.

In Asia, the Japanese Army swept through China, bringing millions of people under its brutal rule. The Chinese, ravaged by a 15-year civil war between Mao Tse-Tung's Communists and Chiang Kai-Shek's Nationalists, could not defend against the Japanese onslaught.

In America, the daily newspapers reported death and destruction around the world. These reports touched many Americans who nevertheless felt safe and isolated from the world's problems. Military preparedness and the building of FDR's "Arsenal of Democracy" created a national prosperity on an unprecedented scale that ended the Great Depression. This brought steady paychecks to more Americans than in the pre-Depression era. Life became good for many Americans who had never known anything other than poverty. The military ranks increased with enlistees and draftees during the nation's first peacetime draft, and the government encouraged the public to invest in America's security by purchasing defense bonds.

During this national prosperity, a wave of bitterness, disillusionment, and desperation swept through America's black communities. African Americans wanted their slice of the national pie of prosperity and to escape poverty. Unfortunately, 75 percent of defense contractors refused to hire African Americans in any capacity, 15 percent offered only menial labor positions, and skilled labor was institutionally excluded. Many craft unions under the jurisdiction of the American Federation of Labor barred African Americans from admission to their local chapters. W.B. Saunders wrote the following letter to FDR:

> Dear President, I am writing you in regard of the job in the Pollack Shipyard and for colored people. The boilermakers union A F of L have the contract for all skilled labor. A Negro can't go to work unless they belong to the union & the union won't accept a colored man. All welders & burners that came out of school can't get a job, so you know how a colored man feels. So in your speech you said bring you troubles to you. They are crying for help, but won't let a Negro work unless he's just a common laborer.[1]

A. Philip Randolph, union leader of the Brotherhood of Sleeping Car Porters, along with other African American leaders, called for an exercise of First Amendment rights by marching on Washington. The march, scheduled for July 1, 1941, was against employment discrimination and segregation in the national defense program. Randolph pledged that 100,000 Negroes would participate.

On June 23, 1941, FDR called Randolph and other African American leaders to the White House for an urgent meeting. The president urged the civil rights leaders to call off the march, characterizing it as "bad and unintelligent." Randolph urged FDR to issue an executive order with enough teeth to compel the defense industry to give all citizens equal employment opportunities. Later that day the president issued Executive Order #8802 forbidding racial and religious discrimination in defense industries and government training programs. Randolph called off the march.

On July 19, 1941, FDR established the Fair Employment Practices Committee. This committee, along with Executive Order #8802, was initially hailed as the most significant executive action toward racial equality since the Emancipation Proclamation. But disappointment followed when discrimination continued due to the committee's bureaucratic inefficiencies and stiff opposition from Southern states. However, FDR was adamant in his warning to withhold defense contracts from companies discriminating against African Americans. White workers around the country rioted against the president's directives.

On June 20, 1943, Detroit, Michigan, experienced the most serious race riot of World War II. White workers enraged by the black participation in the burgeoning war industry rioted for three days. This industrial city, crucial to the war effort, was temporarily paralyzed. More than 600 people lay injured and over 1,800 were jailed. Twenty-five blacks and nine whites were dead. Nineteen of the dead blacks were slain by the police. FDR had to call in federal troops to restore order. Brig. General William Gunther, the commander of the federal troops, reported: "They've been very handy with their guns and clubs and have been very harsh and brutal.... They have treated the Negroes terrible up here and I think they have gone altogether too far.... If they want everyone else to get back to normal then the police will have to get back to normal themselves."[2]

Despite being treated as second-class citizens, segregated in the armed services, and being shut out of most munitions jobs, African Americans embraced World War II with the same patriotic fervor as the rest of the nation. Women knitted socks and sweaters for the troops. Victory gardens sprang up in every vacant lot. Volunteers collected metal and worked as air-raid wardens. World-renowned entertainers put on benefits to raise money. Many young and middle-aged men unhesitatingly enlisted in the armed services.

With the American economy on the rise for the first time in 12 years, the debate over isolation versus intervention in the war intensified. On December 7, 1941, the debate ended when Japan attacked United States forces in the Pacific. Early that Sunday morning, Pearl Harbor, on the Hawaiian Island of Oahu, came under attack without warning. Mess Attendant Dorie Miller, from Waco, Texas, was aboard the battleship USS *West Virginia* when the general alarm sounded.

Miller, age 22, a former high school running back and current heavyweight boxing champion of his ship, went immediately to his battle station. He found it destroyed. Despite intense strafing, bombings, and fire-swept decks, he aided in the removal of the ship's gravely wounded captain from the bridge to a safer location. Although Miller had no weapons training, he manned a machine gun and fired on Japanese aircraft. He was instrumental in blasting several Japanese planes out of the sky.

Public pressure forced the Navy to recognize Miller's heroic achievement. The Navy reluctantly issued Miller a letter of commendation, one of the lowest forms of recognition. After more public pressure, FDR ordered Miller's commendation upgraded to the Navy Cross, second only to the Medal of Honor. African Americans had their first war hero.

Taken by complete surprise at Pearl Harbor, the United States suffered the loss of 18 ships sunk or seriously damaged; 347 aircraft destroyed or disabled; Hickam, Wheeler, Ford Island, Kaneohe, and Ewa airfields in flames; 2,403 Americans dead and another 1,178 wounded. To inflict this terrible damage and pain, the Japanese sacrificed fewer than 100 men, 29 planes and 5 midget submarines. On December 8, FDR asked and received from Congress a declaration of war against the Imperial Japanese Empire. Two days later, Hitler and Mussolini declared war on the United States of America. A stunned America found itself in World War II.

With the hope of the world resting with America, FDR challenged the nation with these words: "We are in this war. We are in it all the way. Every single man, woman and child is a partner in the most tremendous undertaking of our American history. We must share together the bad news, the good news, the defeats, the victories, the changing fortunes of war."

The fear of a Japanese attack on the West Coast, coupled with the built-in prejudices of wartime America, started a deplorable search for scapegoats. This led to the forced removal of Japanese-Americans to relocation centers in the nation's interior. The government claimed it was forced by public hysteria, agitation by the press and radio, and finally, military pressure, to establish a War Relocation Authority mandated by Executive Order #9066 and signed by the president. Under the jurisdiction of the Western Defense Command, approximately 110,000 Japanese born *Issei* and American-born *Nisei* were relocated in the spring of 1942.

During this period Dorie Miller and his mother went on a national tour for the War Department. They went mainly to the black communities, where they encouraged enlistments, sold war bonds, and supported the war effort. Nearly two years later Miller found himself still a mess man, this time aboard the escort carrier USS *Liscome Bay*. Early on Thanksgiving morning of 1943, Miller's new ship rolled over and sank minutes after being struck by two Japanese torpedoes near the Gilbert Islands. Mrs. Henrietta Miller was heartbroken from the news that her son had been trapped inside the burning ship. Dorie Miller was reported missing in action and never heard from again.

Filled with a patriotic zeal, African Americans sought to participate in the crusade to crush the oppression imposed on the world by the Axis powers of Japan, Germany, and Italy. Allowed to participate only under the same humiliating discrimination that was their plight since the Reconstruction period following the Civil War, black soldiers found their assignments menial and unglamorous, such as digging ditches, driving garbage trucks, sweeping out warehouses, and slinging bedpans in hospitals.

Before and during this period of mobilization for war, the Office of the U.S. Army Ground Forces in Washington debated whether or not to use African American soldiers in armored units. The power structure in Washington fostered the attitude that African Americans did not have the brains, the quickness, or the moral stamina to fight in a war. Referring to their experiences from World War I, the commander of the 367th Infantry Regiment, 92nd Division, stated: "As fighting troops, the Negro must be rated as second class material, this primarily due to his inferior intelligence and lack of mental and moral qualities."[3] The commander of the 371st Infantry Regiment, 93rd Division, stated: "In a future war, the main use of the Negro should be in labor organizations."[4] General George Patton, Jr., stated his opinion: "A colored soldier cannot think fast enough to fight in armor." The armed forces embraced these beliefs and recommendations, overlooking the documented fact that African Americans had fought with courage and distinction in every war and conflict ever waged by the nation from the Revolutionary War through World War I. They especially overlooked the fact that the four separate regiments of the 93rd Division served with the French in World War I and that the French government awarded the coveted *Croix de Guerre* to three of the four regiments and to a company of the fourth, and also to the 1st Battalion, 367th Infantry Regiment of the 92nd Division.

Against this mindset, Lt. General Leslie McNair, Chief of the U.S. Army Ground Forces and main proponent on the side to allow African Americans into armor, had to fight. He never accepted the vehement denial of the fighting qualities of the African American soldier. He believed this nation could ill afford to exclude such a potentially important source of strength.

The Negro Press, the National Association for the Advancement of Colored People (NAACP), and the Congress of Racial Equality (CORE) put increasing pressure on the War Department and the Roosevelt administration to allow African Americans to serve on equal footing with white soldiers. Ira Lewis of the *Pittsburgh Courier* inspired the "Double V Campaign" that called for victory at home and abroad. Labor leader A. Philip Randolph, NAACP activist Walter White, educator Dr. Mary McLeod Bethune, and other civil rights leaders fought along with the Negro press for this victory at home that would mean full civil rights for future generations.

The president's wife, ahead of her time regarding the equality of the races, stood up front with the civil rights leaders and the Negro press. Eleanor Roosevelt began her anti-racist struggle in the 1930s. It was she who chastised the Daughters of the American Revolution for their refusal to allow black opera singer Marion Anderson to perform at Constitution Hall. She then arranged for Anderson to sing at the Lincoln Memorial. In 1934, she assisted Walter White in the struggle to place into law the Costigan-Wagner anti-lynching bill. She invited African American citizens to the White House as guests and friends. The treatment of African American servicemen was one of her chief concerns, and she was determined that they would receive a chance to fight in this war. She stated her views clearly: "A wind is rising throughout the world of free men everywhere, and they will not be kept in bondage."[5]

Tuskegee Airman Celes King III illustrates how Eleanor Roosevelt helped to disprove the myth that African Americans did not have the intelligence to fly nor the courage and discipline it took to fight in a war:

> Of the few people that had an impact on the opening up of the U.S. Army Air Forces for blacks in the air, you certainly could not overlook Eleanor Roosevelt. She had no reservations to raising issues she felt were in the interest of this country. There were 2 separate instances where she had a major impact.
>
> One would be when she went to Tuskegee and went to Moton Field where blacks were beginning to train. There she got into one of the aircraft and went around the field for a spin. And of course, needless to say, the Secret Service people just about had a fit. They were on the phone calling Washington to see what to do. There was no controlling her. The next day's news across the country addressed the issue of her riding in a plane being flown by a Negro. It certainly did give impetus to our position.
>
> The other time was when she was sitting in the White House, probably the Oval Office. At that time the President and members of his military staff were discussing the situation of what they were going to do about all the white lads who were being shot out of the sky. At that time Eleanor Roosevelt stepped in and said: "There is no reason not to let the Negroes go over and have an opportunity to fight." That was all it took. We were eminently qualified to fly because we had been spending a lot of time practicing. That was one of our hold cards, this is — we had more of an opportunity to practice.[6]

Secretary of War Henry Stimson had little patience with Eleanor Roosevelt's liberal views and her desire to advance civil rights while there was a war going on. To pull the thorn from his side, Judge William Hastie, an African American, was quickly appointed to handle the sticky issue of race relations for the War Department.

Judge Hastie lobbied for integration in training centers and combat operations. Secretary Stimson, influenced by the strident traditional racism of the South, resisted. At times notations with "not to be shown to Judge Hastie" were attached to papers dealing with phases of Negro troop utilization. Hastie often replied: "I wish again to emphasize the fact that the principal usefulness of this office is destroyed if we are not consulted with reference to such matters." After two years of frustration, Judge Hastie resigned in disgust. Truman Gibson, Jr., succeeded him. *Time* magazine described him as "a less insistent Negro."[7]

Along with the appointment of Judge Hastie, Colonel Benjamin Davis, Sr., was nominated for promotion to brigadier general. The War Department committed itself to these appointments in answer to the promises of the 1940 political campaign. However, African Americans still remained in segregated units.

The contrast between Hastie and Davis could not have been clearer. The 36-year-old judge was an activist by nature. The 64-year-old general, who had served over 40 years in the U.S. Army, had embraced early in his career the philosophy that for an

1. The Double "V" Campaign

African American soldier to survive in the military he had to accept his second-class citizenship. Although Davis became the first African American to achieve the star rank, the message he sent to the black soldier was: "You are my color, but not my kind." This floated through the ranks, causing black soldiers to feel that the general considered himself better than they were.

For a number of years the judge and the general urged the War Department to assign black troops to combat units. In 1942 the War Department appointed an advisory committee for policies on "Race Troops"—a euphemism for black troops. One of the committee's recommendations was that an all-Negro parachute battalion be formed. Army Chief of Staff General George Marshall directed that a parachute company be organized, and designated the 555th Parachute Infantry Company.

Twenty hand-picked enlisted men, selected to undergo airborne training, formed a test platoon. As word of this experiment reached their opposite numbers, bets were wagered. Many believed that black men lacked the courage to become paratroopers. Sixteen of the original 20 earned their airborne wings and formed the foundation of what became the 555th Parachute Infantry Battalion, the "triple Nickels."

In 1943, Japan began launching high-altitude balloons carrying incendiary bombs across the Pacific Ocean. A few landed in Washington, Oregon, Idaho, and Northern California. These bombs caused intense forest fires not disclosed to the American public. The "Triple Nickels" fought these fires as smoke jumpers in the highly classified "Operation Firefly," their only deployment of the war.

Tank tactics of World War I became obsolete overnight with the German *Blitzkrieg* of 1939. The *Wehrmacht* employed rapidly moving mechanized infantry and artillery columns spearheaded by tanks, with close air support. This revolutionized the concept of ground warfare.

In response, just weeks after Paris fell to the *Blitzkrieg*, the U.S. Army activated an armored force consisting of the 1st and 2nd Armored Divisions along with the 70th Tank Battalion, a separate tank battalion. The armored force doctrine called for two separate categories of tactical units. The units organized and equipped themselves for deployment and accomplishment of dissimilar missions.

The armored division category, inspired by the cavalry, was comparable to the *Blitzkrieg*. They operated with large numbers of tanks utilizing firepower and mobility along with mechanized infantry to penetrate deep behind enemy lines. They could operate for at least three days without additional supplies. Once the infantry division with their separate tank battalion breached the enemy lines, the armored division could make their deep penetration. The armored doctrine admonished our tanks to avoid battling enemy tanks and swiftly progress to their objective.

The separate tank battalion category, inspired by the infantry, considered the infantry as the principal ground force. Their role was to provide armored support for infantry operations and come under the command of the infantry division.

In March 1941, 98 African American enlisted men reported to Fort Knox,

Kentucky, from Fort Custer, Michigan, for armored warfare training with the 78th Tank Battalion. The pioneer tankers trained steadily as more enlisted men from other U.S. Army installations joined their ranks. In June of the same year, the Army designated the 758th Tank Battalion (Light), "light" indicating light tanks. The battalion continued to train in tank operations, mechanics, and related phases of mechanized warfare.

Bill Hughes, from Indianapolis, Indiana, recounts the unique events leading up to his introduction to the Armored Force:

> It was during the depression years and life was not easy but the family survived. I attended public schools and graduated from Crispus Attucks High School in June 1941, having majored in music and English. The most cherished memory I have reaching the age of 18 was the love I had for music. I shall never forget the big band sounds of Duke Ellington, Count Basie, Jimmie Lunceford, Andy Kirk, and others. I wanted to go on to college and study music, but financial restraints prevented that. The most hated memory I have growing up in Indianapolis was the segregation and the discrimination that was very prevalent. The schools were segregated, theaters, clubs, churches, and a host of other places. I seriously thought about it and came to one conclusion. As soon as I get old enough (21 years), I am going to get out of Indianapolis. I really believed it can't be like that the world over and I am going to find out. That would be a 3-year-wait so what could I do to earn some money and save for that unknown journey. I took a night job with Indiana Bell Telephone Company checking toll tickets to be charged to customer accounts for calls made during the day. A blessing disguised was about to unfold.
>
> I had forgotten all about taking a civil service entrance examination during my senior year in high school until I got a telegram from the War Department offering me a job in Washington, DC as a clerk/messenger. Reporting date was 28 January 1942; written permission of parents required. I was excited because several of my classmates took that exam on a bet of who would get the highest score. I won with a score of 82 and a neat $25.00, but had forgotten it. This was my first big break to get out of Indiana, but now to get Mom to agree. After 3 days of persuasive argument, I finally got her to agree. It was one of the happiest days of my life.
>
> I reported to the Nation's Capital on January 28, 1942 and was assigned to a waiting pool until I was interviewed for a job in the Armored Force Liaison Office. I was accepted after a brief background check. This office was headed by Major-General Gilbert X. Cheeves. His Deputy was Brigadier-General George Daniels. I was put under supervision of the secretary. The office was very pleasant and it was enjoyable work. There was a constant flow of visitors to the office who were interested in armored warfare. The office was responsible for evaluating tank performances at Aberdeen Proving Grounds, Maryland. One visitor was Major-General George S. Patton, Jr. He had returned from Africa and Italy after victory in battle and was warmly welcomed in Washington. There was something about the man that commanded your attention when he walked in to a room. Those tailor made riding breeches, brown shining leather boots, the waist belt with an ivory handle revolver, and those oversized stars to show his rank just made him stand out from other Generals who visited the office like General Devers, Chaffee, Crittenberger, Walker, Woods, Daniels, and Dean. It was several days before Kay, the secretary, introduced me to Major-General Patton as Billy. He said, "I'll just call you Willie." I did not like the new

1. The Double "V" Campaign

name, but was not about to object so I said that's fine Sir. He was a very colorful person, flamboyant, flippant, and talked tough peppered with profanity. He definitely knew he was somebody special and carried himself that way. I never realized that one day I would see him again on the battlefields of Europe leading the Third Army. My draft number came up again after 3 exemptions in June 1943. Major-General Cheeves was instrumental in getting me assigned to the 761st Tank Battalion located at Camp Claiborne, Louisiana because I did not want to end up in some service outfit. Like many young men I knew, I wanted to get into the fight. Becoming a tanker was my choice and little did I know I was in for some wild rides.[8]

Franklin Garrido from Los Angeles journeyed to Chicago to join the Marines with a friend. They were both refused enlistment and Franklin immediately joined the Army. His friend joined the Navy. Soon Franklin was on his way down South:

Segregation affected me hard. I was born and raised in California and I never knew de facto segregation. I was happy-go-lucky and I didn't know I was segregated. I was shocked as I got off the train in Louisville. I was warned in advance by my parents. When I got off the train again at Fort Knox, the first thing that hit me in the face was the white and colored signs. I was shocked. It was really traumatic. I was prepared for it, but I was not prepared enough.

At Fort Knox everything was segregated, including the training barracks. They had colored and white drinking fountains. They had colored and white latrines. In some barracks they had 3 toilets, one for the officers, one for the white enlisted men and one for the black enlisted men. With all that plumbing and everything the War Department could have built more tanks. That's how I felt about segregation.[9]

James Hamilton from Baltimore, Maryland, portrays the events in his life leading up to his induction into the Army:

At the time I was about 15, in school, and I would caddy at the golf course in the summer. I was the special caddy for Mr. Willy Adams and Charlie Burns. He's the man who had some super grocery stores here in Maryland. And Doctor Wilson and Doctor Pear and Doctor Harmon and all the local famous doctors and big shots. One day I was caddying and the next morning old Willy Adams told me to come down to his house and he took me down to his car. Guess who was there? Joe Louis! He came down and I caddied for him. I went into the clubhouse to get him a ticket and he gave me a fifty-dollar bill and I mean that was great! So when we left there we went to Washington, DC, and when we got to the golf course nobody knew he was there. We did one round and when we went to do the second round, that place was packed. Everybody wanted to see Joe Louis.

The Mills Brothers, I caddied for them at the golf course and I played pool with them at Clark's Pool Hall. Remember Redd Foxx? I talked to him there and we shot a little pool. And, down at the Royal Theater, when they had all of the bands there, Count Basie, Duke Ellington, Stan Kenton, Kirby Williams, and Lionel Hampton. Lionel Hampton rocked that stage. I mean, when he was down there, the lines were around the block. Right across the street from the Royal Theater was Rice's Diner. That's where we took our girlfriends and they served some good food. It was really nice. Our people, black people,

Class of 1942, Spaulding High School, Spring Hope, North Carolina. Jesse Roberts (front row, at left, sitting) and Gerald Mingo (front row, at right, kneeling, hands on ground) both became sergeants in the 784th Tank Battalion. *Courtesy James Baldwin*

had about 15 bars and clubs off of Pennsylvania Avenue at that time and they owned all of them. We owned a few drug stores there. Doctor Weaver was nearby. I knew his son Bobby Weaver who became a lawyer. They had a lot of black doctors in Baltimore who were rich and they were the ones I caddied for. Doctor Pear, he was a beautiful dude, he was sharp. He looked like a Hawaiian! He had 2 great big cars, a Lincoln and a Cadillac, both convertibles. Near the Royal Theater there was another theater called the Strand and they had a dance floor upstairs. We went up there one evening for a dance and Ella Fitzgerald was up there. She sang and I mean that girl put on a show. At Club Astoria on Emerson Avenue, we saw Billie Holiday. Man! That girl was something else and she was beautiful too. And she could sing! They now have a large statue of Billie Holiday at Pennsylvania and La Fayette Avenues. And right on the corner across the street, there is a monument to the Royal Theater. They still have the big sign and logo up there.

In the meantime I was going to school at Carver Vocational. I did well in athletics playing golf, tennis, and basketball. This was around 1942 and I would have had a scholarship to Saint Paul's College but my draft notice came. The draft board was on Edmondson Avenue and from there we went to the armory here in Baltimore and got examined. Then we went back home. They had told us to bring back our toothbrushes and things like that and we went back to the armory and from there we went to Camden Station where Oriole Park is now. We got on the train and went to Fort Meade and from there to Fort Eustace, Virginia, where I went into anti-aircraft. I wanted to be a tail gunner in a B-29 like Clark Gable but because of my color they wouldn't let me. From there they shipped us to Texas; Camp Hood.[10]

Simmons Washington from Mississippi remembers: "I was attending Alabama State Teachers' College, Montgomery, Alabama, music major for about a year before I got drafted. I played in 2 or 3 different bands. We played in the college band and the college orchestra. I left Alabama State into the 784th."[11]

James Baldwin recounts his unique experiences:

I am from Wagram, North Carolina. It's in Scotland County about 32 miles from Fayetteville. We only had one high school in our county for blacks — Laurinburg Institute. I graduated as valedictorian in the class of 1942. I wasn't into sports. I was into the books. I received a 4-year scholarship to North Carolina A & T College in Greensboro. In high school we didn't have counselors. I followed my little group of guys, about 4 of us. They didn't get scholarships so we went to Fayetteville State College together. It is now a university.

At Fayetteville State I enlisted in the Army Enlisted Reserve Corps (ERC) in October 1942. This program allowed male students at approved colleges and universities to enlist in reserve units and complete their education provided they passed a qualifying examination and maintained a satisfactory college standing. In December 1942 President Roosevelt issued a proclamation ordering an end to all voluntary enlistment programs resulting in many male students leaving college for the military.

In March 1943, I along with 38 ERC enlistees at Fayetteville State received orders to report to Fort Benning, Georgia for induction into the United States Army. Jesse Roberts, Thomas Williams, and Gerald Mingo from this group later became members of the 784th with me.

Armored Force Basic Trainees in a February 1942 class at Fort Knox, Kentucky. (A single photograph has been divided to improve reproduction; left half appears at top.) Their commander, Captain Evans (top, front row, tenth from left), L.Z. Anderson (top, second row, extreme left) and Ruben Rivers (bottom, top row, tenth from right) are among those pictured. *Courtesy L.Z. Anderson*

1. The Double "V" Campaign

At Fort Benning we joined in with other ERCs from Negro colleges located throughout the Army's 4th Service Command area: A & T College, Greensboro, North Carolina; Bethune Cookman College, Daytona Beach, Florida; Florida A & M College, Tallahassee, Florida; Fort Valley College, Fort Valley, Georgia; Savannah State College, Savannah, Georgia; Southern University, Baton Rouge, Louisiana; and Tuskegee Institute, Tuskegee, Alabama. After 3 weeks of physical examinations, psychological and IQ testing they finally inducted us.

On or about April 5, 1943, approximately 70 of us were transferred to the Armored Force Replacement Training Center, Fort Knox, Kentucky for armored basic training. I later learned that we had been "hand picked" and if we could complete the training would be transferred to one of the 3 Negro tank battalions.

At Fort Knox we were exposed to the most grueling, intense, informative, training that one could imagine. They taught us to operate and maintain tanks (light and medium), half-tracks, trucks, and jeeps. We became proficient in firing our personal weapons, the carbine and .45 caliber pistol.

In July 1943 we graduated. Within days, they transferred 30 of us to the 784th Tank Battalion (light) at Camp Claiborne. We remained together until deactivation."[12]

The War Department activated five tank groups made up of three tank battalions per group. The 5th Tank Group, commanded by Colonel Le Roy Nichols, was made up of black enlisted personnel and white officers. This tank group became an experiment to see if African American soldiers had the discipline and intelligence to learn armored warfare. With the 758th Tank Battalion (Light) in place, two more experimental tank battalions were needed to complete the 5th Tank Group.

On April 1, 1942, the War Department activated the 761st Tank Battalion (Light). Then exactly one year later, the War Department activated the 784th Tank Battalion (Light). A cadre of enlisted men from the 758th and 761st, along with officers and enlisted men from the Armored Force Replacement Training Center at Fort Knox, formed the 784th at Camp Claiborne, Louisiana. Major George Dalia, a former horse cavalry officer, transferred to the 784th Tank Battalion from the 10th Armored Division to become its commanding officer. In June 1943 he was promoted to Lt. Colonel. He remained the battalion commander throughout its existence. In combat, he would unhesitatingly lead his tanks into battle while on foot and thus commanded the respect and admiration of his men.

This experiment almost ended with the 758th and 761st Tank Battalions. Several weeks before the activation of the 784th, a near mutiny occurred. Several members of the 761st and some from adjoining outfits, infuriated over the persistent bludgeoning of their comrades by the local police and civilian population of Alexandria, Louisiana, decided to fight back. Sergeant L.Z. Anderson (761st) recounts:

It was a Sunday night, I believe. I was in the theater and it was still light, about 6 or 7 o'clock. When they got word back to us at the post that they were beating up on our boys, everyone took off from the movie and went to the motor pool. When we got to the motor pool they had already cranked up those tanks. Captain Wingo was there, up on the hood of his car, begging the guys not to go into town. They had the tanks cranked up at the gate ready to come out. From what I heard they had ammunition. They had broken into our armory where we had live ammunition. They were really going into town to shoot up the place. What distracted their attention was one of them damned old buses that came by. These bus drivers were the ones who caused most of the problems. When the bus came through everybody left the gate and rushed this bus and tried to turn it over. They started throwing bottles and everything they could at the bus. How they stopped this I really don't know. The boys calmed down and everything came under control. I don't remember any charges being filed.[13]

During this constant turmoil, most of the men stayed in the clear while mastering the intricacies of the light tank. The M3A1 light tank (Stuart) had a crew of 4 and a maximum speed of nearly 40 mph with an open road cruising range of approximately 172 miles. After modifications it could move faster. The light tank was employed to provide stinging firepower, mobility, and crew protection in screening and reconnaissance missions.

2

Camp Claiborne

The War Department designated Camp Claiborne on October 28, 1940, from what was formerly Camp Evangeline in the early 1800s and later Camp Beauregard. It was located in Rapides Parish on the west side of U.S. Highway 165 about 17 miles southwest of Alexandria, Louisiana. In the snake-infested swamplands within the Evangeline section of the Kisatchie National Forest, the camp consisted of tents, hutments, and a few permanent structures.

The local communities harbored an unyielding tradition of intolerance, segregation, and a doctrine of black inferiority and white supremacy that they and their ancestors had cherished for over a century. The sight of proud black men roaming the area was an outrage that would not be tolerated. The exasperated white community defended their traditions through intimidation and Ku Klux Klan–inspired violence. The black soldiers who ventured off camp did so at their own risk.

The black soldiers from the North had to learn in a hurry to stay in the black section of town and that they must step off the sidewalk when approaching a white person. They found out the hard way that a Negro could be beaten and tortured to death without any protection and recourse from the law.

When the white police found black soldiers who drifted over to the white section of town, they simply turned them over to the black military police (MP). The black MPs took the black soldiers back to camp and beat the hell out of them before returning them to their unit.

Fifteen months prior to the activation of the 784th Tank Battalion (Light) at Camp Claiborne, Alexandria experienced a bloody race riot. It was Saturday night and the soldiers were enjoying their weekend passes, January 10, 1942. A number of black soldiers from northern states who were unfamiliar with the implications of "Jim Crow" reacted to the violent arrest of a black soldier by white MPs. Hostilities flared in front of the Ritz Theatre when city and state police engaged the black troops. As word spread, additional MPs from Camp Livingston and a mob of white civilians swarmed in. Many black civilians were trapped in the melee along the 4-block corridor of Lee Street, a bustling thoroughfare through the isolated black section of town, where brothels and taverns hosted nightly fistfights and stabbings.

The MPs were mainly from the 32nd Military Police Company. The black troops were from the 367th Infantry Regiment and the 758th Tank Battalion (Light) stationed at Camp Claiborne, and the 350th Field Artillery Regiment quartered at Camp Livingston. Clubbed, tear-gassed, and fired on by shotguns and pistols, the black troops fought back using bricks, rocks, bottles, sticks, and anything at their disposal. By 2200 hours the skirmish was over and Lee Street resembled a war zone. The beaten soldiers left standing awaited transfer back to camp to be confined to quarters. The bodies of the others lay where they had fallen.

The sector of Lee Street where the bloody clash occurred was immediately cordoned off and cleaned up. The Army refused to divulge any information other than prepared general statements, and denied the press interviews with the soldiers who had been involved. The cover-up was perhaps perpetrated to avert further divisiveness on the home front.

Despite the Army's attempt to restrict coverage and the conservative newspapers printing "DON'T BELIEVE THE WORST," word got out that many black soldiers had been killed. The city's police force was described as "The Famous Alexandria Nigger Killing Squad." The riot, it was said, "gave them the opportunity that they wanted, a slight excuse to shoot and beat Negro soldiers, as well as a chance to remind Negro civilians that this is still the South."[1]

James LaFourche, NAACP public relations council and president of the New Orleans Press Club, submitted a report to Walter White, the executive secretary of the NAACP. LaFourche reported that from his "closest informants" he had learned of the deaths of 10 black soldiers in the Lee Street riot. He made numerous references to indiscriminate shootings of black civilians as well as soldiers. He made it clear that in gathering this information he had placed himself in great peril, expounding: "I beg to inform you after a very dangerous undertaking by me, the facts as they happened, and told to me, by persons who miraculously escaped...."[2]

Simmons Washington recalls his arrival at Camp Claiborne:

> That was around April 1943. We stayed there several months in basic training. I had never been in that part of the country even though I am from Mississippi. There was a lot of sand and it was kind of rough on the vehicles. They had mosquitoes and all that stuff down there. Other than that it was not a bad camp. I got all of my basic training there and I was not far from home. I never went into Alexandria because they had some

problems down there before I got there. We kind of stayed away from there. I stayed in camp all during my basic training.³

Bill Hughes recalls his arrival to Camp Claiborne:

I arrived at Camp Claiborne in June 1943, in civilian clothes with a duffle bag full of military gear. I was challenged by 2 white MPs for being out of uniform. I showed them my orders from the induction center assigning me to the 761st Tank Battalion (Light). I told them that I had not been trained to wear a uniform. They escorted me to their building at the main gate and told me to wait outside. I heard one on the phone calling somebody saying "we have one of your boys down here at the main gate in civilian clothes. Come get him."

I waited over an hour before a corporal showed up in a jeep and drove me to battalion headquarters. The road was muddy due to recent rain so I was splashed with mud. I was not warmly received and led to the sergeant major's office. He was shocked and so was the executive officer. I was told that a mistake had been made and I would have to go to a training camp. I was not allowed to leave the building and placed in a room with a cot to sleep on. I was hungry but given no food. That night I talked my way to use the pay phone across the street after forking over 2 dollars and called Major-General Cheeves at home about my plight. He assured me by morning everything would be all right. There was a vending machine with candy bars so that was my dinner that night. Apparently, someone had contacted the battalion and told them they should train me there and I was to remain assigned. The executive officer was furious and transferred me to the 784th Tank Battalion, Company D. First Sergeant Daniels took me in tow and taught me how to wear a uniform, salute, and march.

Camp Claiborne was not a pleasant place to be. It appeared to be cut off from all outside life. The place was stinky and everything looked rather shabby. It was dusty when dry and very muddy after rain. The facilities were very limited and you were not allowed to go to the fine facilities the white soldiers had across Camp. I hated the place. The nearest town of any size was Alexandria. It was a hellhole. People were unfriendly and there was constant friction between black soldiers and white MPs as well as black MPs. Cheap wine, beer, and whisky was available at bars. Prostitution was rampant. They would come into Alexandria by the busload on weekends. It was very sickening for me so I only went one time to Alexandria. It was the worst surrounding I had ever been exposed. Fortunately, for me the stay there was not too long since I was sent to the Armored School at Fort Knox, Kentucky for basic radio communications for a 6-week period and right away again for another 6 week course. This 3-month absence from Camp Claiborne was a great morale booster for me.

One staff sergeant who befriended me was Maurice DeQuier. He was of Creole origin from Baton Rouge, Louisiana. He was our supply Sergeant and saw that I was lonely staying in Camp instead of going on pass to Alexandria. I was there once and hated the town. Staff Sergeant DeQuier was an older man in his mid thirties. He had a young cousin my age also in the Army and they went home together to Baton Rouge on weekends. I was invited to go home with him to meet his family and cousin and made repeated visits to Baton Rouge. We became friends as a result of these visits and daily contacts on supply requisitions and reports at camp.⁴

Franklin Garrido will never forget the hostility there:

> I didn't take any chances by putting myself in a position where I could get into trouble. It was in the air. We knew that at Camp Claiborne and Camp Hood that the bus drivers wore pistols. We knew that if they told you to go to the rear and you didn't they would stop at the nearest sheriff or MP station. I personally did not try them. I just went along with the program. It was a hostile environment."[5]

Sergeant L.Z. Anderson painfully remembers how the mistreatment of his comrades often ended up:

> They would always find one or 2 dead right out from the post. These guys would leave the post and go to the little old towns just outside of the camp. There were a lot of other black soldiers down there. There was an engineer outfit down there and most of the time it was some of their boys. I don't remember us ever having one of our boys found dead, but they found black soldiers dead down there all the time![6]

Anderson went on to describe how he, on few occasions, went into town:

> We stopped going into town on weekends, we went on Mondays to avoid trouble. The bus depot down on Lee Street is where a lot of problems would start. When I got off the bus, I caught a cab and went directly to our USO or to 3rd Street. I didn't spend much time there. I would always go down to lower 3rd Street where it was real quiet. I met a few nice people there and never got caught up in any of the madness. However, I knew what went on. I never came in contact with any whites from there. I remember we had some white soldiers who would go around with us in Alexandria. They would associate with us because they couldn't associate with the other white boys because they were Yankees. They caught hell too.[7]

James Baldwin recalls:

> What I remember about Claiborne, I was very young, 18 or 19. I was used to discrimination because I came from the South but it was pretty rough there. The facilities for blacks were not equal to what they had for whites i.e., the movies, PX, and those kinds of places — especially the movie houses. We didn't have air conditioning. We had benches to sit on with no backs. You actually sat with your feet right in the sand. It seems like every time guys would leave for overseas they tended to tear up what was there.
>
> When you got ready to go into town the black soldiers could only sit in the back of the bus. Only about 10 or 11 black guys could go into town on the bus that held about 45 or 50 people. The guys then started going by cabs rather than be humiliated by that discrimination of standing in long lines when only 11 guys could get on. While at Camp Claiborne my buddies and I went to Alexandria only 2 or 3 times. For the most part we avoided Alexandria. Before leaving Fort Knox we were told about the race riot that occurred there in 1942.[8]

The 784th Tank Battalion (Light), with an initial strength of 19 officers and 99 enlisted men, immediately began receiving fillers. They came from the Armored Force Replacement Training Center at Fort Knox, the Reception Training Center at Camp Shelby, Mississippi, and the Field Artillery Replacement Training Center at Fort Bragg, North Carolina. By January of 1944 the unit made it up to full strength.

The 758th and 761st Tank Battalions provided the nucleus of non-commissioned and commissioned officers essential for the organization and training of this new unit. Sergeant L.Z. Anderson from the 761st served as a hands-on trainer in first echelon "sledgehammer and crowbar" tank mechanics.

The majority of the enlisted men hailed from Mississippi, with the remainder from Illinois, Pennsylvania, New York, New Jersey, Maryland, Indiana, North Carolina, Louisiana, and California.

The training intensified at Camp Claiborne as the new fillers received basic technical training. They moved on to advanced individual training that included crew, section, and platoon tactics. They had so many seconds to get in and out of their tanks. They cross-trained on each other's position and began mastering the intricacies of the light tank and became proficient in tank operations, mechanics, and related phases of mechanized warfare.

Motor marches were conducted at various times during this training. They stressed blackout driving, security (both on the move and in bivouac), and march discipline.

Forced marches on foot were also conducted at various times. Each man carried full field equipment and individual arms. They had a 5-miler and a 9-miler leading up to the big one, a 25-miler to be completed within 8 hours. For the big one, 486 men started and 436 finished.

Franklin Garrido recalls certain individuals in the training program who had a knack for tank driving:

> The Mississippi contingent, the ones from Camp Shelby, made excellent drivers. My best friend, Dewey McFarland, said that was from plowing with mules. He said, "If you can control a mule you can control a tank." He probably was the best tank driver in the 784th. In addition to being a good driver he could also maintain a tank. His engine compartment was always like a refrigerator inside. His tanks were always clean, spotless.[9]

Bill Hughes describes his training:

> After learning the basics of soldiering I became the Company D clerk and took an aptitude test in communications. I was selected to attend the basic communication course at Fort Knox, Kentucky. This 6-week course was another blessing because Fort Knox was very near Louisville, where I could reach my home in Indianapolis, Indiana easily within several hours. The training was very intense on learning the Morse code and keying the line to transmit messages. The code was embedded in my head so much that any sounds I heard like a jack hammer or street car became clear Morse code characters to me. Everything I heard was associated with the Morse code. The pleasant part was going home every

weekend on Friday after 1400 hours until Monday to attend classes at 0800 hours. I finished the course in the top 3 and was granted a 10-day leave at home before returning to the 784th.[10]

On September 6, 1943, the 5th Tank Group received orders of transfer to Camp Hood, Texas. The 784th Tank Battalion (Light) departed on September 14, arriving the next day. They required 2 trains to transport their 33 officers, 451 enlisted men and 150 vehicles.

3

Camp Hood

The 784th Tank Battalion (Light) arrived at Camp Hood, Texas, on September 15, 1943. The terrain was excellent for tank operations, with hills, valleys, woods, open grounds, etc. Back at Camp Claiborne the land was swampy, flat, and densely vegetated. There at Claiborne they became proficient at extricating tanks from the mud. Here at Camp Hood the battalion trained in advanced armored warfare as school troops on constant maneuver. They sharpened their skills against tank destroyer units.

The 784th came from a tent city at Camp Claiborne that looked like an old Civil War lithograph. They took up quarters in permanent structures at Camp Hood, where they occupied the area between 67th and 68th Streets crossing Battalion, Central, Park, and North Avenues. What a difference!

Simmons Washington recalls: "Camp Hood was a pretty good camp. It was a large camp. We had a lot of good firing ranges. It was so large that it had a south Hood and a north Hood. It was ideal for tanks, the only thing, it got cold and it was hot out there during the summer."[1]

On October 29, 1943, a major change in the battalion's organization occurred involving its designation and equipment. The 784th Tank Battalion (Light) became the 784th Tank Battalion. The equipment changed from Stuart light tanks to the M4 Sherman medium tanks. This was going from a 37-millimeter cannon to a 75-millimeter cannon and a small tank with limited use in combat to the main battle tank of the U.S. Army.

Formerly, as a light tank battalion, the 784th Tank Battalion operated around its 3 light tank companies. Each company had 3 platoons containing 5 light tanks each. The light tank had 4-man crews. The standard light tank battalion usually contained 550 men.

Becoming a medium tank battalion, the 784th now operated around its 3 medium tank companies: A (Able), B (Baker), and C (Charlie). Each company had 3 tank platoons containing 5 tanks each. Each company also had 2 command tanks, bringing their total up to 17 per company, the normal fighting complement. The medium tank functioned with a crew of 5. The battalion also had 2 supporting companies — Headquarters and Service. The standard medium tank battalion usually operated with 750 men.

During this reorganization, the table of organization and equipment called for a new company to be added, D (Dog) Company. This additional company would operate with the old light tanks for screening, reconnaissance, and setting up roadblocks.

Also during this reorganization, all the black officers shifted over to the 761st Tank Battalion. Sergeant Simmons Washington points out:

> All of our training came from guys of the 761st, they came as cadre. Sergeant Morris Harris came from the 761st. They trained us. We had good drivers, good gunners, we had everything. Our training was excellent. To survive you had to know what you're doing and you had to be good. A lot of the officers who trained us were transferred before we went overseas. When we went overseas we had 2 black officers, the chaplain, who was a captain, and the doctor, who was a captain. I don't think they ever promoted any of the platoon sergeants with battlefield commissions. But we had excellent noncoms.[2]

Sergeant Simmons Washington, 1944. *Courtesy Simmons Washington*

Between November 6 and 7, 1943, the battalion took their new vehicles on a 90-mile road march to North Camp Hood. About 135 vehicles took part in this road march. They exercised in night-blackout marching. It was difficult maintaining visual contact with the tank in front with the Texas dust swirling around the very small dim red taillights. The field exercise went without incident.

In early January 1944, more new equipment arrived. Dog Company exchanged their M3 Stuart light tanks for the updated M5 Stuart light tanks. This modified tank had twin Cadillac engines, hydro transmissions, and a gun stabilizer. The light tank weighed approximately 15 tons, not much for a tank.

However, with its lightly armored body, it was extremely maneuverable and fast, and cornered easily. This faster and more maneuverable M5 could fire its 37-millimeter cannon on the run. It had a .30 caliber machine gun mounted to fire along the same axis as the main armament, the 37-millimeter cannon. When the tracer bullets from the .30-caliber showed they were on the mark, the cannon could be fired for theoretically a direct hit. The M5 was also armed with 2 more .30 caliber machine guns, one on the turret for anti-aircraft fire and one in the bow for anti-infantry fire. The model number skipped M4 and went directly to M5 in order to distinguish the Stuart from the M4 Sherman medium tank. Also during this period, orientation on the new M4A1 Sherman medium tank began.

At this stage of the war, the Sherman medium tank came in 3 variations, the M4, M4A1, and M4A3. The M4 and M4A1, powered by air-cooled aircraft engines, could push their 34-ton medium tanks approximately 30 miles per hour. The new M4A3, powered by water-cooled Ford engines, performed even better.

Training continued to intensify at Camp Hood, with an emphasis on road marches and fire missions (direct and indirect). The Sherman Medium Tank (75 millimeter), Stuart Light Tank (37 millimeter), Mortar Platoon (81 millimeter) and Assault Gun Platoon (105 millimeter howitzer) received intense engagement. Much of what was learned dealt with aiming and firing, the use of azimuth readings, triangulation, etc.

Headquarters Company employed 3 platoons: the Assault Gun Platoon, the Reconnaissance Platoon and the Mortar Platoon.

The Assault Gun Platoon operated with 3 self-propelled 105-millimeter artillery pieces mounted on Sherman chassis. This was mobile firepower at its best — High-Explosive Anti-Tank (HEAT), larger HE rounds, and White-Phosphorous (WP) smoke rounds. The big guns possessed that extra punch needed for the heavier-armored German Panther and Tiger tanks. The short-barreled guns had direct sights. Each crew had 5 members, similar to a Sherman tank crew. Because the ammunition was conveniently stored in racks around the sides and on the floor, the crews could fire 8 to 10 rounds per minute. Positioned in a strategic location, the assault gun could fire over the tanks at enemy defenses.

The Reconnaissance Platoon operated with jeeps and any fast-moving vehicles they could get their hands on, including motorcycles. Their duty was to take point, draw fire, reconnoiter, and report back on what the unit was up against. This would be extremely hazardous duty, "Purple Heart work."

Sergeant Simmons Washington describes the Mortar Platoon:

> I was assigned to the 81-millimeter mortar platoon. We had all of the tank training, firing range, all of that, we could have gone into either one. They needed to build it up, it was a good platoon, a dangerous platoon and they could do some damage. In the mortar platoon you didn't have to work quite as hard as you did in the tanks. The tanks kept you dirty and they kept you going all the time. The 81-millimeter mortar was good for indirect firing, laying down smoke screens, just about anything, high explosives, supporting the tanks, supporting the infantry. We had 5 men in a squad, a gunner, a loader, and 3 ammunition handlers. Mainly everyone could do the same job just in case someone got

taken out. I was the squad leader, the same rank as a tank commander, a buck sergeant with 3 stripes.3

Other areas covered entailed the capabilities and limitations of armored vehicles, assault on fortifications, close combat and street fighting/cleanup, tank/infantry coordination, booby traps, decontamination of vehicles, hand grenades, personal small arms, swimming, foreign map instruction, gas mask, censorship/sensitivity, use of compass, first aid, individual cooking, malaria control, rocket launcher firing, and 10-mile conditioning marches. All individuals and platoons underwent a series of proficiency tests to establish combat eligibility.

Corporal Bill Hughes, Dog Company, 784th Tank Battalion recalls this training:

During the spring of 1944, I along with a group of others was sent to Camp Hood for a big maneuver involving infantry, tanks and tank destroyer units as well as artillery. I was sent to be a messenger jeep driver for a liaison team of observers. I never got to know the camp very well at that time because we were out in the field just about all of the time. I do remember the camp was much better equipped with barracks and other facilities. The entire 761st Tank Battalion was there for this maneuver; having moved from Camp Claiborne in the latter part of 1943. It was exciting to see their new M4-A1 Medium tank. I thought they may be going to see combat after all. Surely all that money would not be spent for tanks, especially on a black outfit and why the big maneuver. My stay was cut short there when I was told I was being sent back to Fort Knox, Kentucky to radio school. Prior to leaving, I got a chance to ride in that big monster and was very impressed with its speed and maneuverability, not to mention that big 75 mm gun. Although Camp Hood was better kept, it was still a place of segregation and discrimination. Noticeable was the close contact made between black and white soldiers in the field. They mingled, played games and supported each other during the maneuvers; and oh yes shot craps together which was forbidden and in hidden places, but let the dice roll. The heat was unbearable and those rattle snakes kept you awake out of fear most of the night. There were constant rumors that someone had been bitten, but I don't know if this was true. I saw several in the daylight but they went on their merry way unless you were within striking distance and suddenly came upon them without heeding their warning. So was my encounter with white soldiers. They would sometimes let you get near but you better stay away when you got an unwanted warning. I

Sergeant Bill Hughes in 1944 (one month before his promotion to sergeant). *Courtesy Bill Hughes*

had the feeling that a lot of those guys wanted to be in closer contact with blacks but peer pressure ruled since most of the troops were out of dear old prejudicious Deep South.[4]

Tech-5 James Hamilton remembers Camp Hood:

I went into the 669th Tank Destroyer Battalion. There we started training out in the field and then I went to school at South Camp Hood, a mechanics' school, and I was doing good there and then I came back to North Camp Hood. And then they transferred us to a tank battalion and all along we were learning how to destroy a tank and ironically they put us in a tank battalion — the 784th.[5]

James Hamilton goes on to recall running into a "homeboy":

A cook in the 784th by the name of Fields lived on McCullough Street in Baltimore. And man! I was glad to see him. We would come back from town in Texas and he would go in the kitchen and open it up. We'd fix some steaks and stuff and we would just lay back. We had a good time.[6]

Corporal Bill Hughes remembers his commanders, key individuals, and friends in his unit:

I was assigned to Company D, commanded by Captain John T. Powers. The First Sergeant was George Daniels who had ministered a small Baptist church in New York. He was a kind fatherly man who kept close watch over his flock. I got to know him very well since I was assigned duties as the company clerk. His approach to disciplining the men was not harsh but fair. He was not the loud barking first sergeant who instilled fear in the men. His approach was to make you feel ashamed of yourself for not doing the right thing and giving a soft worded lecture. Captain Powers was only 23 years old. He was respected and did not rule with an iron fist. He left most of the everyday care of the men up to the platoon leaders, first sergeant, and platoon sergeants. I got to know many of the men primarily by making up the duty rosters, preparing morning reports, writing correspondence, preparing passes, preparing extra duty lists, and too many reports. Lt Colonel Dalia was well liked by all the men. You did not see much of him unless there was a Battalion formation or during inspections. I did not have many close friends. There were several however I had known from my school days in Indianapolis who also graduated from the same High School. They were Sergeant Hubert Dabner and Sergeant David McMurray, both tank commanders. We vowed to look out for each other. I became friendly with battalion Sergeant Major Freddie Dobbins because of many trips made daily to battalion headquarters. He was my idol and well educated. He was sharp in appearance and carried a baton crop at all times. First Sergeant Daniel and I were very friendly since we had all day contact in the orderly room.[7]

The 784th made a temporary change of duty station from Camp Hood to Camp Swift, Texas, from May 19 until June 29, 1944, for additional combat training. The entire unit jumped off from their training area west of Clear Creek. All battalion vehicles traveled by Highways 190 and 81. They moved through Georgetown, the outskirts of Austin, and Bastrop, arriving at Camp Swift on May 20, 1944.

The battalion traveled in the column formation until they hit the open grounds. There they spread out into the desert formation, a formation used when the tanks are not confined to the narrow roads. They learned that an armored formation is an effective force only when moving from point to point, overcoming obstacles along the way. Standing still meant becoming targets.

Training emphasized individual tank crew training. The driver and bow gunner/assistant driver sat in their positions in the lower level, driver on the left. Their seats moved up and down, giving them the option of driving with their hatches unbuttoned for better vision. The entire tank crew wore earphones for constant communication with the tank commander. There were 3 men up inside the turret. The tank commander and the gunner were both near the main hatch to the right of the big gun, and the loader/assistant gunner was to the left near the secondary hatch. The tank commander stood behind the gunner, where he received commands over the radio from the platoon leader and/or the

(Left to right) R. Woodard, Frank House, Harris, unknown, and L.Z. Anderson (reading), Camp Hood, Texas, 1944. *Courtesy L.Z. Anderson*

platoon sergeant. From this position in the turret the tank commander functioned as the eyes and ears of the tank. He guided the gunner to the target, estimated the distance, ordered the type of projectile, etc. For example, the tank commander instructed the driver: "Slow down." "Turn left." "Maintain position." Then he commanded the entire tank: "Get ready!" He received an instant reply: "Loader ready!" "Gunner ready!" Then he directed the gunner: "AP! Traverse left, up 5 degrees!" The gunner adjusted the 75-millimeter and turned to loader: "AP!" The loader slammed and locked an AP (armor piercing) round into the breech. Then the tank commander bellowed the order: "FIRE!" The gunner smashed on the solenoid button on the floor and fired the big gun. Then they heard a tremendous detonation, a hollowed ring, followed by the loud clang of the instant recoil as the empty casing ejected onto the steel floor. The loader, on command of the gunner, loaded another round as fast as he could and then ducked away from the mighty recoil. The noise in the tank became deafening. The gunner then switched his foot to the other solenoid button on the floor and fired the .30 caliber machine gun mounted coaxially with the big gun. When the tracers hit a target, he could theoretically fire the big gun for a direct hit. Both .30 caliber machine guns rattled away, dumping hot empty shell casings on the steel floor while the loader slammed home another round. The action was fast and furious and the red-hot 75-millimeter and .30 caliber shell casings piled up high, increasing the temperature inside the tank. The smoke and noxious ammonia odor choked the tank crew. It cleared only when the hatches opened. The goal of this exercise was to pierce an opening into the interior of an armored target with the AP round (shot), then with the big gun stabilized on the target, a second round of HE (shell) would follow its predecessor through the same hole and produce a spectacular flash explosion. Target destroyed!

The big guns were mounted on a gyrostabilizer unit that floated the guns and kept them trained on the sighted target even when moving across uneven terrain. The American tanks could fire on the move and thus had a distinct advantage over the German tanks. In order to fire accurately, the Germans had to stop their tanks before firing their big guns. The gyrostabilizer was top secret and had to be removed or destroyed every time an American tank was abandoned.

Not to be outdone, the Mortar Platoon brushed up on some indirect firing. Corporal James Baldwin points out:

> We relocated to Camp Swift for what some of us felt was definitely a "dry run" for actual combat. Training intensified! All of our activities became combat simulated. I was the gunner of the 2nd squad. Sergeant Simmons Washington was our squad leader. Sergeant Washington from his vantage point gave me concise and clear commands: "Traverse right! Traverse left! Steady! Commence firing!" I followed his commands and hit the target almost every time. We fired from the half-track. At times we fired from the terrain where we removed the tube, tripod, and plate and set it up while being timed. We supported our tanks by lobbing high explosive rounds and laying down smoke screens.[8]

The tank crews would soon find out that the Sherman tank had a grave tendency to catch fire and burn completely out of control when hit. Their training conditioned them to swiftly exit at the first sign of fire. By stopwatch they were timed to the second. The Sherman's use of gasoline engines versus diesels, along with the electrical wiring and ammunition storage, could turn it into a blazing inferno within seconds.

The training at Camp Swift included firing of all battalion weapons, zeroing in on targets and destroying them with the least amount of fire. This training stressed tank/infantry coordination. Tank platoons would split up into 2 sections. One section would advance ahead of the infantry and the other section would stay behind, providing covering fire. When the advancing section came to a halt and found a defilade (cover from enemy fire) position, the other section would advance. This leapfrog tactic closely resembled "Cover me, Alpha.... Move out, Bravo!"

Almost as bad as having your tank knocked out by enemy fire was having it break down at a crucial moment in combat. Each tank crew spent a considerable amount of time performing first-echelon maintenance, routine and preventive. The Sherman tanks were temperamental, high-maintenance vehicles and the tankers stayed grease-smeared.

Carbon monoxide poisoning was another hazard of the Sherman tank. When its exhaust became blocked, the buildup of carbon monoxide backed up into the turret.

Communications was vital to successful tank/infantry coordination. Bill Hughes points out:

> They had an intercom system where all crew members could talk freely to each other. However, another form of communication was necessary in case there was a malfunction of the intercom. Tank crews were taught to respond to foot pressure on the shoulders and heads if the intercom system failed. As an example, the tank commander could instruct the driver to turn left by putting pressure with his foot on the left shoulder of the driver. The harder the pressure meant a sharper turn. The same held true for right turns on the right shoulder. A tap in the center of the head meant stop. Pushing the head forward meant go forward and back by pulling the head back. It was a simple form of communicating, but it worked and [was] often practiced.
>
> Radios were tuned to frequencies by installing crystals and beating them with an oscillator. Further fine-tuning was necessary to get maximum strength readings. Each radio was given a call sign for reporting in or out which also identified the tank or vehicle. Crews were taught radio protocol for uniformity and brevity in transmission time. In case of radio failure, a fluorescent panel was displayed on the tank or a flashlight signal could be given at night if permitted. It was my responsibility to train crews, practice radio protocol with them, and most of all, to keep those radios properly working at peak performance.
>
> The tank radios were equipped with whip antennae in several sections on the tank. It could be tied down when necessary. When erected at full length, it could be dangerous if it came in contact with any high-tension wires. The tank commander and crew were taught to look out for this danger of being electrocuted.
>
> Infantry troops had backpack radios that tuned to our tank frequencies, normally carried by the platoon leader, platoon sergeant or squad leader.
>
> Radios were very useful in directing fire, identifying targets, alerting others of dangers, spotting enemy locations, over running machine gun nests, pockets of troop resistance etc.
>
> Some form of communications is essential at all times when tanks are operational.

Highly desired are radio communications. However this may not always be possible due to interception, jamming or other interference, or breakdowns. Tanks were equipped with radios in the SCR 500 series.[9]

During this brief stay at Camp Swift, Captain Gustave Burant, the battalion's supply officer, moved 350 men and their vehicles to Magnolia Beach, Texas, for anti-aircraft target firing at the Indianola Firing Range. The .50 caliber anti-aircraft gun on the turret proved awesome. The Germans had no weapon comparable to it. The massive slug would virtually create an explosion inside a human body and if an arm or leg were struck, the entire limb would be severed. The Germans were terrified of it.

In the field the tankers ate 10-in-1 rations. Each box contained 10 meals for one person or one meal for 10 persons. Each tank turret contained a single-burner gasoline camp stove.

The D-day invasion of Fortress Europe took place while the 784th Tank Battalion participated in the Camp Swift field exercise. June 6, 1944 (D-day): in the early morning hours, more than 1,000 air transports dropped paratroopers and inserted glider-troopers to secure the flanks for the pending assault. Amphibious crafts landed over 100,000 troops on 5 beaches along 50 miles of Normandy coast. The British and Canadians landed on Gold, Juno and Sword beaches, while the Americans landed on Utah and Omaha beaches. After bombing enemy targets along the coast, the U.S. Army Air Forces and British Royal Air Force controlled the skies. Rangers climbed cliffs, engineers destroyed beach obstacles, and quartermasters stockpiled supplies in the largest beach invasion in military history.

The battalion arrived back at Camp Hood on June 29, 1944. During June through September 1944, the 784th Tank Battalion continued to train in all phases of armored warfare and continued upgrading their skills. This additional training gave them a distinct advantage for combat. During this field exercise, they had been put on alert for overseas movement.

Corporal Bill Hughes recalls:

> I was very excited about it because of several reasons. First I wondered where we were going. Would it be Europe or the Far East? Second what would my family and friends think? Third, I envisioned combat and danger and wondered what lies ahead. Fourth it confirmed my earlier thoughts that it would happen one day when others were in doubt. Much to my surprise I was selected to return immediately to Fort Knox to take the advance course in communications after being back only 3 days with the battalion. I was really overjoyed that I would get another 6 weeks of training and again weekends at home. The course revolved around fast speed operations in Morse code, operations of field radios, antennae set ups, line of sight, message handling and delivery, security, etc. I finished at the top of the class and asked for another leave at home. The answer was NO! Everyone is being given a 10-day leave at home because we have been alerted for overseas duty. I could not believe it because none of us thought we would ever see combat. I was told to report back to duty and go on leave for 10 days. My argument that I was already near home did not matter. So again, travel back to Camp Hood, for a week before returning to

784th Tank Battalion officers at a night club in Dallas, Texas, 1944. Left to right: Capt. Donald Carman (Commanding Officer, C/784th); his fiancée "Charlie"; Lt. Don Brown (784th); unknown; Lt. Art Solow (C/784th); unknown. *Courtesy Mark Carman*

Indianapolis for a 10-day leave. All of this took place in the spring and summer of 1944. Upon return from leave I was assigned the MOS 542, Communications Sergeant and promoted.[10]

It was extremely difficult to leave their loved ones behind knowing that they may never return. Sergeant Simmons Washington describes: "I married my childhood sweetheart at Camp Hood. We came all the way up together and we are still at it. This year it will be 61 years. My daughter, Sandra Joyce, was born the day I left the States. That was rough on me.[11]

Mrs. Washington adds:

Simmons and I were married at Camp Hood (Temple, Texas) on December 26, 1943. We lived back and forth during the year of 1944. Simmons shipped out in October 1944 and our daughter Sandra was born on the day he left the USA. It was hard because I thought he was coming home for the birth of our daughter. He was gone for 14 months. This was hard because the fighting was going on and you didn't know what might happen. I was blessed because I lived with my family until Simmons came back.[12]

4

Destination ETO

During the preparations to join the great battle to liberate Europe, the 784th Tank Battalion received the distressing news that Lt. General Leslie McNair had been killed in action. Unknown at the time, their benefactor became a victim to friendly fire. During a bombing raid over Normandy, the wave of American bombers targeted the billowing smoke and dust rather than the enemy lines. Thus their bombs fell "short." Lt. General McNair had visited the front that day when "shorts" claimed his life among many other Americans. The planes flew over like rush hour traffic and left the targeted fields burning and smoldering. The grave registration specialists identified the general only by the 3-star lapel pin found on a mangled, smoldering, unrecognizable corpse. McNair was the second highest-ranking American officer killed in action during World War II.

The 784th Tank Battalion departed Camp Hood on October 3, 1944, after turning in all of their vehicles to Ordnance and boxing up their organizational equipment for shipping. The unit had an overage of enlisted men, due to a change in the Table of Organization and Equipment, who were transferred to the 669th, 679th and 827th Tank Destroyer Battalions. The 784th traveled by rail to Camp Shanks, New York, arriving on October 7.

Sergeant Bill Hughes expressed:

> I was hoping we would be bound for Europe although we were not told where we were going. The shades were pulled down on all windows of the train so you could not see where you were going. The word soon got around that we were heading east in a round about way. My family and friends were sad of course but I was not. Naturally, they were worried about my safety. I felt some discomfort because I knew we were going to kill

someone or get killed. I wondered if I could really point a gun at someone to kill. All sorts of things came to my mind about combat and danger, which haunted me for sometime. Although now confirmed that it would happen, I thought about where were our tanks and equipment? They are not on the train after all that cleaning up process. Others were also wondering and thought perhaps we would not see combat but used as service troops. That feeling prevailed until we went to the port at Cardiff, Wales and found all new tanks waiting to be fine-tuned as well as other equipment. We were delighted.[1]

The unit proceeded by rail and ferry from Camp Shanks to New York Harbor's Pier 97 on October 30, 1944. They embarked on Ship NY559/CU45, slipped away from the dock, and sailed past the Statue of Liberty into the dark blue waters of the Atlantic. During this voyage their training consisted of calisthenics, military discipline, aircraft recognition and the foreign languages of French and German. They slept in hammocks hung from ceiling hooks. For safety they were required to wear life jackets at all times while on deck and were not allowed on deck after dark. They disembarked 10 days later. They arrived in Liverpool, England, in the late hours of November 10.

Picadilly Circus, New York City, October 1944. Five 784th Tank Battalion officers celebrate before departing for the European theater of operations. Left to right: Lt. Tom Redditt, Capt. Gus Burant, Capt. John Powers, Capt. Donald Carman, and Lt. Don Brown. *Courtesy Mark Carman*

4. Destination ETO

Sergeant Bill Hughes describes this sea voyage:

It was the worst trip I have ever made in my life. I have not been able to recall the name of that British ship made up into a troop transport. It was old and squeaky and looked weather worn. I was very surprised that we would be sailing on a British ship. It was very crowded with hammock bunks slung over each other. They were very uncomfortable and very easy to fall out of them as many did. The compartments were smelly with little ventilation. The food was terrible and the water tasted awful since it was laced with some sort of treatment. The ocean was very rough most of the time so many became seasick day and night. There were daily boat drills where you had to put on life jackets and go to an assigned station. I noticed right away that the ship did not have a sufficient number of boats. I thought if something should go wrong, how does one survive in frigid waters. We started our voyage the night of Halloween in October 1944, and I thought this must be a trick because there sure was not a treat in sight. Here I was in the middle of the Atlantic Ocean and could not swim which everyone was supposed to know. Prior to going overseas everyone had to go through several tests. One was swimming so with guards close by you had to jump into the pool and start swimming. I jumped and down I go to be rescued by the guards. First Sergeant Daniels said "PASSED" and checked me off as being able to swim. I told him later you know I can't swim. He said "Look Hughes, even if you could swim, how far do you think you could go in the middle of an ocean." When I looked out over all that water and high waves I thought by Golly he's right so we are all in the same boat. There were many details as usual but nothing really meaningful to do for almost 2 weeks. We could go on deck at times and do exercises. Card and crap games were the plays of the day and night. At times we could see other ships so we knew we were in a convoy with destroyer escorts. We were told by members of the British crew that several supply ships had been sunk by German submarines therefore our route was not a direct one to Great Britain. They did not know where we would be landing so not knowing did not help. The seasick pills did not help much so many of us avoided the problem by just not eating much of anything. I lost a good 5 pounds. We hardly saw any of the officers as they were quartered separately. The senior NCOs were tasked to keep watch over the men. In spite of the discomfort, the men made the best of it. We finally landed in Liverpool on 11 November 1944, currently known as Veteran's day. What a great feeling it was to touch solid ground again? It was a very bad experience I hoped I would never have to repeat.[2]

Corporal James Baldwin adds: "The *Moreton Bay* was an old ship and was a rough ride. The ship was very uncomfortable: overcrowded, bad food, and seasickness."[3]

Tech-5 James Hamilton describes this same sea voyage: "We went to Camp Shanks, New York, and from there we shipped overseas to Europe. That was a pretty rough ride going across that ocean. We had submarines and destroyers there to protect us. When we hit England, we looked up, and we were in Liverpool. It was pitch black dark. No lights or anything. We got on a troop train and from there we went to Pontypridd, Southern Wales."[4]

Sergeant Simmons Washington adds:

We went across the Atlantic and it took us about 10 to 14 days. We had to run a course to stay away from the submarines and we would change courses often. There were a lot of ships in the convoy. The water was kind of rough because it was in October and the weather was bad. The Atlantic was rough out there. We landed in Liverpool and caught a train to South Wales. We stopped at South Wales and then went back to Liverpool to pick up our tanks and equipment. Then back to South Wales to the port of embarkation into France.[5]

From November 12 until December 18, 1944, while at Pontypridd, South Wales, the unit trained in the parks and the Mortar Platoon did some brush-up firing. The people were very different from back home, Sergeant Bill Hughes recalls:

The people were reserved but friendly. I had to listen very closely because their English sounded very different from American. The left hand drive on the streets and roads was a surprise, not to mention the difference in words for their meaning (e.g., a truck was called a lorry, a boy was called a lad, a lawyer was called a solicitor and so on). There were many words that were quite different from our English words, but meant the same thing. You just had to get use to them. Very noticeable was the respect people gave you and their politeness. It was a good feeling of getting away from segregation and discrimination and being treated on an equal footing. I thought we would not be staying in Wales for a long time but one day I must come back to see the rest of Great Britain and its people. I was impressed by just how orderly they were and the care they gave their homes and villages. We were located to Pontypridd, Wales and came into very close contact with the populace. Company D orderly room was located in the basement of a church where I slept. I will never forget being awakened early one morning hearing the singing of beautiful male voices. Pontypridd was located in a valley and when I jumped up from my cot bed and looked up into the hills, I could see men carrying candles and singing while walking to the pits (coal mines mind you). Their voices were ringing down into the valley so loud and clear. It looked like the whole hill was moving with flickering candlelight. I learned later that a very impressive Hollywood movie was made in Pontypridd called *How Green Was My Valley*. Singing was a great past time in Wales. There were many clubs and competitive recitals all the time. We were invited several times to join in singing at events. I participated having been much into music while in high school including the senior choir.
 A certain percentage of the men were permitted to go out in the evening between 7–10 PM on pass without restrictions to attend public places and meet people. The men behaved very well and got along well with the people. I noticed the children to be ahead of American children in school in subjects such as math, English, and history. They also showed more discipline at home and school and had better manners. The people had a lot of tradition behind them and were very proud to join in with their dances and festivities. I had not experienced this feeling before of community belonging. We stayed very busy during the day checking our new tanks and equipment, inspections, tank drills, marches, classes. We had to march to and from our tank area through the middle of the village. This was an impressive sight for the people to see as it was done with a singing cadence and quick time prances etc. The people loved it and so did the men. Our stay in Pontypridd was not that long, approximately 6 weeks. I did not get to know England really until after the war when I spent almost 9 months in a university and technical college there while still in the service waiting for time to discharge from the Army. I remember particularly one family that befriended me in Pontypridd. Owen and Gwen Cooke,

who had 2 young daughters named Brenda and Pamela. Owen was a professional baker and his goods were fantastic. Gwen was a good cook so I was there very often to have dinner with them. They treated me as a long lost son and I will never forget their kindness and care. Brenda was 10 yrs old and a very good ballet dancer. The younger daughter was 8 yrs old and was taking up acting. I often wondered about them but have not been successful in locating them. Pontypridd records reveal they moved to London in the 1950s. Not much here. The old buildings, street layout, and creek running thru the village gave it a nice peaceful flair where everyone knows each other and got along so well.[6]

Staff Sergeant Franklin Garrido adds:

I felt hostility from white American enlisted men and officers because they didn't want the English girls to go after the Negro soldiers. They told them stories, just like Johnny Holmes said, we had tails, we were ignorant, and the only reason we had tanks was because we were bringing them up to the front for the white boys. They were the ones! The ones who put out the bad rumors, but I will say this, they failed. Many of the black soldiers had English girlfriends, some of them got married.[7]

On Thanksgiving Day, the men were the grateful guests of the Saint Catherine's Church in Pontypridd. The Reverend G. Shelton Evans, LD, delivered the address. The men furnished music for the occasion. Captain William Van Nortwick played the organ and First Sergeant Morris Harris led the choir. Sergeant Bill Hughes comments:

Staff Sergeant Franklin Garrido, 1944. *Courtesy Franklin Garrido*

I sure do remember the day but not the Service. I had sergeant of the guard detail that day and could not get another one to volunteer a swap with me. All the guys told me it was great and the Reverend made some very nice comments about our being in Pontypridd and prayed for our safety as well. I wanted to go so bad but my day was ruined checking guards for duty and their posts.[8]

December 18, 1944: the 784th departed Pontypridd and traveled in their newly issued vehicles to Weymouth, England, the port of embarkation (PE). Along the way they were forced to discontinue their road march due to severe weather in an area around Amesbury, England. On the 20th they continued with most vehicles intact. They arrived at the PE on the 22nd after traveling 217 miles. There they boarded Landing Craft Tanks (LCT) to cross the English Channel bound for Rouen, France.

Tech-5 James Hamilton illustrates:

> And then we went down to the beach and took our tanks with us and we had no ammunition. We had to clean the guns — the machine guns and all of the big guns. After we got them all clean they told us we were going to ship across the channel. Then the LCTs came there and pulled in to the shore. We ran our tanks on the LCTs, secured them and backed out going across the channel. The water was rough and one of our tanks broke loose in our boat and we had to go down there to grab it and chain it down again. It was dangerous! It almost knocked a hole in the ship. Then we landed in France by the River Seine.[9]

Christmas Day, 1944: Rouen, France — the 784th Tank Battalion, with 693 men (40 officers and 653 enlisted men), rolled ashore on the continent of Europe with their new M4-A3 Sherman tanks.

A problem that loomed on the minds of the tankers was that their Sherman tank could not go toe-to-toe with the German Panther and Tiger tanks, especially at long range. They were relieved to learn that engaging those massive battlewagons would not be a typical activity of an infantry support tank unit.

A war correspondent with the 3rd Armored Division noted later in the war that captured German tankers had a common joke: "*Von off our tanks iss besser zan 10 off yours, but you alvays haff elefen.*"[10]

Army regulations had prohibited vehicles wider than 124 inches because of shipping constraints. This maximized the number of Sherman tanks that made it to the ETO, far exceeding the number of German tanks, especially Panthers and Tigers. Besides, tanks were not supposed to get bogged down fighting other tanks. That was the job of the Tank Destroyers.

5

Baptism of Fire

December 26, 1944: the 784th Tank Battalion began a long road march towards Germany. During this period, the Battle of the Bulge raged through Belgium and the weather was miserably cold with overcast skies and intermittent snow flurries.

Sergeant Bill Hughes, Dog Company, 784th Tank Battalion relates:

We had learned the Germans were making an all out effort to stop our fighting forces in a last ditch stand to keep us from crossing the Rhine. I knew we were headed for the front and I wondered where we would start fighting. Many thoughts passed through my mind about how well we and our equipment would stand up against seasoned enemy troops. I thought about how well the men kept the tanks and guns in great condition. I thought about how much time I had spent tuning the radios, over and over again. With that thought in mind, I wondered what would happen if we were ordered to maintain radio silence. I hoped that would not be the case because all tanks would not be in view and you could not warn others of enemy locations and where to direct fire. I wondered if we would be fighting against tanks, foot soldiers, artillery, etc. I hoped we would not be tasked to fight the German Tiger tank with that 88-millimeter gun. I thought about the men getting wounded or killed and not getting back to their families. It was a very nagging thought and I wanted to get it off my mind, but it never entirely went away. I thought about a direct hit on the tank or losing a track disabling the tank. What would be the best course of action? Well, I thought I am not going to be a sitting duck so the best thing is to get out of there; preferably through the hatch but kept in mind the bottom escape panel that could be removed as another means of getting out. I thought about the things to take with us if we had to abandon the tank like personal weapons, ammunition, flares, flashlights, maps, ID panel, and that .30-caliber machine gun as well as rations. Many things ran through my mind about family and friends, with prayers to keep every one safe from harm. I knew that would not be likely. Someone is not going to make it back home. Who will it be and how terrible it would be to see one of the men die? Finally, I thought about having to shoot someone. Could I do it? Would it be right? How can I pray to keep us safe and kill someone who may have also prayed for a safe return home? It was a very disturbing thought. The morale of the men was very good and I knew they could be depended upon so that was a very comforting thought.[1]

December 26, 1944: approaching Soissons, France, en route to join the 104th Infantry Division, the 784th heard bomb blasts. As the explosions increased in intensity and rapidity, the troops discovered the source, a flaming ammunition train. An ammunition company officer requested and received their help in saving the un-detonated rail cars. Using tanks as recovery vehicles, the men worked all afternoon while the explosions from heavy caliber ammunition continued. Shrapnel fell all around as they saved 160 of the original 300 rail cars. For their efforts and bravery, they received several cases of champagne for the coming New Year's celebration. After this diversion, the unit performed maintenance on their vehicles and immediately continued their road march.

Tech-5 James Hamilton, Charlie Company, 784th Tank Battalion recounts:

> As we were trying to get some ammunition, Bed Check Charlie came over trying to bomb the ammunition dumps. Our commander, Lt. Colonel Dalia, he went with one of the recovery vehicles and hooked it onto one of the freight trains and pulled 5 cars out. That guy was something else! Then we got our ammunition and everything and started up to Germany."[2]

Sergeant Bill Hughes gives his account:

> I definitely remember this incident because we heard the explosions and at first thought the city was being bombed or artillery rounds were being fired on the city of Soissons, France. That thought was dismissed when we were halted and in haste a team of tanks and other vehicles were gathered to make an attempt to save some of the cars of ammunition from exploding. My company, "D" was not directly involved because our tanks were too light to pull heavy ammunition cars. Medium tanks were used and some tank recovery vehicles. I did monitor some of the radio conversations and learned the men were being successful in attaching cables to the cars and pulling one after another to safety. Fortunately, it was daylight so the operation went very smooth. There was no panic although the danger was there. I don't know how many cars were saved but it could have been over a hundred. The men had no time for rest and worked until the early evening. I heard they did get a good meal and some great French wine that night. I was surprised to hear later that a bomb may have set off the first explosion, which was followed later by rapid explosions one after another. The main thing is no one got hurt. We continued our drive to meet up with the 104th Infantry Division.[3]

Sergeant Simmons Washington, Headquarters Company, 784th Tank Battalion adds:

> It was a little scary because after we pulled out from England, we started seeing what war was really all about. Then we landed at Le Harve and we saw everything torn up, ships

sunk, houses blown apart, it was really nasty. By the time we arrived, the Germans got on us. They started bombing our ammunition. We had to try to save our ammunition. That was near Soissons. That was our first taste of battle. Then we moved from there and went north. We were not in the Battle of the Bulge but we were near that area. You could tell because it was rough all over the place — cold, snowing, it was bad. That was in December 1944.[4]

At night each tank crew member had to complete a 2-hour shift of guard duty while the others slept in their seats. At times they would sleep on the engine compartment absorbing the last remnants of heat from the cooling motors — a comfortless existence.

The 784th had endured a tedious 6-day road march across France and Belgium and through portions of Holland at Maastricht to reach Eschweiler, Germany. They traveled over icy roads and through dense fog and biting cold. Vehicles with metal tracks did not maneuver well on the ice and slid in every direction. The tanks had been pushed to extremes. The tank drivers and assistant drivers performed first echelon maintenance while the rest of the crew cleaned and maintained their weapons. The road-weary outfit broke up and started attaching to units within the 104th Infantry Division.

Tech-5 James Hamilton recalls reaching the 104th Infantry Division: "We made it up to Aachen, Germany. There was a forest out there and we lined up our tanks and they told us that at 0300 hours we were going to level that forest. They put microphones and everything out there telling the Germans to come out but they didn't come out. So at 0800 hours we leveled it. The whole forest was leveled there like a lawn mower went across it.[5]

Sergeant Simmons Washington adds: "The 104th Infantry Division was a good outfit. We never had any problems with them and we worked well together. Our battalion was always split up. We went our separate ways. Sometimes we didn't see each other for a month. Our 81-millimeter mortar platoon always stayed together while being attached to different tank and infantry units. We always come back to Headquarters Company."[6]

Dog Company and their M5 light tanks found shelter in an abandoned factory complex that shielded them and their vehicles from the harsh winter elements. Sergeant Bill Hughes gives a painful account:

> We were on the move to join the 104th Cavalry Reconnaissance Troop and after a tiresome drive it was decided we should do first echelon maintenance and take rest in a town called Eschweiler (near Aachen, Germany). Company D was assigned to bed down in an old bombed out factory. We were told it was used earlier as a factory that made coal briquettes used to heat many homes instead of coal. Earlier the place was a coal mine-processing factory. The place was large enough to shelter our tanks and vehicles. As far as I can recall, it was New Year's Eve because some of the men had obtained cases of champagne on the drive through France and celebrated. The officers closed their eyes on this activity because they also celebrated with forbidden fruit. The next day we were up early performing

maintenance checks on the tanks. About 10:30 AM on Jan 1st 1945, a formation of bombers flew over us heading toward Aachen or Koln. There were a total of 12, I remember counting. A half hour later the ground beneath rumbled and shook. Another half-hour and they were on the way back passing over us again heading I thought must be England. Twenty minute later another wave would appear. This constant bombing kept up all morning and most of the day. The flyovers were so regular you could time it. You could see some bombers were missing or limping back out of formation. About 1430 hours someone yelled "TAKE COVER AND CLOSE YOUR HATCH, THEY ARE DROPPING BOMBS ON US" Sure enough it was true. I saw the first one hit about 300 yards away and ducked in the hatch and closed the cover. The second one was closer because I could hear bomb fragments hitting the side of the tank. I thought oh my God, I have to get out of here because the next one might be a direct hit. This was false thinking on my part because bombs fall in a skipping pattern; not several in the same spot unless more than one bomber is involved in a strike. How could I know this? I climbed out of the tank to make a run for it when the next bomb hit some 200 yards away. The pressure knocked me to the ground and I ran in a half crouch position toward an exit. All of a sudden, a .30-caliber belt of ammunition went off in the company commander's jeep. The driver Corporal Curly was riddled with bullets as he was loading the gun. I fell to the ground and crawled for "dear life" as did several others behind me. We made it to a building about 50 yards away and climbed down some basement steps. I was shaking all over and incoherent for several minutes. I cried "bitter tears" as several men carried not only the Corporal, but also another body past me. Needless to say, there was chaos for about a half an hour. Finally a formation was called to see who was accounted for or missing. There were only 2 and I believe Company D suffered the first casualties in the battalion on 1 January 1945. I have been deeply bothered by this event because the company clerk who took my place much earlier was not allowed to type the death reports. No one was allowed to see the bodies. No comforting remarks from the company commander, no prayers of mourning which really upset the men. About 2–3 hours later, I saw a marked ambulance carrying the bodies away. To this very day, I wonder where they are buried, if their loved ones were properly notified, and if they were told the truth that they were killed by our own American bombers. I learned later that bomber pilots were given primary and secondary targets. If they missed both, they were told to drop them on any signs of enemy activity or structures. Above all, "DON'T BRING THOSE BOMBS HOME!" If you crash with that load, it will destroy the runway. I guess this makes sense but why Company D? We had fluorescent air ID panels all over the place because the German air power was nil. It was a bright clear day so the pilot had to see the friendly panels. I wish I had those 2 men's serial numbers and full names; but I don't and that bothers me.[7]

The 784th Tank Battalion quickly learned that they would have to fear their own air forces. "Friendly fire" attacks against tanks had been reported with some consistency since Normandy, and they continued until the closing days of the war.

In an area between Duren and Murken, along the west bank of the Roer River, the 784th Tank Battalion linked up with the 104th "Timber Wolves" Infantry Division. There they supported this division as they held and defended their position. The tanks fired alongside the artillery in a coordinated fire mission directed across the river. Each tank platoon was given an aiming point, the proper elevation, and deflection for its guns. Observing the bombardment through binoculars, the field of death appeared to be boiling with its building melting into it.

At times some targets could not be engaged due to the shortage of ammunition that went to priority units in the Ardennes (Battle of the Bulge). The "Timber Wolves" held their ground and constantly maintained their aggressive defense by patrolling and executing stinging raids on enemy positions on the east bank of the river.

Sergeant Bill Hughes explains this attachment:

> As far as I can recall, this was the first infantry division we were attached to in combat. The battalion became fragmented since companies were assigned to various elements of the 104th Infantry Division. We were not in a cohesive fighting force posture and this surprised the men. As an example, the companies were assigned to various units of the 104th. I can't remember their exact assignments; but D Company was assigned to some reconnaissance outfit of the 104th where other companies were assigned elsewhere with different mission objectives. I think I can safely say we did not like this because we never knew exactly where the other companies were or who was in charge of the battalion. Orders came down from division elements; not the battalion so the men were uneasy about this.[8]

Dog Company, severely bloodied and still staggering from the friendly fire attack, linked up with the 104th Cavalry Reconnaissance Troop (CRT) to support them with their light tanks. Sergeant Bill Hughes recalls:

> It was along the Roer River where we met up. The 104th CRT had set up a command post (CP) near the river but I can't remember the closest village. The CP was in a wooded area in a house belonging to the State managed by the Forest Master. It was nice and cozy with a log fireplace, bunk beds, game records, and a stockpile of game feed. Well water, lamplights, and no toilets. The woods were it if nature called. I was there twice. The first time was with Platoon Leader Waters. We drove the jeep along the river road and on the other side of the river you could see enemy troop movement. We were covered fairly well but there were openings where you could be seen. I was driving the Jeep so whenever we were exposed, Waters directed me off into the woods. We returned to the road without incident and finally reached the CP. The only thing bad about the CP was that it must have been known to the Germans because they would send in mortar and artillery fire. It was very nerve wrecking. When we left the CP Lieutenant Waters said they did not like his being there as a platoon leader. They directed that Captain Powers, Dog Company Commander, be there the next day at exactly noon. We reached Captain Powers who directed that I go the next day with him since I knew the route. About 1030 hours the next day we took off. Captain Powers insisted on driving the jeep. When we came to a clearing, I told him we should take out into the woods. He said for WHAT? We will be across here in no time. Twenty-five meters later WHAM! There came a mortar shell behind us. I shouted again to turn into the woods. He said "DAMMIT! Sergeant Hughes! I am driving this jeep! You just stay with that machine gun in the ready." The next round, WHAM was not a direct hit but landed in front of the jeep causing it to tip over on to its side. We managed to scramble out to the woods and crawled until we thought it safe and walked to the

Private Pullens (left) and Sergeant Spencer of the 81 Millimeter Mortar Platoon, HQ Company, 784th Tank Battalion, in Germany, 1945. *Courtesy James Baldwin*

CP 10 minutes late. The colonel was furious until he learned why? He directed a halftrack with a winch go recover the jeep and I had to go along. The jeep was still drivable but the windshield was shattered so we had to return to the company area with it turned down. I was the designated driver on the return trip needless to say. There are several things that annoyed me about this incident. The captain not heeding my warnings, which could have gotten both of us killed or seriously injured. Then too, I was very unhappy that Captain Powers purposely left the colonel with the impression that I was to blame for the delay since he said "MY DRIVER and I got into a little trouble coming up here." I am sure the colonel thought I was driving that jeep. Even in combat, reports have to be made so I saw that report on the Jeep damage. One Line Told IT ALL! "DRIVER OF THE VEHICLE: SERGEANT William M. Hughes." It listed Captain Powers as the COMMANDER OF THE VEHICLE. We supported the 104th CRT in prodding to test the enemy defense posture.[9]

Headquarters Company wasted no time moving out. Corporal James Baldwin, Headquarters Company, 784th Tank Battalion recounts:

The 81-Millimeter Mortar Platoon would get briefings but they would not tell us too much. It was rumored that we were going into combat. It was on a Sunday and we moved out that morning about 0530 hours in our half-tracks. We rode in a line formation, one vehicle behind the other. After riding in a line formation for hours, we were ordered into a wedge formation, something like a triangle. The lead vehicle went ahead and we flanked it. About an hour after that we heard gunfire and we were in combat just that quick. We got those rounds off fast. Sergeant Washington gave me commands to fire that mortar: "Zero in on this! Zero in on that!" I was the gunner.[10]

January 28, 1945: the Battle of the Bulge was been declared officially over and the Germans began slowly withdrawing toward the Rhine River. Hitler had pulled his Sixth *Panzer* Army out of the Ardennes and sent them to slow down the tide on his eastern front. This action left huge gaps along his western front.

The 784th Tank Battalion ended the month of January 1945 with 91 reported casualties. Most came from frostbite caused by the extreme European winter and arduous operating conditions in the cold tanks, grimly referred to as "armored Frigidaires."

Three men were reported as wounded in action and 4 as non-battle injuries. The battle casualties were light due to the inactivity at the front.

There is no mention of anyone killed in the 784th Tank Battalion's journals or reports. However, the American Battle Monuments Commission reports something different. There is a Private Curley J. Ausmer (Service Number 4626994) from Mississippi, reportedly killed on January 10, 1945. This is the same name that Sergeant Bill Hughes remembered 59 years later. They also report 2 men listed as missing in action whose dates of death are unknown. Then there are 5 other men killed in action whose remains are unaccounted for by the American Battle Monuments Commission. They most likely had been shipped back home for interment.

February 3, 1945: somewhere near Eschweiler, Germany, the 784th Tank Battalion was released from the 104th Infantry Division and assigned to the 35th "Santa Fe" Infantry Division.

Staff Sergeant Franklin Garrido illustrates an incident during which he fought as an infantryman while on his way to the 35th Infantry Division:

> One of the things that can happen and usually does happen to tankers when spearheading without stopping to lube the bogy wheels is that they burn out. That's what happened to me. We were spearheading, going as fast as we could without stopping when the bogy wheel, at least one, in my tank burned out. We pulled over to the side where an armored division was bivouacked. Two other tanks from the battalion also pulled over because they too had burnt out bogy wheels. I was the highest-ranking noncom there so I took charge. The first thing we did was beg the armored division for a couple of cases of ten-in-one rations, which they gave us. The next thing we did was to get "Preacher," who was a member of another crew, to evacuate civilians in a house so that we could use it as a command post. He was a preacher. He was always quoting the gospel. He is the one person who could really evict people from their houses. Within minutes he had them flying out the door. While we were there waiting for Service Company to come up and put on our new bogy wheels, an infantry lieutenant came up to us and asked if he could borrow one of our machine guns. I was a little bit leery because I might not get it back. I told him, how about us taking it and going along with you? I'll ask my gunner if he will go with you. That was okay with him just as long as he had the machine gun. They were notified that on a hill a few kilometers away was a German encampment. He was ordered to capture the hill. The lieutenant had a squad of infantrymen, which we call doughs, from doughboy. When we had to shoot at German infantrymen coming toward us, we referred to them as doughs. Any infantry, we called them doughs.
>
> We loaded up on a weapons carrier and drove to the base of the hill. We spread out and charged. I was in armor, the whole time being in tanks. I was not used to running against the enemy without any protection around me. I felt naked. We were ordered to fall and fire. We fired. I had my grease gun with me and fired along with the machine gunner I was commanding. I fed ammunition to the machine gunner. We did that about 3 times before reaching the top of the hill. There were 2 Germans there. One was intact and the other was lying on the ground groaning. The wounded man was shot by a dough. He just walked up to him and dropped his M1 on his temple and let go. The other must have been drinking a lot of schnapps because he acted as if he was intoxicated. We left the dead on the top of the hill and took the other German prisoner. On the way back, one of the doughs took his canteen and smelled it and sure enough, he smelled alcohol.[11]

February 8, 1945: Geilenkirchen, Germany — the 784th Tank Battalion attached to the veteran 35th Infantry Division. The Division's After Action Report put it this way: "We received the 784th Tank Battalion which soon proved itself as an effective, courageous, and dependable unit which earned the respect and admiration of the infantrymen who worked together well with the tankers."[12]

The following 2 paragraphs are intended to aid the reader unaccustomed to terms used in this book regarding military organizations:

The 784th Tank Battalion was composed of Companies Able, Baker, and Charlie.

Sergeant Walter "Pop" Hall's tank dozer extricates a 784th truck mired in an underwater bomb crater near Merode, Germany, February 13, 1945. *Courtesy U.S. Army Military History Institute, Carlisle Barracks, Pennsylvania*

In support they had Dog, Service, and Headquarters Companies, along with a medical detachment. Companies Able, Baker, and Charlie operated with the Sherman medium tanks, the embodiment of the battalion. Dog Company, the "Mosquito Fleet," operated with the Stuart light tanks. Service Company took charge of maintenance, administration, transportation, mess, etc. Headquarters Company had the 105-millimeter Assault Gun Platoon, the 81-Millimeter Mortar Platoon, and the Reconnaissance Platoon.

The configuration of the US Army at this time was the "Tri-system." With some exceptions, each unit had 3 elements along with supporting units. For example, each army had 3 corps; each corps had 3 divisions; each division had 3 regiments; each regiment had 3 battalions; each battalion had 3 companies; each company had 3 platoons; etc. The 784th Tank Battalion, a medium tank battalion, operated with 3 medium tank companies, Able, Baker, and Charlie. They also had 3 supporting companies, Dog, Service, and Headquarters. When the 784th attached to a division, each of the medium tank companies would get assigned to one of the division's 3 regiments.

The attachment to the 35th Infantry Division started out as follows: Able Company attached to the 134th Infantry Regiment, Baker Company to the 137th Infantry Regiment, Charlie Company to the 320th Infantry Regiment, and Dog Company to the 35th Cavalry Reconnaissance Troop. Soon platoons, sections, and individual tanks shifted among different units within the division. The company commanders took orders from the infantry commanders. Yet no one ever forgot that they proudly belonged to the 784th Tank Battalion.

This battle-hardened division, commanded by Maj. General Paul Baade (USMA 1911), had landed on Omaha Beach in July 1944 and fought in the Normandy hedgerows north of Saint Lo. Then, for the next 126 days of almost continuous combat, the division fought through Northern France and into Germany. After a brief rest they participated in the Battle of the Bulge. Elements of this unit were among the first American troops to reach the beleaguered 101st Airborne Division trapped in Bastogne. Now the 35th Infantry Division, with the armored support of the 784th Tank Battalion, would help spearhead the U.S. Ninth Army's drive into the German heartland.

Sergeant Simmons Washington remembers the "Santa Fe" Division: "We stayed with them longer than we stayed with any other infantry division. They were a very good outfit too. They were really some fighting guys. We got along fine."[13]

Geilenkirchen is situated within the northernmost reaches of the infamous Siegfried Line, approximately 14 miles northwest of Aachen. Here the 784th Tank Battalion, in a coordinated effort, assaulted Hitler's previously penetrated but still formidable Siegfried Line. This defense system stretched from Kleve, Holland, down along the western border of the old German Empire, to the Swiss border. This 392-mile stretch contained bunkers, tunnels, tank traps, and pillboxes. Many of these pillboxes had walls as thick as ten feet, designed to withstand direct artillery fire. Natural vegetation grew over them for years, making them nearly impossible to detect. Other pillboxes were constructed to appear as houses, barns, haystacks, and even outhouses that blended harmoniously with the natural landscape. Many of them contained anti-tank guns and other direct fire weapons. These strong points had further protection by patterns of mines and barbed wire; complicated mazes of zigzagged anti-tank ditches; and concealed enemy tanks and artillery waiting behind reverse slopes.

Most of the tank traps, also known as Dragon's Teeth, had reinforced concrete blocks standing in several irregular rows on a single concrete foundation. However, in this area of the Siegfried Line, the concrete tank obstacles could not be used effectively due to the soft muddy terrain. Instead, water-filled dugouts and trenches proved effective in delaying tanks.

This area of the Seigfried Line had several *Volksgrenadier* (people's grenadier) Divisions defending it. The *Wehrmacht* had suffered exorbitant losses of men and divisional

5. Baptism of Fire

structure on both fronts. Fair estimates approximate the loss of 25 divisions, 200,000 men, and 30 generals. In response, they created completely new divisions — the *Volksgrenadiers*. They built each new division around the remnants of a regular infantry division. They simply added stragglers, boys, old men, and 'anyone whose seeing-eye dogs didn't have flat feet." The name grenadier implies elite warriors — simply propaganda. These new units made their offensive debut in the Battle of the Bulge and failed miserably. After that they were used exclusively for defensive operations mainly behind the Siegfried Line.

Infantryman Murray Leff, Easy Company, 137th Infantry Regiment recalls fighting with the tanks of the 784th:

> The tanks were such a large target and of course the 88s made them very vulnerable. The Tiger tanks, they were really no match for a Tiger tank with an 88. A lot of Shermans got

The remains of a German soldier appear as snow melts near Merode, Germany. Members of the 784th load shells into their tank, February 13, 1945, *Courtesy U.S. Army Military History Institute, Carlisle Barracks, Pennsylvania*

taken out that way. I know that. But, when they talk about the effectiveness of the Sherman against the Tiger tank, certainly the Tiger tank had the big advantage. But as far as we were concerned, there weren't that many Tiger tanks around. So we were the beneficiaries almost like there was no other opposition because most of the time there wasn't any. So when we go across the field with the tanks we really feel somewhat invulnerable. Anyway, that was a high morale booster when you have those Shermans along with you.

Most of the shooting I saw from the tanks came from their machine guns rather than the cannons and that was really very heartening for us because we were so exposed and even for us to shoot would be revealing our positions. Of course they were very obvious where they were and their shooting would keep the Germans' heads down so we could move. They threw a shell every once in a while and that was very discouraging to the Germans but of course improved our morale.

I was probably a little unusual in the way I would advance across an open field. I would run from one depressed area to another, or somewhere to get cover. I would run out ahead and stay there until the tanks passed and run some more until I could find something. I was always looking for a place where I could get some protection.

At one point prior to beginning an attack across an open field, I was in a ditch and there was a Sherman right above me and he let a round go from his 75. I was right under it! It knocked me around! I couldn't recover for a little while from the concussion.[14]

Infantryman Murray Leff went on to point out the advantages of being in a tank:

The tankers carry their foxholes with them. They don't have to dig holes. They take their shelter from the wind and the rain with them. I envied them being inside something, they were out of the weather at least. I had been wet and that was cold enough, but when the cold wind hit me, I really looked at the tanks and thought gee I really wish I could get in there. And I did ask and they told me there was no room and of course there isn't. Another thing I envied about the tankers is that they could carry stuff with them such as the 10-in-1s. We had them only when it got very quiet and it could be brought up to us, and also when we were in reserve. The tanks could also carry water, which was very heavy. For water to be brought up to us was quite a thing. I know this because I was on water-carrying detail on occasion. The 5-gallon Jerry cans of water felt like 50 or 60 pounds. To carry that up at night over bad terrain could really be a hard thing to do. The tankers could almost always have water.[15]

6

The Raging Roer River

Early February 1945: along the west bank of the Roer River — the 784th Tank Battalion stood ready to support the 35th Infantry Division's assault to cross this narrow and winding passage of water. In the skies above, bombers passed by daily on their way to drop lethal tonnage on enemy industrial and strategic targets. Behind the east bank, the enemy frantically continued to improve their defenses by herding in civilians and forcing them to dig anti-tank ditches. The enemy held a tight grip on the floodgates of the dam.

February 10: Operation Grenade was scheduled to jump off with Lt. General William Simpson's U.S. Ninth Army crossing the Roer River to link up with the Canadian First Army coming from points north. British Field Marshall Sir Bernard Montgomery directed Operation Grenade as commander of the Twenty-first Army Group. He controlled the Canadian First Army, the British Second Army, and the U.S. Ninth Army at this, the northernmost front facing Germany.

This narrow and slow-moving river meanders southeast from the Maas River at Roermond, Holland, and flows through scenic German countryside. The unseasonably warm weather melted snow and swelled the river, causing it spill over. The Wurm River and the tributary creeks in the area also rose to such an extent that the U.S. Ninth Army postponed Operation Grenade for 24 hours. To complicate matters more, the Canadians attacking southeasterly along the west bank of the Rhine River, planning to link up with the northward-attacking U.S. Ninth Army to put a pincer around the enemy Roer River defenders, were cut off. When it seemed it could not get worse, all hell broke loose! The Germans opened the floodgates at the mighty Schwammenauel Dam and also destroyed the power-room machinery, making it impossible to stop the flow of water. Tons of raging water gushed out, sweeping away men and equipment from both sides. The entire Roer Valley became inundated, making the grounds impassable for tanks. The river, normally 25 to 30 yards across, had spread out to 300 to 400 yards across with sharp currents. In one area it spread out like a lake, approximately a mile wide. Operation Grenade had to be postponed indefinitely.

Combat Engineer Robert Martin, 208th Engineer Combat Battalion remembers making preparation to construct a bridge:

> My company stopped at Maastricht, Holland. The company commander sent me and my squad to Mariadorf to get the pilings ready for the bridge on the Roer River that wasn't even taken yet. So after we were out there for 2 weeks and gathered all of this here material and put points on them, like telephone poles, so they can drive them into the ground to make a base for the bridge. They drove the pilings in with a machine with a boom on it and a weight. The captain came out to see us and brought our mail. He was amazed that all of the guys in my squad were busy, clean-shaven, looked like soldiers and just clean — period! This one boy was a cook, he went around and gathered enough stuff to make a pot of stew with cabbage and I don't know what else. The captain, he took the lid off of it and he started laughing. We asked him if he cared for a dish of it and he said no. Anyhow, he was really happy. When he went back to the company that night he had a meeting and he said: "Damnit! I wish I had more soldiers in this company like Sergeant Martin!" I didn't know he was going to say that but when we got back to the company all of the guys were asking questions — what were we doing out there? Well, he must have had a lot of faith in me to let me take my squad out 60 miles away from the company for 2 weeks.
>
> We kept camouflaged during the daytime or whenever we were not doing a job. We would put our equipment in a place where it was naturally camouflaged and then added nets and whatever to it. In Julich, Germany, is where I got the piling ready for the fixed bridge and one of the other platoons in my outfit were clearing a beachhead and checking it for mines and a young lieutenant had the guys with their bayonets down on the ground. One guy hit a mine and it blew up. It blew part of his ears off, part of his nose, blinded him, deafened him, and blew some of his teeth out. I saw him and what a sight! I never thought the man would live. They rushed him back to the hospital. A friend of his who was in my outfit, he got word that Junior Horack had made it back home but he had to stay in the hospital for a long time. After that when his wife saw that he wasn't any good to her and she must have seen someone else she liked better, she dropped him like a hot potato. That was a shame, I thought — a sad story.[1]

Infantryman James Graff, Charlie Company, 134th Infantry Regiment recalls waiting to cross the Roer River:

> Our first day here light bombers of the Ninth Air Force came over to bomb Hilfarth, the only German-held position on the west bank of the Roer River. German AA guns shot one down. The next day over they came again, but this time they dropped their bombs short, right on us. The concussion was terrific and a 500-pound bomb landed on one of the pillboxes occupied by the 1st platoon. Alex Cameron (Michigan) suffered a broken shoulder and later was injured during a buzz bomb attack while in the hospital. All told we suffered 9 or 10 casualties (fortunately no fatalities) in this bombing. Some would

6. The Raging Roer River

dismiss this incident as accidental, but we cannot believe this. We were 1,500 to 2,000 yards from this town, it being all bottom ground and timber between our lines and the Germans. We knew that the Air Corps doesn't get credit for a mission unless they get rid of their bombs. The loss of a plane the day before led us to believe they unloaded the bombs short of their target and got out so they wouldn't have to face the German AA fire — Just another reason for the bad feeling between the infantry and the Air Corps. Not that we didn't appreciate the support we received from them, but in this case there was no excuse for it. We were supposed to jump off and cross the Roer River on February 10, but the night before zero hour the Germans opened the flood gates of huge dams below us sending millions of gallons of water to flood the Roer Valley. The Krauts had opened them just before the First Army could capture them.[2]

Combat Engineer Robert Martin, 1944. Courtesy *Robert Marin*

February 11: the 784th Tank Battalion and the enemy watched each other through binoculars across the raging flood. Even though tanks operated rarely at night, the infantry went at it nonstop. Enemy and 35th Infantry Division patrols continued to engage each other. Flare activity intensified during darkness. At one point an enemy patrol followed an American patrol back to the American lines and engaged them in a fierce firefight.

During this stand-down, the 784th Tank Battalion, along with the 35th Infantry Division, received several crushing artillery and mortar barrages from the other side of the river. Some of the shells, believed to be from 280-millimeter railway guns, landed and shook the earth and everything around it. These shells had dual action in that fragmentation could be obtained by either airburst or super-sensitive point detonation. They wreaked havoc upon the entire 35th Infantry Division sector. Then, to make matters worse, V-bombs, primitive ballistic missiles better known as buzz bombs, sputtered overhead before going silent and then smashing into random targets. The frantic buzzing unnerved many soldiers, always mindful that there is one single bullet or bomb out there addressed personally to them, but the buzz bomb was addressed to whom it may concern.

55

Combat Engineer Robert Martin recalls: "The buzz bombs had some big charges in them. When they ran out of fuel and hit, they blew up. They would take out almost half a block. They were powerful! No wonder England got tired of them. Jeeze!"[3]

The tanks of the 784th Tank Battalion fired alongside division artillery in coordinated fire missions directed across the Roer River. Infantryman Murray Leff, Easy Company, 137th Infantry Regiment points out:

> I saw the tanks used as mobile artillery where they were placed on a reverse slope of a hill to shoot high trajectory like all the conventional artillery does. I wondered all the time how they could spot their targets. I knew about the forward observers. All the artillery had that. I didn't know how they could correct their aim in the way all the other artillery did. I knew about mortar fire that was based on seeing an aiming stake for a point of reference. In other words, once they could fix the aiming device or whatever it is they had on this aiming stake, they would know how much deflection from that aiming stake they needed to be consistent in every shot they made. There is also the elevation. I know with mortars the elevation would give a very close approximation of how far that round would go. Mortars, unlike the other artillery, had little powder charges that they could add to the tail of the mortar round before it was slipped down the tube. They had charts showing this much elevation and how much power charge would go, say 1,500 meters. I can't remember if it was meters or yards but I know afterwards meters became standard. On machine guns they have an inclinometer, which goes on the receiver. It has a little bubble, like the carpenter's leveling tool, and once you had that centered, you then knew by the inclination how far the rounds would go. A range chart was made in daylight, aiming the machine gun at a target you wanted to hit later in the dark. Notes on elevation and deflection are made to bring the gun to bear in the dark. I didn't know how the tanks did it but apparently they must have had a way.[4]

To add to this barrage, the U.S. Army Air Forces bombed during the day and the British Royal Air Force bombed during the night. The enemy received no rest as the planes kept coming overhead like a conveyor belt dropping bombs in carpets. They left the fields burning and smoldering and the front lines resembled a landscape on the moon. This put many German soldiers out of action — dead, wounded, or in shock.

The 35th Infantry Division continued its aggressive defense of its sector on the west bank as sporadic enemy artillery fire and probing infiltration patrols continued. In a rear area the infantrymen received assault boat training. They also received training on concrete fortifications, the type directly across the Roer River in the Siegfried Line. The 784th Tank Battalion trained with the infantry in combined infantry/tank team tactics and the combat engineers received specialized training on enemy mines and booby traps. Infantryman Murray Leff recalls:

> We had some training back there to break the Siegfried Line. They formed us up into 10-man teams, one man to carry a flamethrower, another to carry explosives. We actually attacked the Maginot Line as practice. My job was the flamethrower and I'm a small guy and they gave me this heavy thing. But we never actually did it. I don't even remember the Siegfried Line. We must have crossed a road at a point where it was not visible.[5]

6. The Raging Roer River

On the night of February 13–14, several extremely large groups of British bombers flew over the Roer in waves. Destination: East Germany. Mission: plunge tons of incendiary bombs on the Saxon city of Dresden, the Florence of the Elbe. Key strategy: "disrupt and confuse" the German civilians on their home front and in effect weaken their resolve to continue fighting. The bombers rained horror on this city for half a day. What the British started at night with incendiaries, the Americans continued in the morning with conventional bombs. A vast firestorm ensued as a result of hundreds of smaller fires joining in a single massive inferno. This sucked up huge masses of oxygen to feed the firestorm and suffocated those cowering in nearby basements and bomb shelters. Those outside flew directly up into the inferno. This resulted in the obliteration of this historic city and the annihilation of approximately a third of its inhabitants, mostly women, children, wounded and recovering soldiers, and the elderly. A recent flood of refuges fleeing the Soviet advance, only 60 miles away, swelled the famous cultural center and got wedged up into the firestorm. After 14 hours of hell, long-distance Allied fighters added a finishing touch by strafing rescue workers and those who had huddled together on the banks of the Elbe during the hellish night. The exorbitant civilian death toll could only be estimated. Ranges varied from 135,000 to half a million. Some in the press called it one of the greatest atrocities ever perpetrated against a civilian population and later compared it to Hiroshima and Nagasaki.

Back at the Roer River, when the water level began to subside, the combat engineers resumed constructing pontoon bridges made up of long airtight floating drums. They attached steel cables strung across the river and solidly anchored on each shore. They placed treadways on the pontoons to provide tracks that allowed the tanks to cross. In the rear, fully loaded C-47 supply transport aircraft sat ready for airdrops.

The 134th Infantry Regiment sent a patrol to probe the town of Hilfarth, the last enemy stronghold on this side of the river. It had strategic importance because of an intact stone bridge that crossed over to the east bank. Infantryman James Graff recounts:

> The next night I was picked along with 11 others for a combat patrol. Our new lieutenant (Conley Cox, Texas) was to take us close to Hilfarth where we were to open up on the Germans and draw their fire, and he was to radio back to a couple of tanks that would fire on any automatic weapons. He would adjust their fire. We moved out and up a road until we came to a knocked-out pillbox. We then cut right and moved through waist-deep water until we were within about 300 yards of the town. Lt. Cox wanted to move up to another tree line closer to town, but as there was a lot of open ground to cover, which was probably sown with mines; Baker, Christopher and I refused. As most of the other men were new, they also hesitated. We waited in the mud and water and then opened up with 6 BARs and 6 M-1s on the town. The tank fire knocked 2 Krauts out of a church steeple and also knocked out several more automatic weapons.[6]

February 23, 1945: the Roer River subsided enough for the U.S. Ninth Army to launch its drive to cross it. This entire army had spread out approximately 50 miles along the Roer River with the strength of over 300,000 men and approximately 2,000 tanks. At 0245 hours, more than 2,000 guns opened up at once in an ear-splitting Time-on-Target (TOT) barrage aimed at the east bank. The purpose of a TOT is to have shells from different guns arrive at the same time. This would catch more of the enemy out in the open, pinning them down to allow the attacking force to close with them, in this case, to cross the Roer River.

Forty-five minutes later the 320th Infantry Regiment jumped off. They crossed the Wurm River on improvised footbridges and consolidated their positions with the rest of the 35th Infantry Division along the Roer River. Other U.S. Ninth Army divisions were already in action on the east bank.

Combat Engineer Robert Martin recalls:

We were there to build a footbridge across the Roer River. Julich, Germany, was nothing but rubble and the streets were full of bricks. All of the buildings were down. There were no roads through there. We had to clear roads to get the vehicles through. Anyhow, the

A Pontoon Bridge crossing the Roer River at Julich, Germany. February 23, 1945. *Utah State Historical Society*

footbridges are built during the night, like at 0300 hours you start, and it doesn't take long. It all depends on how wide the river is and the Roer wasn't very big. It takes about an hour to build a footbridge if it's a normal size river. We struck a bridgehead by pinning down a base or something to start by. Then we put a cable on the other side and brought it back and studded it up. Then we just kept adding sections (prefab) to it to the other side. Anyhow, they were built and another outfit would come down, the infantry, to cross on that bridge. So here comes a new lieutenant and he has a squad of men, about 14. He sent 7 of them across the bridge and the Germans were dug in on the dike on the other side and they went "burrrrrrpt!" And that was the end of them. Before the lieutenant could think, he sent the other half of the squad across, which he never should have done. And got them killed! So then he said, "I guess it's too hot here for us, we'll go down to the next bridge site to cross." That's what he did and when he left Sergeant Huffacre said, "Let's all synchronize our watches. If I have any volunteers, I'll go across first." They went to see if they could get behind the Germans and throw hand grenades and whatever it took to stop them from shooting up our men. So that's what happened, we synchronized our watches and at that certain minute, we all started firing from the dike we were on to the other dike where it looked like the Germans were. And it must have been the right place because the Germans didn't fire any while the guys were going across. They went one at a time, not 7. They threw hand grenades where they could see the openings in the dike and they killed the Germans. When it was all over there were 9 Germans that had been dug in with machine guns set up. They pulled them out and left them on the bank for 2 days. Anyhow, that action probably saved more Americans. Sergeant Huffacre and the guy who went across with him, they had nerve enough to do that when they didn't have to.[7]

2200 hours, February 25, 1945: elements of the 134th Infantry Regiment assaulted Hilfarth in force. 784th Tank Battalion's Able Company along with the Assault Gun Platoon fired into Hilfarth in direct support of the infantry as they moved in under this fire. The barrage ceased when the Doughs made it in and around the burning structures. They began clearing the town and took the stone bridge intact before the Germans could blow it up. Two combat engineers, Tech-5 James Stanislau and Private Harold Wright, braved automatic weapons to cut the demolition wires and drop the explosive devices into the river. Access to the bridge had been denied to the enemy by the 161st Field Artillery Battalion's skillful use of interdiction artillery fire. They fired at a rate of one round per minute; that kept the enemy away from the bridge and surrounding area for days. Able Company, 784th Tank Battalion rolled into Hilfarth early the next morning and provided armored support in the mop-up operations. Next they crossed over into Doveren and attacked northeast.

After crossing to the east bank, elements of the 134th Infantry Regiment encountered several pillboxes and took numerous prisoners against moderate resistance as they captured several small towns. Each infantry platoon had 2 intrepid assault engineer soldiers attached who would move in under the tank and heavy weapons fire to plant ear-splitting blockbuster-type high explosive devices near the entrances of the pillboxes. The blast blew the pillbox occupants out of this world. The concussion from the tank's

75-millimeter high explosive shells stunned the pillbox occupants long enough to allow the combat engineers to plant these devices.

The following morning, Item Company, 134th Infantry Regiment, loaded up on the back of the 784th tanks for an assault on the town of Wassenberg. On the road into town, they encountered 3 deadly anti-tank guns that destroyed one 784th tank. That entire tank crew, less one man, escaped the inferno. Corporal Earl Morgan perished inside the blazing tank. The infantry captured 2 of the enemy anti-tank gun crews while the third crew escaped after destroying their weapon and ammunition.

On the following day, Able Company led elements of the 134th Infantry Regiment towards the crossroads at Birgelen. Anti-tank mines and roadblocks held up the advance. One tank hit a mine with minimal damage. The combat engineers moved forward and removed the mines, and the tanks blasted away the roadblocks. The enemy left their equipment and rations behind in their hasty withdrawal.

Meanwhile, Baker Company, 784th Tank Battalion supported the 137th Infantry Regiment in their crossing of the Roer River on a bridge in the 84th Infantry Division's sector. They went immediately on the attack to clear wooded areas and small towns while under a deadly barrage of intermittent fire from enemy artillery batteries that occupied positions along high grounds east of Gerderath.

Infantryman Bernard "Jack" Kirsch, Fox Company, 137th Infantry Regiment explains:

> We didn't cross on February 23rd, we crossed on the 26th, about 2 or 3 days later. We crossed and went north. That morning when we jumped off, our squad leader went back. He happened to be carrying a Thompson submachine gun. How he got it, I have no idea. It wasn't issued. He was afraid someone was going to take it. So he said to me, "Give me your rifle, and you take this Thompson till I get back." So we went up and then all at once, they called all automatic weapons to move forward. Well, I had that machine gun. And so here they made us a patrol to go out to draw fire. The purpose of the automatic weapons is to lay down as much firepower as we could.[8]

The 137th Infantry Regiment's After Action Report put it this way:

> Continuing the attack a second day, the 137th Infantry shoved ahead on February 27 and pitched the enemy out of Gerderath, Fronderath, Gerderhahn, and Almyhl. The regiment received exceptional work from Company "B" 784th Tank Battalion, a Negro unit which was attached to the 137th for this operation.... The 2nd Battalion launched its attack from K1 Gladbach at 0600 with the 784th tanks and tank destroyers from the 654th battalion. Spearheaded by Company "F" the battalion fanned out and went through the woods southwest of Gerderath, moved across the stream, and cleaned out a patch of woods 500 yards wide, below Myhl.... The work of Company "B" 784th Tank Battalion had been exceptional all day, and the Negro tankers supported the regiment in an excellent manner all day.[9]

Charlie Company, 784th Tank Battalion, in ready reserve with the 320th Infantry

Regiment, jumped off and joined the rest of the 35th Infantry Division. Infantry Intelligence Officer Orval Faubus, Staff/320th Infantry Regiment, recounts:

> The 134th is across the river on our right and has made good progress. Other forces push on toward Cologne farther south. Looks like it might be a wild day for us tomorrow and the following days. Seems we are to work with the 8th Armored Division. We are to cross the Roer River and cut north — work behind the Siegfried defenses in a move to entrap German forces there and still farther open the line.[10]

Infantry Reconnaissance Officer John Walsh, Cannon Company, 320th Infantry Regiment adds: "The 3rd Battalion, 320th was to lead off in crossing the Roer River. Lt. Colonel Joe Alexander from Chicago, snuck his battalion across by about 0300 and sent word back to call off the artillery. In his words, 'The shelling would only wake the Germans up.'"[11]

Between February 26 and 27, the 35th Infantry Division had routed the enemy out of 23 towns and villages. The "Santa Fe" Doughboys and the 784th Tank Battalion in coordinated assaults had routed the enemy from concrete strongholds, cellars, woods, and towns along the road to the Rhine River.

Operation Grenade came to a successful conclusion when the U.S. Ninth Army advanced up the western banks of the Rhine and linked up with the Canadian First Army advancing down the western banks.

The 35th Infantry Division's commanding officer, Maj. General Paul Baade, ordered the formation of Task Force Byrne, named after Colonel Bernard Byrne (USMA 1918), the commander of the 320th Infantry Regiment.

During the month of February 1945, the 784th Tank Battalion suffered 12 battle casualties and 48 non-battle casualties. Included in the battle casualties is Corporal Earl Morgan of New Jersey, killed in action, on February 27, 1945.

7

Task Force Byrne

March 1, 1945: in *Blitzkrieg* fashion, Task Force Byrne jumped off. Colonel Bernard Byrne's 320th Infantry Regiment executed the leading role. Support came from elements of the following units: the 216th Field Artillery Battalion, the 275th Field Artillery Battalion, the 654th Tank Destroyer Battalion, the 60th Engineer Combat Battalion, and the 110th Medical Battalion. The 784th Tank Battalion (less Able Company) spearheaded this task force with the objective of liberating the Dutch town of Venlo and pushing towards the Rhine River to their final objective, the town of Drupt, Germany.

Reconnaissance Officer John Walsh, Cannon Company, 320th Infantry Regiment sums up:

> In the late winter of 1945 Task Force Byrne was formed to make a dash for the Rhine River and expedite the crossing. Our mission was to gain a road to the vicinity of Venlo, Holland. The 320th Infantry Regiment was the core unit. Attached were an engineer battalion, an armored artillery battalion and a tank battalion. We also had the support of a trucking unit and all troops were mounted. As the reconnaissance officer of Cannon Company, 320th, I was part of the task force staff and traveled with the command group behind the leading battalion of the 320th mounted on the tanks. The tankers led the way and roadblocks were established at crossroads. In my recollection our sector of attack was narrowed to about several hundred yards on either side of the axis of advance. The tankers were aggressive in pushing forward and we moved along rapidly. My relationship with the tankers was minimal although I did witness the results of their aggressiveness. My own duties were to locate battery-firing positions for Cannon Company and communicate the locations to my commanding officer, so that timely forward displacements could take place. On at least one occasion I recall seeing a tank engaged in a firefight which resulted in the tank being set on fire and having to be abandoned by its crew.[1]

Able Company, 784th Tank Battalion, along with elements of the 134th and 137th Infantry Regiments, followed task force Byrne. They mopped up bypassed enemy forces and secured the flanks of the task force.

This motorized force dashed along the Roer River's Siegfried Line defenses on their way to liberate the Dutch people approximately 20 miles north of the U.S. Ninth Army's zone. Bypassing resistance, except in towns and villages, the task force moved so swiftly that the stunned enemy had no time to destroy bridges. The close coordination between the infantry and the tanks quickly wiped out any resistance. They passed barbed wire entanglements, abandoned foxholes and gun emplacements. They shoved aside the roadblocks or simply ran over them.

Infantry Platoon Leader Royal Offer, King Company, 320th Infantry Regiment recalls: "We went through so fast, the Germans would try to surrender and put up their arms, but we couldn't stop. The rear echelon had to take them. We would go right on through and the Germans with their hands in the air would soon take them down in disgust. Nobody would take them."[2]

Tech-5 James Hamilton, Charlie Company, 784th Tank Battalion will never forget this fast pace: "When I was driving, Irby was on my side. I was the bow gunner—.30-caliber machine gunner. So when I was on his side, man, we were moving so fast that when we came around a turn in a town, I slide right through a house. I mean we tore the whole house down."[3]

With the mission of reaching Venlo and making contact with the British, the task force outflanked and cut off a large segment of the Siegfried Line defenses as the overcast sky broke and began raining, making the off-road grounds difficult for tanks to maneuver.

Infantry Intelligence Officer Orval Faubus, Staff/320th Infantry Regiment, following behind the column recounts: "The hundreds of abandoned fox holes, trenches, emplacements, barb-wire entanglements, etc. which were part of the Siegfried defenses. The bridges over the AT ditches and small streams were not blown because the speed of our advance caught the enemy away from their prepared demolitions. Our engineers removed the charges and the bridges remain intact."[4]

The 784th Tank Battalion spearheaded in march-column formation with the light tanks as advanced recon (bait). They encountered light resistance until they reached the town of Niederkruchten, where roadblocks and sniper fire halted the advance. The resistance crumbled under the tanks machine gun fire that allowed the pinned-down infantry to remove the roadblocks. Without much delay the column knifed right through. The next major resistance came near Bracht but again was quickly wiped out. The task force moved on to its next obstacle, this time at the outskirts of Kaldenkirchen. Here more roadblocks, and sniper fire came from all directions. The tank crews, when buttoned up, had limited vision and relied on the infantry's hand signals to point out targets. The tanks blasted holes through buildings where enemy fire came from. This gave the doughboys access into those buildings and they mopped up. The tanks fired at anything that didn't seem right. Dutch Resistance Fighters pointed out enemy strongholds. This well-coordinated tank/infantry task force captured over 20 small towns and villages before they reached Venlo on March 2, 1945.

The task force began to meet smiling and waving people. Some gave the V-sign. At first this puzzled the American infantrymen. The black tankers immediately responded with the "Double V."

Infantry Platoon Leader Royal Offer recalls:

> I remember riding those tanks, that's for sure. I had a lot of respect for that officer in charge of that first tank. He really had control. Anything that was suspicious on the side, like haystacks or anything that could be a gun emplacement, he would say, "Tank number so and so." We could hear everything riding on the back. That tank would take off and he stayed after that tank until it got that mission completed. They were good. It was a mighty fine outfit. The commanders really took charge. That was the only time we rode on the back of tanks.
>
> That action was the most interesting part of my whole time in combat. We really moved and once you broke through the main line of resistance, all you had was back-up people, like supply, not the top troops. On these tanks we moved so fast that we didn't have many casualties. Anytime the bullets started to fly or something the tankers would button up. One of the fellows next to me on the tank called down to them, "Be sociable!" We were like sitting ducks on the back of those tanks.[5]

Meanwhile, Able Company, 784th Tank Battalion, not with Task Force Byrne, moved to the Dutch border in their support of the 134th Infantry Regiment. They headed towards the southern edge of Venlo with the mission of protecting the flank of Task Force Byrne. The 134th Infantry Regiment's After Action Reports put it this way:

> After the removal of anti-tank rails in the streets, men of Company I climbed aboard the tanks of Company A, 784th Tank Battalion, and the colored tankers, full of "vim and vigor" drove their "iron horses" up the highway toward Wassenberg. When a group of enemy dared fire upon the tanks, it brought on the fire of all tanks in the column (and in the process they pinned down Company L which was marching along a parallel railway to the right). An anti-tank gun did knock out one of the tanks, but that was the extent of the defense of Wassenberg.[6]

After Wassenberg, the tank/infantry team met stiff resistance. High-pitched, heart-stopping shrieks of *nebelwerfer*, 105-millimeter multi-rockets (aka screaming meemies), were fired almost simultaneously in clusters. The reverberation instilled terror in anyone within earshot. This battlefield became a horror-filled caldron of flashes and shrieks. An infantry battalion commander was severely wounded and his vehicle demolished. The shaken driver walked away unscathed in one of the many freak occurrences of the war.

Infantryman James Graff, Charlie Company, 134th Infantry Regiment relates:

> Later that night we moved out of Wassenberg on tanks and TDs. It was a long and eerie ride at night — no lights and a tank isn't the easiest thing to ride on at best. You had to

keep your head down or you might get it jerked off by a low hanging utility wire. One fellow did get his helmet knocked off by one.

A couple of miles down the road we came upon the recon (35th Reconnaissance Troop) and they had about forty Krauts corralled in a big house. They were firing with a tank and we were momentarily held up. We were sitting at a road intersection when a small convoy of vehicles approached it. They stopped as we were blocking the road both ways, and then one guy with a jeep pulling a trailer pulled out on the shoulder of the road setting off a mine. There was one hell of an explosion. The motor of that jeep flew at least 15 feet in the air and came down right through the jeep. An officer standing nearby had both legs broken and Landrum, Sokolowski, and Sanborn were all wounded. They were sitting on the left side of the tank I was on and they all got hit. Sanborn's wound was pretty bad, a big chunk of mine shrapnel in the upper leg, and the other 2 fellows' wounds were slight. The jeep driver walked off with help, but I believe all his damage was from concussion as I could see no blood on him....[7]

At the outbreak of World War II, the Dutch government declared itself neutral, as it did in World War I. However, on May 10, 1940, Germany launched a *Blitzkrieg* and quickly defeated the poorly armed Dutch army. Initially they destroyed the Dutch army and left Holland in turmoil with close to 1,000 civilians dead and tens of thousands homeless.

The Germans established a government that placed the Dutch citizens under the sinister and crushing rule of *Reichskommissar* Arthur Seyss-Inquart, an overt anti–Semite from Austria. Earlier he had received the "honorary" SS rank of *Gruppenfuhrer*. He immediately removed Jews from positions in the government, media, and commerce. Then he established a "Jewish board" as a way of organizing and identifying them for deportation. He promised them safety if they registered, and most of them did. The overwhelmed Dutch people offered very little resistance at this point because an Allied liberation seemed impossible, unlikely, or far away at best. When the Nazis gathered enough information, they dropped their façade and broke all promises. Their anti–Jewish measures intensified in 1941 with the confinement of registered Jews to ghettos and makeshift camps. In February 1941, they deported them to the Buchenwald and Mauthausen concentration camps and later to Auschwitz. The unregistered Jews went into hiding. One of the victims, Anne Frank, became posthumously famous from her diary that she wrote while in hiding. The Dutch people reacted with a strike known as the "February Strike" to protest the deportations. This strike became a major setback for Seyss-Inquart's success because the Nazis had planned to win the Dutch people over to their cause. At this moment all remaining façades fell and the Nazis treated all of the Dutch citizens with contempt and brutality. In the area of Putten, Holland, the entire male population was summarily executed after an assault on a Nazi officer.

Seyss-Inquart imposed the *Arbeitseinsatz* (labor draft) that obligated every man between 18 and 45 to work in the German war factories and in manual labor groups to build fortifications along the Atlantic Wall, Siegfried Line, and other defenses. The ones who would not be subjugated went into hiding. The Nazis took food and other goods out of Holland and rationing became a way of controlling the people and flushing out those in hiding. Any infraction meant the immediate forfeiture of ration cards and those hiding Jews or able-bodied men were punished by death. Nutrition became a life or death struggle that turned the Dutch people violently against each other.

The Nazis placed strict censorship on radio and newspapers. They reported only the positives of the Nazi regime and their military victories. Their broadcasts romanticized the war and depicted the Jews as the root of evil. Soon these victories started coming closer and closer to Germany, giving hope to the beleaguered Dutch people. Listening to *Radio Oranje* (Radio Orange), broadcasted from England, and possessing the illegal newspaper from *Radio Oranje*, became a punishable offense. The color Orange symbolized their deliverance.

Not all Dutch people offered resistance (active or passive) against the German occupation. Some collaborated passionately. Many voluntarily joined the *Wehrmacht* (German military) and some became members of the dreaded *Waffen SS*.

On March 2, 1945, the American Liberators received cheers by thousands of liberated Hollanders, many wearing orange after 4 years of Nazi occupation and brutal rule. Sergeant Bill Hughes, Dog Company, 784th Tank Battalion recalls:

> Rolling into Venlo, Holland to liberate it with all those infantry men atop our tanks sure brought back memories. We would drop them off at selected street intersections and strategic points; then race like mad to set up roadblocks to keep the enemy from escaping. In the meantime the infantry would go door to door to clean up any resistance. We nick named their cleanup operation "HOUSE CALLING" and the guys loved it. It soon got around in the entire infantry division as one of the tactical operations. Everyone knew what "HOUSE CALLING" meant; thanks to the 784th.
>
> Task Force Byrne was tasked to liberate Venlo, Holland. We did not meet too much resistance, which was a surprise. On the outskirts of one village, a guard in one shack came out to challenge our tank column. Henry Coffey, gunner in a half-track was very alert and fired one round from his .50-caliber machine gun to silence him. When we entered the outskirts of Venlo, we could hear music and laughter in a hall. The German soldiers scattered when they realized we were there but they were too late. Venlo was taken without too much resistance. The infantry did a fine job of mopping up. By early evening, we had Venlo under control and the people were delighted. We were sheltered in their homes over night and had long over due baths. The Germans did some periodic shelling but it proved harmless. The next day we went to the town square as the Queen of the Netherlands was flown in from England to congratulate the troops for liberating Venlo. We wasted no time in moving on as the Germans were on the run.[8]

Tech-5 James Hamilton adds:

> We went to Venlo, Holland. We moved in there so fast we captured 13 towns in 2 days and the Germans didn't even know we were coming. When we were coming over a bridge into Venlo with our tanks a German was coming across from the other side on a motorcycle. He threw his hands up and we took him. We went into town and a lot of them were in the houses eating and didn't know we were there. Then we opened the gates of a camp

in Venlo and those poor people came running out of there. Some of them were dropping dead on the road. It was awful!"[9]

Infantry Platoon Leader Royal Offer adds: "When we went into Venlo we got off the tanks and started cleaning out the town. The Germans didn't give us much opposition. I guess when they saw that tank column it discouraged them. In Venlo I was so surprised. I expected we were going to encounter stiff resistance but we didn't lose a man in Venlo."[10]

Infantryman James Graff adds:

> We came to a large town and as we were dismounting, crowds of civilians began to surround us. As one man approached Loos in a forward manner, he received a rifle butt to the head. Quickly we were told that we were in Venlo, Holland and these people had just been liberated after almost 5 years of Nazi rule. They meant us no harm and a nasty situation was narrowly averted. We should have been told these people were Dutch earlier.
>
> We stayed here a couple of days and these people were in a bad way. The British had been on the west bank of the Maas River since September and the city had been under virtual siege since then. All they had to eat were a few rotten potatoes and a little grass that was just beginning to green March 1. We met one man who had been hiding from the German labor draft for a couple of years. He had lived in a room lined with firewood in an eighteen inch crawl space beneath the floor, daring to venture out only at night; and we thought we had it bad.[11]

Task Force Byrne continued its rapid advance eastwards. The enemy blew the road passage on the approach to Straelin after the tanks had passed and thus had cut off the rear elements. Inside Straelin *Panzerfaust* fire destroyed a tank in the column. The combat engineers could not repair the roadway due to heavy shelling. Able Company's tank-dozer came in and repaired it and the tank/infantry combat teams regrouped and moved on. Sergeant Bill Hughes remembers:

> We moved pretty rapidly through a lot of villages and ran into resistance here and there. It did not impede our progress even though the enemy did blow up a few bridges. One tank did get a direct hit from a weapon called a *panzerfaust* (similar to our bazooka). It caught fire as the crew scampered out and was picked up by a half-track. Good thing they got out of there because the disabled tank received more fire until the ammunition went off. It was the first time I saw a tank being blown up. I think this was the first tank lost by enemy fire in our battalion. Sergeant Smith in the lead tank hollered over the radio that the fire came from a church steeple and he was going to direct one of the medium tanks to blast it. The first shot missed but the second round struck home and the steeple just toppled. The infantry confirmed they found 2 bodies they had seen trying to escape from their perch on the steeple. Task Force Byrne met much success capturing the town of Straelin and the small village of Nieukirk. The enemy managed to dig a roadblock ditch outside this small village, which held up our tank advancement. The roadblock area was being heavily shelled by constant mortar fire. Despite this, Sergeant Hall used a tank-bulldozer to fill the ditch wide enough for the tanks to cross. He saw the enemy nest that was firing on the column and ran over it with his tank-bulldozer.[12]

Tanks of the 784th move out of Venlo, Holland, on March 3, 1945. *Courtesy U.S. Army Military History Institute, Carlisle Barracks, Pennsylvania NARA-111-SC-337936)*

Infantry Platoon Leader Royal Offer recounts:

That's where they blew the bridge. As far as the town names, one town was just like the other. We are just expected to take them. But as far as remembering towns, I remember Straelin. After the tanks went in and the bridge was blown, I had 4 men wounded. When we got into town we didn't have any opposition right then and we carried the wounded into a house. There was a little German gal there. The staff sergeant was badly wounded, he was bleeding from the mouth and anytime I saw that I knew it was curtains. The medics couldn't get in for 3 hours to take care of the wounded. I had one of my men who could speak German to ask if she could get a doctor for us. And she took off and no time

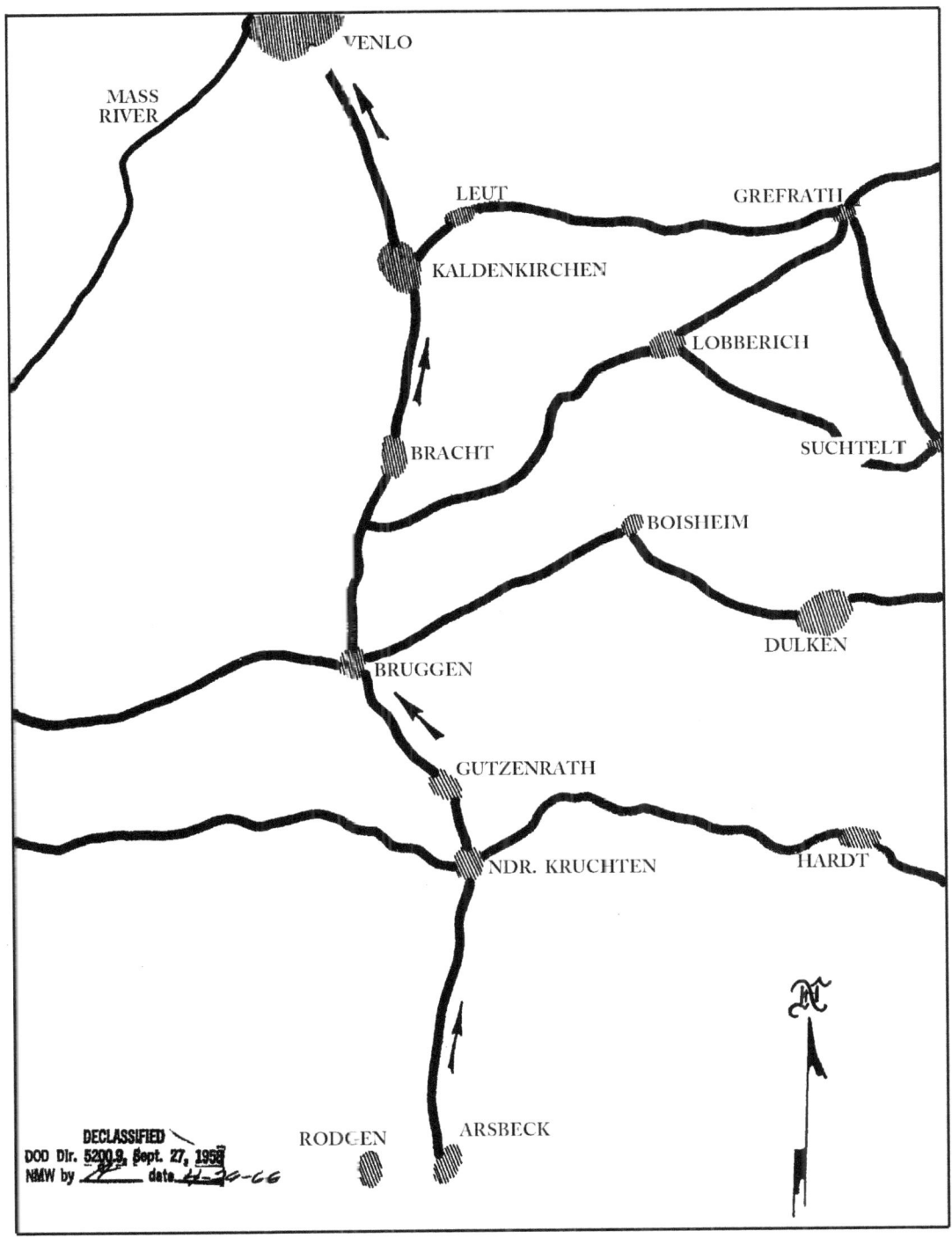

Route followed by Task Force Byrne as it struck north from the Roer River bridgehead at 0700 on 1 March 1945. Advancing rapidly, the task force seized Venlo by nightfall. *35th Infantry Division map, courtesy National Archives and Records Administration*

flat here comes a doctor with a little black bag and he really worked to try and save the wounded. He stayed right there until the medics arrived. The staff sergeant died before they got there. The others were still alive when the medics came in. One of the men badly wounded, he and I were good friends. He loved to smoke a pipe. He had a pipe and a pouch of tobacco all of the time. Anytime we set up and had a little time, he would start smoking that pipe. I said, "Jim, when you get hit, your body won't even get cold and I'll have that pipe and that bag there." He just laughed. So that night after the medics got in, the medic came over to me and he said we got something for you. He offered me Jimmy's pipe. Jimmy said, "I'm not going to need that anymore, just give that to Offer." I don't think he made it because I'm sure he would have written me from the hospital but I never heard anything from him. I thought of that a million times.[13]

With little delay, the task force knifed through Straelin and continued towards the other German towns, advancing almost 50 miles in 3 days.

Elements of the 134th and 137th Infantry Regiments spearheaded by Able Company, 784th Tank Battalion continued following Task Force Byrne, mopping up bypassed enemy forces as Task Force Byrne set out in the direction of Sevelen and Rheinberg. The 784th had little trouble moving ahead except for scattered resistance and blown bridges. Soon another tank got knocked out. The crew, less one man, ejected safely. Sergeant Charles Jefferson perished inside the burning hulk. Other tanks pushed his burning tank aside and the advance continued as the crew members took up positions with the infantry.

This is where the dreaded *Panzerfaust* (tank fist) began extracting a heavy toll on 784th tanks. The white star that identifies American vehicles provided an excellent target. This arm-held or shoulder-fired, single shot, rocket-propelled, anti-tank weapon easily destroyed Sherman tanks. They had an effective range of 100 to 500 feet, depending on model.

The *Panzerfaust* had a deadly back-blast of 6 to 10 feet and if fired too close to a structure it would kill or injure the firer. Thus it could not be fired safely from the protection of a bunker. In red embossing on the end of the tube appeared the following warning: "*Achtung! Feuerstrahl!*" (Warning! Fire Jet!)

When this warhead struck a tank, a fuse triggered a rear charge that detonated an intense heat upsurge that at ballistic velocity melted out a path that allowed the slug to penetrate the armor. The Sherman tank's high-octane gasoline fuel and electrical cables would turn the tank into a firetrap. Sherman tanks were labeled "Ronsons" after the famous cigarette lighter with the advertising slogan: "They light every time."[14]

The inside of a tank, potentially an iron coffin, was a hell of a place to be. When an armor-piercing shell penetrated a tank, slivers of white-hot metal fragments flew throughout the tank's interior, striking everyone. These flying fragments would rip a man apart and splatter blood and human flesh all over the tank's white interior. The hellish part about it is that once it got in there, there wasn't a damned thing that could be done about it.

Staff Sergeant Chester Jones from the 961st Tank Ordnance Company points out:

> When you open the hatches of the wrecked tanks that could be repaired, some of the most ghastly sights you could imagine were exposed; what were once human beings were scrambled all over the interior of these tanks. You didn't stop to figure out which leg or arm went with which remains, if there were a whole torso. You just put it in a plastic container and cleaned the spattered brains and blood from the inside of the vehicle. I was a tank mechanic, but cleaning out those wrecks went with the job.[15]

Infantryman James Graff recounts the coordinated tank/infantry assault in great detail:

> March 3 we mounted tanks for an attack on Geldern, Germany.... Our division tank battalion had been replaced with a new battalion, the 784th Tank Battalion, which was made up of colored tankers. As this was our first combined attack with them (although they had transported us to Venlo) we were wondering how things would go.
>
> As we moved out, a member of the tank crew opened the hatch of the turret and asked if anyone knew how to man a .50 Cal. Machine gun. I said I could and he answered, "They done told us to button up and for you to watch for bazooka men along the road." As usual, when the words "no opposition expected" were heard you'd better look out as hell is liable to bust loose.
>
> As our column approached Geldern we came under heavy mortar and rocket fire. As the lead tank approached a bridge over a canal at the edge of town, the bridge was blown up. A bazooka round hit the lead tank and knocked it out and the road was now effectively blocked. The tanks were road bound because of mines along the shoulder of the road. Captain Chappel escaped injury when a bazooka round hit the tank he was on. A piece of shrapnel cut his pistol holder and lodged in 2 plugs of tobacco in his hip pocket. Several other men were wounded and we all dismounted and got down in a ditch along the road. The colored tankers were really laying down a barrage. The muzzle blast of the tanks firing over us was terrific. The colored boys hollered out the tanks, "Hey, white boy, pick them out and we will shoot them." The combination of the mine explosion and the muzzle blasts of that day has continued to affect my hearing (left ear) to this day.[16]

Meanwhile, an advanced force of Task Force Byrne that consisted of a company of light tanks, a platoon of medium tanks, a platoon of assault guns, and accompanying infantry sped towards Sevelen. They passed through prepared anti-tank positions south of the town. The Germans seemed to allow the swift-moving tanks to cross a bridge over a deep railroad cut and enter Sevelen unopposed. When the tank force reached the middle of town, the enemy blew the south entrance bridge, trapping the tanks there. Intense small arms and *Panzerfaust* fire broke out. A barn door opened and an anti-tank gun fired and knocked out the lead tank. The other tanks immediately silenced that anti-tank gun. Many Germans stayed just outside of town and poured in mortar, machine gun, and artillery fire throughout this ordeal. They had key points inside Sevelen zeroed in and their shells hit with deadly consequences. The tankers, nearly out of gas, had to refuel in a hurry. Every time they got out to open a jerry can, mortar fire fell around them, but they kept right at it until the tanks were refueled. When the .30 caliber machine gun ammunition ran out the tankers climbed out on top of the tanks and opened up with their .50 caliber anti-aircraft machine-guns.

Major Gustave Burant, Executive Officer, 784th Tank Battalion remarked: "Bazookas and shells came in from all sides. There must have been a bazooka shell every minute all night. In the midst of the melee with street fighting going on all over town the Germans blew the bridge behind the tank force and they were on their own."[17]

Sergeant Bill Hughes adds in great detail:

After a short period to refuel and perform maintenance checks the task force commander ordered a night attack to take the town of Sevelen. The attack force consisted of all D Company light tanks, some medium tanks, a heavy gun platoon, with a major in command. A blackout was ordered except for the cat eyes on the tanks and vehicles. We were ordered to maintain radio silence for the march, which took about 2 hours to reach the outskirts of Sevelen. We halted for a few minutes to make a final check on all weapons.

For some reason Captain John T. Powers, Company D's commanding officer ordered 1st Lieutenant Waters, to take charge and lead the tank columns. I was told to go with him in a half-track and man the field radio since I knew Morse code and how to operate that radio. Corporal Henry Coffey manned my .50-caliber mounted machine gun and the driver was Private Walter Smith. About 6 Infantrymen also boarded the half-track. The tanks were on the main road leading to the village with some infantry riding atop the tanks and others on the ground to the left and right flanks. Periodically, we came across small arms fire but no real encounter with the enemy, which was rather surprising. We reached the center of town and crossed a bridge near a railway track. About 12 minutes later, after we were all across the bridge, there came a big explosion. The bridge blew up leaving us trapped. Shelling and mortar rounds came in almost immediately. An orange flare was ignited to signal radios are to be turned on by our task force. All vehicles checked in by radio and were ordered into various positions back to fields just before the small town's entrance. The infantry dug in so all knew this was going to be an all night stand. A defense perimeter was set up to protect the rear and front from any possible surprise attack. The enemy kept shelling the small town for sometime thinking we were there. The major sent a runner over to my halftrack with a message telling me to contact the task force operations officer to advise that the bridge was destroyed behind us; heavy shelling was encountered; and gave position coordinates and stating reinforcements may be needed before the attack could continue and that we were pinned down. The operations officer responded in about 5 minutes. Ordered a hold on our position; reinforcements were preparing to move; and to advise of further developments. I had to run this message over to the major since the runner had departed and I thought he was still there to take the message back. He did not tell me where the major was located so there I was running, ducking and diving into infantry dug outs until I found a lieutenant who reached the major by radio. He told me, don't read that message. Just bring it to me about 200 yards away. Again, more ducking, running and diving to avoid those shells. The major asked could I bring that half-track closer to him. I told him it was too dangerous without lights since his men were scattered all over and could get run over. He told me to make sure I stayed awake because he would be sending runners over often. I thought I had better let Lieutenant Waters know what was going on so I located his tank and told him about the messages. He said, "OK but tell his runner, he has to wait and carry the messages back to the major unless you get a direct order to do so otherwise. On the other hand I want to be kept informed so run any messages you send or receive over to me." I had no problem getting the runners to wait after that but throughout the night I made about 6 trips back and forth between the halftrack and Lieutenant Waters' tank to keep him advised. I was glad the distance in making those runs were shorter because this was very exhausting and those shells coming in were scary with fragments flying in the air. Several times I heard screams for medics from the infantrymen as someone got hit. They sure looked out for each other. Our bulldozers helped by digging deeper and wider dugouts. This gave more protection to the infantrymen. Our tankers were safe inside their tanks although shell fragments splattered against them.

The reinforcements had not arrived. We could not go back so as it began to get light, the decision was made to fight our way out of there and move forward to take the small town. It was decided to rapidly advance on the main road into town, continue through it until the outskirts were reached. At the same time, 2 other columns would go through the roads on the left and right of the main road. This proved successful although we lost one tank led by a Lieutenant McNutt who I really never got to know except by name. He was wounded by shellfire as he climbed out of his disabled tank. The rest of the crew escaped unharmed and scampered to a building where they were picked up. My halftrack was behind the main column through the town and Henry Coffey kept that machine gun blasting away with a sweep high and low at any potential target. The barrel got so hot you could not touch it. Shortly before noon, the town was taken with many prisoners, food stores, ammunition and more than 50 enemy dead. All the tanks were accounted for except that one led by Lieutenant McNutt.

The reinforcements arrived from the north and took over mopping up. Our spirits were very high because we knew our company could fight seemingly winless odds and win. After a couple hours of sleep and maintenance, we hit the road again. A signal corps photographer came on the scene and shot some photos of the guys from Company D. Our morale was very high. The force had blasted its way out of a trap that was designed to seal its doom. The Battalion motto "It Will Be Done" became so clear and we were proud.[18]

1st Lieutenant Thomas Redditt, Charlie Company, 784th Tank Battalion adds:

I remember the battle of Sevelen. This town was not very large but it had a church with a high steeple. While we were in this town we were getting artillery every now and then until somebody said, "Shoot the steeple off the church. That might be where the forward observer is." So somebody backed a tank up and shot the steeple off.

Then I was in a basement looking out a window and here comes a bunch of men running down the street. They were all coming back carrying a case of wine. They found a boxcar at the railroad station and broke into it. They had taken some of the shells out of their ready rack in their tanks and replaced them with wine bottles. They were all human beings.[19]

The 320th Infantry Regiment's After Action Report put it this way:

"The Company I platoon and the Negro tankers who attacked Sevelen at night were isolated from the rest of the column when the Germans blew up a bridge after they crossed. In house-to-house fighting the men had largely cleared the town by morning when more tanks and men could join them. Sevelen was secured despite the deadly observed fire from mortars and artillery just outside the town."[20]

In April 1945, Wes Gallagher of the Associated Press described this skirmish in newspapers across the country: "Negro Tank Battalion Fights Miniature Bastogne All Alone."[21]

March 3, 1945: reinforcements discovered 53 enemy soldiers dead, and a large supply of food and ammunition. One of the structures hit by enemy artillery contained German prisoners and several were killed.

While clearing the town, Task Force Byrne discovered stacks of Nazi propaganda leaflets addressed to the 35th Infantry Division. The leaflets warned of the Roer defenses:

WELCOME MEN OF THE 35th DIVISION! Considering the fact that you are newcomers, we would like to do everything to make you feel at home. We extend to you a cordial greeting and a hearty welcome to the Roer Valley! You have tried to veil your arrival here by doing such things as removing your divisional insignias. Nevertheless, a little bird told us about it. Before you arrived, there were other divisions here who didn't fare so well; namely the 84th, the 102nd, the 29th, and, not to be forgotten, the British. They all got knocked about a bit. You can see that you won't have any easy time of it against the Roer defense lines. We said before, we shall try to make you feel at home. We hope to make every day here seem like "the glorious Fourth"— there will be plenty of fireworks.[22]

Sergeant Bill Hughes looked back on how his specialized training paid off:

I was also trained to setup, install and operated a field radio using Morse code to key the line as a high-speed operator. The learning process is very intense although I only used it once in battle and that was at Sevelen when we were trapped behind a blown out bridge. However, to keep on my toes, I was often at battalion headquarters using the field radio to send administrative traffic. It is not easy to forget the code because it really sticks, but you can get rusty. It really paid off having that know how at Sevelen.[23]

Task Force Byrne consolidated its positions before continuing its road march through the Roer defenses towards the Rhine River to their final objective the town of Drupt, only 4 kilometers from the Rhine.

Sergeant Walter "Pop" Hall, as commander of a tank bulldozer, filled craters in the roads, extricated mired tanks and vehicles, and dug trenches for the infantry while under fire. In one action he knocked out an anti-tank gun and ran it over and buried it. At the age of 47 and a veteran of the last war, the men looked up to him like a father and thus gave him the nickname "Pop."

In another action Sergeant Ambrose Hicks went back to help guide a supply convoy through. He personally saved 3 trucks parked near a flaming ammunition vehicle loaded with over a ton of high explosives. The battalion commander, Lt. Colonel George Dalia, singled these 2 men out for special recognition.

7. Task Force Byrne

Sergeant Simmons Washington remembers Hall and Ambrose: "Sergeant Hall was an older fellow. From what I remember he was in World War I. He had a maintenance tank and he took care of the tanks that got knocked out. If he could pull them in, he did. He was quite a guy, old 'Pop' Hall. He taught us a lot. Sergeant Hicks was the custodian of arms for our company. He was quite a guy too."[24]

Infantry Intelligence Officer Orval Faubus, following closely behind the task force, recounts:

> Never to be forgotten. The night ride through the German countryside, lit up by the light of burning hay stacks, houses, and barns, and the flashes of guns and shells. The slanting flames alternately glowed red and white as the freezing wind waxed and waned. In the fluid situation one could not always be sure if he was meeting a friend or a foe....
>
> Once we came to a fork in the road with no idea which road to take. As Lanier halted the jeep I looked at a line of fires glowing brightly across the countryside and indicated the road that led in the same direction. It was the right way. Those Negro tankers fired on everything—houses, cows, men, vehicles, haystacks, barns, houses, and other buildings. The line of fires marked the path of their advance.[25]

March 4, 1945: one platoon of Baker Company tanks assisted elements of the 320th Infantry Regiment in an assault on the town of Kamperbruck, Germany. The initial assault failed due to superior enemy forces and a lack of coordination. The tanks fired with caution, believing friendly infantry operated in the eastern section of town, when in fact the infantry unit had been forced out of there by a strong enemy counterattack. The tank platoon, on a road zeroed in by the enemy, lost 3 tanks to direct anti-tank fire. In one action, tank commander Sergeant Douglas Kelly ordered his crew to stay in the tank after it was hit. They returned fire until their ammunition began to explode. Finally they dismounted and Kelly made his way to a forward observer's post under mortar and small arms fire, where his direction of artillery knocked out 4 enemy anti-tank guns. Before he could do this, 3 tankers from the other tanks perished: bow gunner, Tech-5 Albert Harte; tank driver, Private William Hogue; and loader, Tech-4 Arthur Whitbeck.

Sergeant Walter "Pop" Hall, tank-dozer commander, March 28, 1945. A U.S. Army Signal Corps photograph. *Courtesy National Archives*

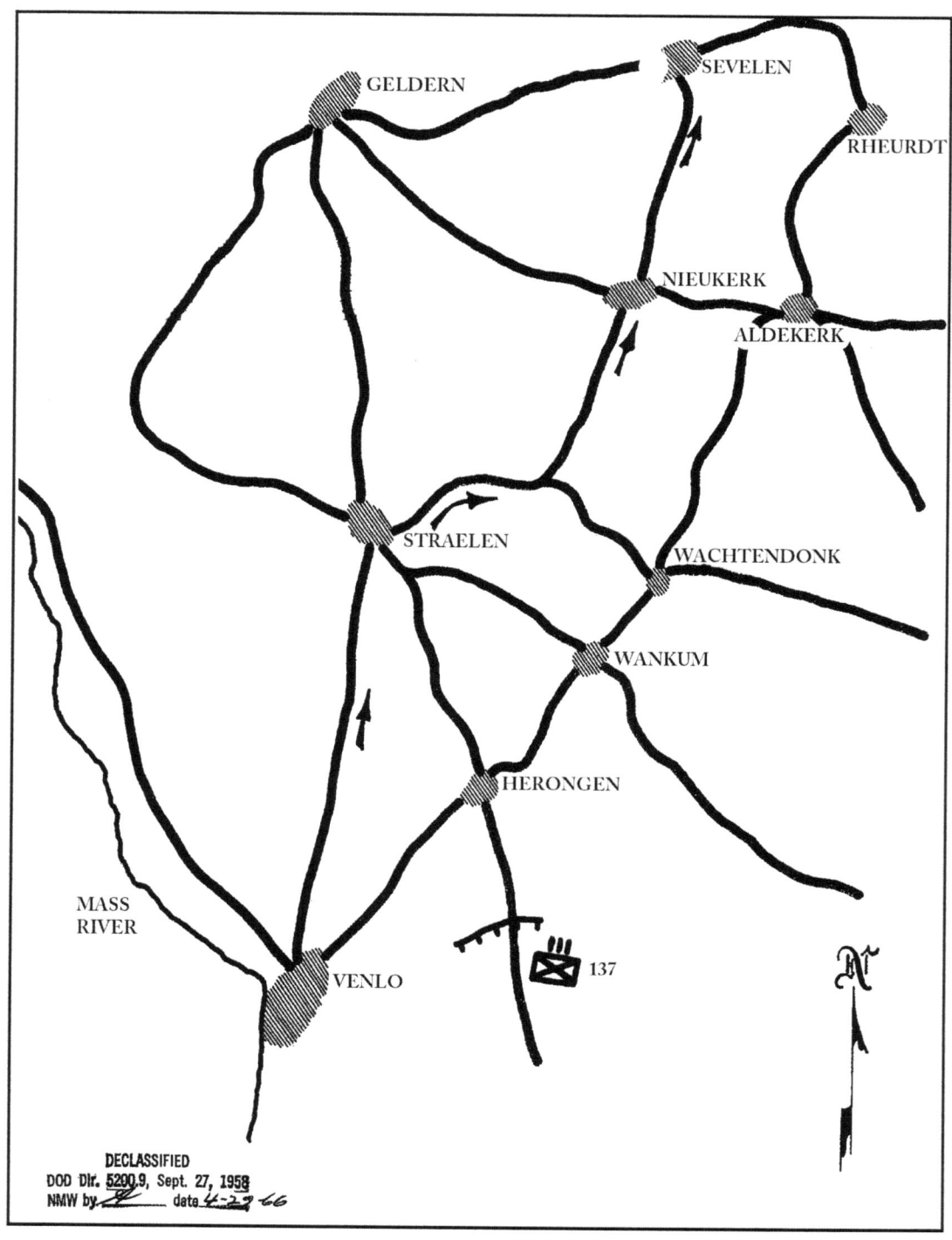

On 2 March 1945 Task Force Byrne continued its rapid drive to Sevelen where it encountered its first stiff opposition since breaking out of the Roer River bridgehead the day before. *35th Infantry Division map, courtesy National Archives and Records Administration*

7. Task Force Byrne

Sevelen, Germany, March 4, 1945. Sergeant Bill Hughes of the 784th recalled, "I am in that photo and remember it being taken during a maintenance break. Across from the jeep, tall Lieutenant Waters with hands in his pocket. Next to him with a cigarette in his mouth is Sergeant Alfred talking to Sergeant Williams. Between them in the background, me coming out of that building where you see the half-track. I had just finished checking a radio." Infantryman Keith Bullock (HQ/137th) adds, "Note the jeep in the foreground marked 35-134!" *Courtesy U.S. Army Military History Institute, Carlisle Barracks, Pennsylvania, and National Archives*

Sergeant Simmons Washington relates:

A high school friend of mine was in B Company named William Hogue. His tank was hit and he got killed. The tanks got hit on a mission with an infantry company. I didn't know too much about Private Hogue except that he was in B Company and they caught it pretty bad. A lot of other guys from other companies, I can't remember all of their names, a lot of their tanks got hit. It is rough when you soldier with guys and you go on a mission and come back and they say somebody didn't make it. So I can sympathize with the soldiers of today, I know what they are going through. It's a different type of war but you still lose people and it's rough. We were fortunate that we didn't lose more people.[26]

Staff Sergeant Franklin Garrido, Baker Company, 784th Tank Battalion recounts:

Kamperbruch is where our tanks got knocked out, 2 light and 1 medium tank. This was in the afternoon, possibly 1600 hours. We were ordered to make up a platoon of tanks plus 2 light tanks for reconnaissance. Captain Abernathy ordered the formation of a second platoon, which I was the number-5 tank, the last tank in the column. The 2 light tanks were scouting ahead of us. Our orders were to join C Company because they were in trouble. On the way there, we passed a company of doughs from the 35th Infantry Division. We continued on another 2 miles when the lead tank, a light tank, was hit in the transmission. The 4-man crew jumped out uninjured. The lead tank blocked the road. In tank warfare, if you're shooting at a column, what you should do is knock out the rear tank first so the other tanks can't turn around and retreat. My tank was the rear tank. I ordered my driver to back up and I guided him around a building. The tank in front of me became the last tank and it was hit and knocked out. The crew ejected safely. That's when I was ordered by Lieutenant Peterson to pick up men who were wounded in a burning building. We put one on a door and carried him back to where our tanks were.[27]

Staff Sergeant Garrido and Tech-5 Dave Adams received the Bronze Star Medal for devotion to wounded comrades. Garrido went on to recount:

Lieutenant Peterson then ordered me to go back to the infantry and tell them that we lost 2 tanks and needed help. I loaded up with hand grenades and clips for my machine gun and I took off running. I probably broke [miler Roger] Bannister's record before he did. I ran and everything that moved I threw a grenade at or a blast of submachine gun fire. The infantry was eating upon my arrival. I told them essentially what happened. They insisted that I eat with them. I guess that was the first time the 35th Infantry Division was integrated. I had beans, bread, and a cup of coffee. We finished and lined up, I as infantry, and we marched up to where the tanks were. Evidently, the German anti-tank gunners retreated. By that time it was getting dark. The M5 light tank, the first one hit, its motor was still running. The infantry captain asked me if I knew how to shoot that thing and I said yeah. The first thing, I said, the engine is still running, maybe it can move. The M5 had twin Cadillac engines. The transmission was in the front and there was a neat hole in it. It had been a long time since I fired a 37-millimeter, but you just don't forget those things. He pointed to a haystack and said knock it out. I did. He then pointed to another target and I knocked it out too. That was it.[28]

March 4, 1945: Charlie Company departed Sevelen to assist in the attack on Kamperbruch with the 2nd Battalion of the 320th Infantry Regiment. They were stopped dead in their tracks by a sustained fury of anti-tank fire and lost 3 tanks. Hatches opened and men, accompanied by smoke and flames, scampered out. Three tankers perished inside their blazing tanks: tank commander Sergeant James Laurie; tank driver Private Willmore Mack; and tank driver Private Raymond Womack.

Tech-5 James Hamilton recalls: "When we got hit, me and Irby (the driver next to me) got out of there together. His right arm got split all the way up. The lieutenant said he never saw anyone who could run that fast. He said. 'They were shooting at you and they couldn't even hit you.'"[29]

Charlie Company withdrew and spent the night on the road northwest of Lintfort. The platoon of light tanks attached to Charlie Company set up road blocks along the road to Rhineberg. The prisoners taken in this area were mostly *Fallschirjagers* (Paratroopers), who put up stiffer resistance than any other troops encountered thus far.

Infantry Intelligence Officer Orval Faubus recounts:

> On the 5th Captain [James] Watkins of F Company was killed while his company was leading the advance with the colored tankers. The tank company commander [Captain Donald Carman, C/784th] had a leg blown off and a tank platoon leader [1st Lieutenant David Crawford, C/784th] was wounded. By yesterday afternoon one company of our tanks had lost all its officers except the maintenance platoon leader [1st Lieutenant Thomas Redditt, C/784th], whose duties were more or less somewhat to the rear of the front elements. The company also lost 8 tanks, 5 yesterday, 3 day before.[30]

The tank/infantry teams attacking past Kamperbruck in the direction of Rheinberg had been stopped in their tracks by fierce direct anti-tank fire. Then indirect artillery began thundering into the area from

1st Lt. Tom Redditt (Maintenance Officer, C/784th), Capt. Donald Carman (Commanding Officer, C/784th), and 2nd Lt. Alexander Carr (Platoon Leader, C/784th). Geilenkirchen, Germany, February 1945. *Courtesy Tom Redditt*

across the Rhine. The enemy desperately protected their main forces withdrawing to the east bank of the Rhine River.

At intervals throughout the cold night, rifle shots rang out, cracking the moonlit stillness. Entrapped enemy soldiers were trying to slip past the American lines to get back to their forces attempting to cross the Rhine River. Several desperate groups succeeded. One even captured 2 American infantrymen before they crossed the main road from west to east.

Early in the morning, the remainder of Charlie Company once again attacked Kamperbruck, but this time the enemy had withdrawn the night before. Then they assisted in the assault on 2 small villages — Alpsray and Bauern until they reached Millingen. There they broke up into a 2-pronged assault. One tank platoon went along a soggy, rutted road leading through a German forest of evergreens, now heavy and dripping with rain. The lead tank got knocked out on the approach to this village by a cleverly concealed self-propelled anti-tank gun. Then they became sitting targets for well-organized automatic, small arms, and mortar fire from prepared entrenchments and buildings. The other tanks provided covering fire to affect a withdrawal.

The other Charlie Company tank platoons didn't fare so well either. They went straight down the main road into Millingen. Then all hell — in the most vivid meaning of the term — broke loose! Well-concealed anti-tank guns and *Panzerfausts* appeared from out of nowhere. Muzzles flashed all around. These anti-tank rounds had tracers and could be seen streaking from the enemy, hitting the tanks, and the ineffective ones careening hundreds of feet into the sky. Then the thumping sound of the *Panzerfaust* roared and swished as its rocket-like projectile unsteadily streaked towards the tanks in perceived slow motion. The ones that hit the road threw up dirt and rocks along with searing pieces from their phosphorus warheads. The tanks directly hit by this deadly fire shuddered and stopped in the middle of the road before erupting into flames. Smoke hissed from the neatly pierced holes in the armor. The enemy anti-tank guns, in typical fashion, knocked out the lead tank to block the advance, then took out the rear tank to prevent the others from backing out. One by one they went after the other tanks, destroying 4. In the lead tank, Platoon Leader 2nd Lieutenant Ernest Mikus, commanding a platoon of light tanks attached to Charlie Company, was hit. His younger brother gave a second-hand account: "They proceeded through a town, he was in the lead tank, when a barn door swung open and his tank was hit with an anti-tank round. He was wounded and pulled out of the tank by a soldier from another tank. He subsequently was hospitalized and after a month was assigned to an MP unit guarding German prisoners as the war was almost over."[31]

Charlie Company suffered the loss of 4 tanks. Tank gunner, Corporal Wilson Griswell and Platoon Leader 1st Lieutenant Art Solow perished. Platoon Leader 2nd Lieutenant Alex Carr along with 3 other men went missing in

7. Task Force Byrne

action.* Platoon Leader 1st Lieutenant David Crawford and others medically evacuated. This left Charlie Company without officers. Fighting continued at a fierce and savage pace as this tank company regrouped and launched several assaults to liberate their trapped comrades and officers.

Infantry Intelligence Officer Orval Faubus observed:

> A great part of a platoon of Negro tankers were either killed or captured when they spearheaded into a town and were cut off. The bodies of some were found, badly beaten about the face, and one shot through the forehead. One was recovered alive after other troops fought into the town. He was badly bruised from beating. He said the Nazis beat them after they were made prisoners. He was in too bad a condition to question further and was rushed on back to the hospital.[32]

1st Lieutenant David "Shorty" Crawford, a Charlie Company platoon leader, updated Captain Carman on the aftermath of this battle:

2nd Lieutenant Ernest Mikus, 1944. *Courtesy Wayne Mikus*

> Hello Don, Boy I sure sweated out that letter from you, and don't have to tell you that I was glad to get it. I know how you felt when you heard about Art & Alex, Don! It hit me like a ton of bricks, and I'm not over it yet. So far I haven't heard from Alex, but I have tried to find out if they have retaken him yet. As soon as I hear anything, you can be sure I will let you know as soon as possible. I just read part of your letter to the men, and they were glad to hear you are getting along o.k. Sgt. Willie and Sgt. Fields want me to send their regards also! About your question on Sgt. Laurie, yes, he was killed the same day that Carr was missing! I guess they had a pretty rough time, the next two days after you and I were evacuated! Sgt. Burus took over the Company after Art was killed and did a damn good job. The Colonel asked me to recommend him for a battlefield-commission for his good work. I did, but his I.Q. wasn't high enough. He took it over again yesterday, but still couldn't quite make the grade. I was hoping he would make it, because he had

---

*1st Lietenant David "Shorty" Crawford was wounded and evacuated.

done darn good work. I don't know whether you knew it or not but he made two attacks with the company to try and get Art when he was first wounded. I have recommended him for the Silver Star, but haven't heard as yet whether he will get it or not.[33]

1st Lieutenant Thomas Redditt, Charlie Company's maintenance officer, recounts:

Lt. David "Shorty" Crawford (left) and Lt. Alexander Carr in Geilenkirchen, Germany, February 1945, before Carr went missing in action. *Courtesy Mark Carman, Esq.*

Alex Carr was a platoon leader in C Company when he was killed. His leg was shot off and I believe he was captured by the Germans because I found some of his clothing away from the tank. They got him out of the tank and left his leg in there. The next day when I went up there with the adjutant we happened to look in the tank and I found his leg. It was almost up to the knee. We got it out of the tank and I got a shovel off of the tank and went over to the field, dug a hole, and buried his leg. The army contacted me several years after the war and tried to identify him but could never identify Lieutenant Carr's body so they buried him as an unknown. He was from Boston, Massachusetts.

Another platoon leader, Art Solow, was killed within 50 yards of Alex's tank. I didn't go out and visit his tank because it was in a field and I didn't want to step on a mine. His body was returned from Europe and buried in North Dakota.

Art and Alex were killed and the other platoon

leader was shot in the neck and went to the hospital. With Don Carman hit; Solow and Carr killed; and the other officer in the hospital, I was made company commander and promoted to captain.[34]

Charlie Company, nearly decimated, went into reserve to refit and reorganize. Despite reports that Captain Carman lost his leg, the doctors saved it.

Sergeant Bill Hughes commented on getting captured: "It was rumored. Based on that rumor many of the guys thought for sure they would not be treated well or survive in the hands of the enemy. In fact many said, 'I will always save that last bullet for myself.' I personally thought the rumor came about to get the men to fight as hard as they could and instill as much hatred as possible toward the enemy."[35]

Infantry Intelligence Officer Orval Faubus went on to describe the lull following this battle:

> While I stood briefly in a church, now being used as a shelter by our troops, a GI was playing the chapel organ and a Negro solder was singing with deep feeling an old familiar religious hymn — strange assemblage and a strange scene for such a place. Other battle-strained GIs listened with weary, strained faces turned toward the singer and the player. Another Negro trooper slept the sleep of exhaustion upon a soiled, silken pallet."[36]

The wounded were removed from the battlefield to aid stations. From there they went further back to battalion aid stations and triaged into 3 groups: the lightly wounded, the critically wounded, and those who had little or no chance of recovery.

Ambulance Driver Wayne Martin, 60th Field Hospital points out:

> I would at times pick up wounded at battalion aid and collection stations and deliver them to our hospital. To give you an idea of the size of our hospital, we could set up and pull a major operation within one hour. We would set up 2 12-by-12 tents, use one as an operating room and one as supply, sterilization ward tent until our other 6 tents would arrive. I would deliver patients to the Evac hospitals. Each of the 3 platoons made a hospital."[37]

Along with delivering patients and nursing, the drivers at times assisted in the operating rooms. A good surgeon and a good enlisted man, with the help of an anesthetist, would explore and adequately mend abdomen, chest and other injuries. The enlisted men would fix up packs, run the autoclave, and lay out the necessary equipment for the major procedure. After it was over, they cleaned up without losing forceps, needles, scissors, etc. A sterile supply was imperative to the operating rooms at all times.

March 10, 1945: Captain Donald Carman sent word home to his fiancée that he was alive:

> Dearest,
> This is quite an ambitious undertaking but will undertake it anyway. Hope you got the

Tech-5 Wayne Martin, 60th Field Hospital, May 20, 1944. *Courtesy Wayne Martin*

note that the Chaplain wrote for me earlier in the week. Well, Charlie, I believe this war is over for me. I don't think the army will have such high regard for my physical capabilities after they finally fix me up. I'm sorta propped in bed & at not too good an angle so forgive if the words seem to run all over the paper. I'm a little shaky myself too. I wonder when your letters will catch up with me. I am in a field hospital now, & it is the third I've been in! But I expect to go further back yet. Got to get your picture, haven't a thing except what was in my pockets when I was hit. You are probably wondering what is the matter with me, honey. Well, I'm not in too good a shape at present. An 88 went thru my tank & also my leg somewhere below the knee, shattered the leg and also ankle. I believe the records call it multiple facture and number of other things I can't decipher. They put one of those plaster casts on it for time being. It's going to be a long time before I'll walk again, I guess. Just a tough break. You should see the wounded. A lot aren't so bad but it is tragic. One doesn't realize how horrible war is till you've been there and seen this side of it. Seen plenty of killed but they are at least thru suffering. All the boys do best they can & joke & try to build up the other fellows' spirit. These nurses over here are working harder than anyone can imagine & doing a swell job. Do you remember Benham? He's the guy who stayed in the hotel room because he was afraid of the colonel. He got hit a couple of days before I did. Had a number of casualties, but were going great guns when I got hit. Really had the Jerries on the run.[38]

Infantry Reconnaissance Officer John Walsh, Cannon Company, 320th Infantry Regiment provides a glimpse into the post-traumatic stress from this battle:

7. Task Force Byrne

Later after our objective had been met I became ill with hepatitis and was hospitalized at the 191st General Hospital in Paris. Following the custom of patients, I pinned my 35th division patch on my bathrobe. A soldier approached me one day and identified himself as a member of the tankers who had been with us in Task Force Byrne. We chatted a bit and reminisced about our exciting dash to the Rhine. He had been in the tank that was set afire. Later, one of the nurses or doctors who had seen us together asked me if I knew the man. It seems as though he was having nightmares that would cause him to roll out of bed

Master Sergeant Harold Maddox (left) and Sergeant Jack O'Neil, 784th mechanics, weld brackets onto Sherman tanks to hold extra bogie wheels, March 28, 1945. A U.S. Army Signal Corps photograph. *Courtesy National Archives*

and across the floor of the ward. I told the doctor about the burning tank and apparently he used that information to treat the soldier.[39]

The Wesel pocket, the Nazis' only remaining stronghold west of the Rhine, was now well contained. Kamperbruck, Kemp, Hogenhof, Saalhof, Alspry, Schmetshof, Millingen, Huck, and Drupt had been seized. The 320th Infantry Regiment reported:

> Mostly it was brutal, nerve-wracking going. One crew sailed into battle manning their 3rd new tank in a week. This relentlessness was effective. Second Battalion though sustaining heavy losses, captured 300 prisoners in 2 days of fighting at Milligen. And there were clean-cut strokes, like the perfectly timed action at Hillmanshoff by a platoon of F Company led by battle-fielded commissioned 2nd Lieutenant Vivian G. Palmore of Mattox, Virginia: "We didn't have a casualty," reported Palamore. "The Kraut positions were in 2 houses completely surrounded by a thick hedge and we had to cross 1,000 yards of open ground covered by their 2 88s. Our artillery poured in a 10-minute barrage, pinning them down. Then our tanks smashed up to within 100 yards, letting loose with everything they had, and then we ran out in front of the tanks laying town a terrific marching fire. The Krauts just couldn't get started."[40]

Meanwhile, Able Company, still attached to the 134th Infantry Regiment, battled through light resistance west of Geldern, where they made contact with the King's Royal Rifles of the British 8th Armored Division. They were then released from the 134th Infantry Regiment and prepared to join another task force being prepared.

Able Company received a letter of commendation from the regimental commander through the division commander for a "splendid performance" and proving "indispensable to the 134th Infantry Regiment in the assaulting of Hilfarth and the Roer River and the dash to Wassenberg, Bergenlen, and Geldern. Their high morale, aggressiveness, and willingness to fight deserve commendation."[41]

The task force commander, Colonel Bernard Byrne, commented: "Those tankers gave a good account of themselves and our doughs say they can fight with them any time. They stay right up with the doughs and the foot soldiers like that."[42]

8

Eighty-eight Alley

While Task Force Byrne wheeled northeast toward the Rhine River — March 5, 1945 — some 30 miles away Task Force Murray, in close coordination with Combat Command B (CCB) of the 8th Armored Division, jumped off. Colonel William Murray's 137th Infantry Regiment executed the leading role. Support came from various artillery, tank destroyer, engineer, and medical units, along with elements of the 8th Armored Division. Able Company, 784th Tank Battalion spearheaded the 137th Infantry Regiment's drive with the objective of striking north to take Ossenberg and then crossing the Rhine River with Wesel as its final objective.

If the Germans wished to continue the war, they had to stop the Allies at the Wesel pocket on the west bank of the Rhine in order to protect their primary industrial region, the Ruhr Valley. The German strategy: Hold the Wesel pocket as long as possible, cross the Rhine, and then destroy the remaining bridges behind them. They had orders to fight to the end if necessary or face reprisals against their families. The SS roamed the area executing any German soldier or civilian in dereliction of duty.

Dog Company, 36th Tank Battalion, of the 8th Armored Division turned north at Lintfort on the road leading to the Fossa Canal. They passed elements of their 49th Armored Infantry Battalion who were bogged down in mopping up the northern edge of the town. When their light tanks cleared a road crossing, an enemy infantry company dug in just north of the intersection opened fire, blasting into the rear of the column and working their way to the front. As they returned fire, 2 tanks from the 784th Tank Battalion, who were assisting the 49th Armored Infantry Battalion, came from the south and drove north directly into the enemy's dug-in position. They crushed enemy soldiers in their foxholes and drove the rest of them off.

Dog Company, 36th Tank Battalion continued north and ran directly into "88 Alley." Their light tanks, without the support of infantry, had made crucial mistakes that later the surviving sergeants critiqued. They lost all of their company officers, either killed or seriously wounded in action. The light tanks backed out of the intense artillery fire while firing at every possible place where a concealed anti-tank gun could be hidden. The enemy's artillery fire continued nonstop. During the withdrawal several more tanks fell. When they finally reached safety, they found a medic from the 784th Tank Battalion. He treated and loaded one casualty on his jeep and the others on the back of a 784th tank for evacuation.

The 137th Infantry Regiment followed elements of the 8th Armored Division in a single file column towards Rheinberg and encountered practically no opposition. Every house and building appeared to be an enemy fortress. Machine guns, mortars,

Troops of the 137th Infantry Regiment follow tanks of the 784th as they clear their way to Rheinberg, Germany. Note censored road signs. *Courtesy U.S. Army Military History Institute, Carlisle Barracks, Pennsylvania*

88-millimeter guns, and an extremely large caliber unidentified weapon opened up on the already zeroed-in road. The entire column took heavy casualties as they braced themselves and returned fire while the infantry scattered and dug in. Later, military intelligence determined that the enemy employed another one of its stealth weapons, the *Sturmmorser* Tigers. These mobile superstructures brandished a 380-millimeter assault rocket mounted on a Tiger I chassis. They normally operated in a company of 4 tanks.

CCB, 8th Armored Division recounts being trapped on that road: "'All we could do was sit there and sweat,' remembers Tank Commander Sergeant Vernon McLean, Towson, Maryland, of the Rheinberg battle. 'We were hemmed in. We couldn't turn.'"[1]

By many accounts, the deadliest weapon the *Wehrmacht* employed was their legendary and fearsome 88-millimeter cannon. This versatile weapon could appear on a tank, as an anti-tank gun, as an assault gun, or as an anti-aircraft weapon. With relative ease, it knocked out Sherman tanks with its extremely high muzzle velocity. Even without armor-piercing ammo it could penetrate a Sherman tank. The trajectory would fire so flat that the rise of the warhead in its direct path would seldom get higher than the height of its target. It also proved lethal as an anti-infantry weapon when it fired short-fused shells to create airbursts. The sharp ripping whine of an incoming 88 was intended to unnerve everyone who heard it.

Meanwhile, elements of the 137th Infantry Regiment attacked Lintfort and then at dusk took the lead position in the column relieving elements of the 8th Armored Division. The 35th Infantry Division's After Action Reports put it this way:

> A night attack was planned to capture Rheinberg, a plan which only a veteran, experienced unit could fulfill. In a daring and shrewd move, the 3rd Battalion entered Rheinburg at 1930, and the 2nd Battalion at 2012. After dismounting from trucks, the battalions made contact and worked their way down the main street, the 2nd Battalion on one side and the 3rd Battalion on the other. After flushing out dark cellars and buildings, Rheinberg was nearly cleaned up by 0300. Firefights continued until 0600 when the city was mopped up and securely out posted. The tankers of the 784th added a touch to the victory by prefacing their entry into the city with a sensational dash, through 5 miles of enemy lines, to the Rhine River itself.[2]

Infantryman Bernard "Jack" Kirsch, Fox Company, 137th Infantry Regiment illustrates:

> Rheinberg was very intense fighting. We took that town in a night attack and it was dark and I'm telling you it was so dark that we had to almost hold onto each other to keep from wandering off. That preceding day had been a huge tank battle at Rhineberg. It was so dark that we could not see but there were still tanks burning. It was really a ferocious battle so they decided to try to take it with infantry at night so that is what we did. The next morning the 784th came with us. They went on about a 4 or 5-mile dash through there. We got into Rheinberg and on the other side were blown bridges in Rheinberg itself and that stopped the tanks and it stopped us.[3]

The prized captured trophy for Task Force Murray in the taking of Rheinberg was the luxurious mansion in the town square. Regimental Headquarters and the 3rd Battalion located their command post (CP) there.

Meanwhile, elements of Task Force Byrne along with elements of the 8th Armored Division entered Rheinberg. Staff Sergeant Franklin Garrido, Baker Company, 784th Tank Battalion recalls:

> Rheinberg, Germany, is where I was wounded. Rheinberg was a little town on the Rhine. We cleared the way for the infantry under small arms and mortar fire. I was riding uncovered with my hatch open for better vision. We were in a line formation about 50 to 100 yards apart. It was just a platoon of tanks, 5, possibly 6. We moved in on Rheinburg and captured it. Prior to moving into Rheinberg my tank was hit by a mortar shell and fragments flew up and hit me in the face. It felt like a baseball bat or something. I fell to the floor. It hurt and I told my crew I was hit, I was hit, I was hurt and I was going to kill the first Kraut that I see. That was a trickle-down that we heard from General Patton. He admonished all of his troops to not call the German soldiers Jerry because Jerry sounds too friendly. "If you have to call those SOBs anything, call them Krauts!" That was the first time I used the word Kraut because I was in pain. I told my crew, just keep going and I'm going to kill the first Kraut I see. We skidded into the town square. On the cobblestones we skidded to a stop where the doughs were rounding up prisoners. As the first prisoner walked past my tank, I climbed up and out of the turret and cocked my submachine gun and I leveled down on the first one I saw. I was going to kill him. The prisoner screamed, he fell down to the ground in the fetal position and started screaming: "*NEIN! NEIN!* (NO! NO!) *BITTE! BITTE! BITTE!* (PLEASE! PLEASE! PLEASE!)" I was concentrating on whether I was going to shoot him in the head or in the belly. I was thinking, if I shoot him in the head, it will kill him instantly. If I shoot him in the belly, his guts will fall all over the place and he'll be screaming even more. I was aiming for his head and he kept saying, "*NEIN! NEIN!*" He then said, "*KINDER! KINDER!* (CHILDREN! CHILDREN!)," I turned away. In the meantime my crew was yelling at me, "Don't do it! Don't do it!" The doughs were yelling at me, "Kill him! Kill the SOB! Kill him!" My crew won out. I couldn't shoot the man.[4]

For the remainder of the day, the combat teams waited in and around Rheinberg due to the blown bridges. Without the support of tanks, the infantry couldn't move against the heavy enemy fire directed at them from across the flat expanses of terrain and the tanks couldn't cross the stream until a bridge was built. The drive continued as soon as a bridge was assembled, with Ossenberg as the next objective. American artillery pounded Ossenberg day and night so that it could be taken and an end put to the enemy's retreat across the Rhine River above the town. The infantry had a bitter struggle clearing the Haus-Heideberg Woods west of Ossenberg.

Infantryman Murray Leff, Easy Company, 137th Infantry Regiment noted the mood:

> In Rheinberg I was able to find a camera. I traded, I forgot what for it, and it was with this camera that I took pictures of the 784th and the action that day. I had taken a miniature

camera with me to Europe. It took 2 frames on a 127-size film. I took some great pictures coming up to the front line with that camera. My mother would send me film in packages so I would be able to continue taking pictures. But unfortunately when I got up to the front line they asked us to put everything in a barracks bag that we didn't want to lose because the conditions on the front line were unpredictable. Among other things I put that camera in the barracks bag. We were on the line for a week or 2 and when we got back I asked for the barracks bag and lo and behold, there was no barracks bag. The things I put in there had just disappeared. So I had no camera until Rheinberg. We didn't fight for Rheinberg. Some other unit had taken it. We had come in there to get ready for the assault the following day on Ossenberg. In Rheinberg we were able to get some beer, there was a beer hall where we could help ourselves to the beer, which we did. Everybody enjoyed that. In general it was a relaxing kind of day but the following morning was a different story.[5]

March 7, 1945: Task Force Murray found itself at the outskirts of Ossenberg, absorbing all sorts of intense interlocking enemy artillery fire. The road from Rheinberg to Ossenberg, dubbed "88 Alley," is where they encountered their heaviest artillery and mortar fire. Infantryman Bernard "Jack" Kirsch recalls: "It was fierce! We had them pocketed and they were fighting for their lives to get out of there and to cross that bridge at Wesel. They moved up artillery on the other side of the Rhine. I mean they just laid it on us. One day it was so intense that we had to lay low in the basement most of the day. That's when we were out of Rheinberg going to Ossenberg, a part of '88 Alley.'"[6]

Infantryman Murray Leff describes in great detail the infantryman's most valuable implement:

We were always digging holes. The entrenching tool, the shovel we carry had more significance and importance than the rifle because our opportunity to shoot the rifle was limited. You have to see the enemy to shoot at him and they weren't showing themselves. Most times when we where shooting, we shot where we thought they were, in trees and in windows, but not actually seeing the German soldiers themselves. The way I saw it, we would attack a position, they would shoot at us, we would dig in, and our tanks and artillery would shoot at where we drew the fire. I came up with this feeling that we were mostly targets, out there being targets for them to shoot at. In that role, digging in to the ground gave us protection like nothing else could. The feeling that I got when I got into a foxhole that was fairly deep was relative safety. The shell would have to hit very close to do any damage to me when I was at the bottom of a hole. When you think about it, 10 feet of earth would stop nearly anything. A shell hitting closely by would be very unnerving but in a couple of minutes you would recover from that and you don't get hurt. What I'm getting at is the constant digging of holes. As soon as we stopped anywhere, we would start digging right away.[7]

The enemy also resorted to every conceivable trick in their desperate attempt to keep the Allies from crossing the Rhine River. Some even clothed themselves in American uniforms and fired on unsuspecting Allies.

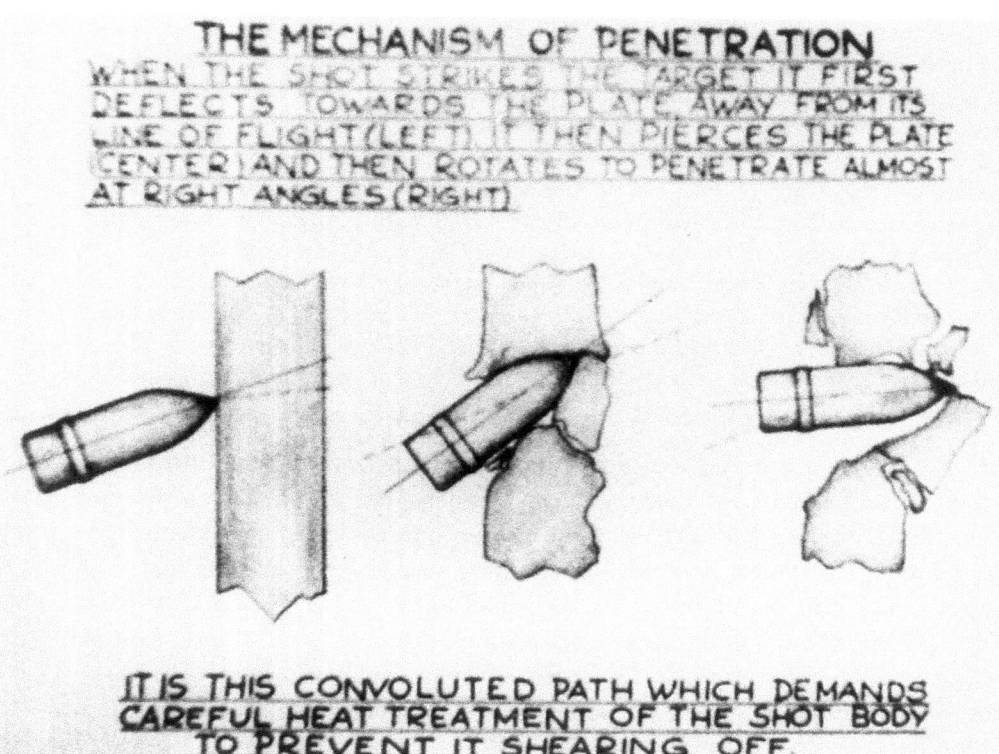

Diagram of the mechanism of penetration. The original caption reads, "When the shot strikes the target it first deflects towards the plate, away from its line of flight (left). It then pierces the plate (center) and then rotates to penetrate almost at right angles (right). It is this convoluted path which demands careful heat treatment of the shot body to prevent it shearing off." *Courtesy U.S. Army Ordnance Museum, Aberdeen Proving Ground, Maryland*

March 8, 1945: Task Force Murray hammered away at the enemy pocket in and around Ossenberg. There they organized into 3 combat teams for a sustained assault.

Combat Team One, commanded by Major Fink, consisted of the 1st Battalion, 137th Infantry Regiment; a platoon from the 654th Tank Destroyer Battalion; a platoon from the 60th Engineer Combat Battalion; and a platoon from Able Company, 784th Tank Battalion. This combat team jumped off prior to dawn with the mission of hitting the highway between Ossenberg and Millingen, then attacking northwest to take the town of Menzelen. They battled 18 hours before they came upon a huge slag pile and brickyard southwest of Ossenberg. Before dawn the next morning they jumped off behind the support of artillery fire that scattered the enemy defenders and left them crazed with panic and running for their lives. Then the column opened up with a murderous hail of machine gun fire that cut into them and bounced them around like puppets. The rest were ineffectually crawling for cover. The combat team captured the slag pile by 1400 hours. Then they went around the slag pile and attacked the yard with its numerous piles of bricks. By 2000 hours, they cleared the area with the exception of determined enemy snipers.

Combat Team Two, commanded by Lt. Colonel Butler, consisted of his 3rd Battalion, 137th Infantry Regiment; Baker Company, 809th Tank Destroyer Battalion; elements of the 36th Tank Battalion; and Baker Company, 53rd Engineer Combat Battalion. This combat team jumped off in the predawn hours with the mission of taking Ossenberg. At daylight they reached the town only to get pushed back by a counterattack. The combat team pulled back and then jumped off once more. They reached the Solvay Works, where they ran into fierce enemy fire coming from every building and shack. They destroyed 2 enemy tanks and one assault gun before out flanking the enemy.

Combat Team Three, commanded by Lt. Colonel Roseborough, consisted of his 49th Armored Infantry Battalion; 2nd Battalion, 137th Infantry Regiment; elements of the 654th Tank Destroyer Battalion; Baker Company, 36th Tank Battalion; elements of the 80th Engineer Combat Battalion; and 2 platoons from the 784th Tank Battalion. This combat team jumped off before the first light with the mission of attacking along the highway west of the Rhine River. They continued northeast up the highway to Buderich, where they got pinned down by heavy artillery fire from the eastern side of the Rhine River. The enemy's artillery fire fell incessantly and accurately in "88 Alley" as the ground shook with concussion after concussion.

Infantryman Bernard "Jack" Kirsch with Combat Team Three points out:

> Task Force Murray had 3 groups and we were in the third group. Our assignment was between the river and the first group as we were adjacent to the Rhine River pushing up. The enemy was looping around and that is how we got a lot of intense artillery fire. That was the most intense artillery shelling we had ever experienced. At least, I had experienced. It was fierce! So when we went to Ossenberg, we went along a road without tanks. We were not in Ossenberg center, we were by the Rhine River and they brought up the tanks and we were talking to them, we had a conversation. We all had pistols we had picked up from the Germans. They shouted out: "Hey! We never get any pistols!" We shouted back: "We'll get you some!" I say this because the 784th hadn't been with the 35th for very long. They had been assigned sometime before that. Our guys really liked them. They really were very commendable. They were a lot more aggressive than the other outfit that had been with us. "Hey, we ought to get some prisoners today and we'll get you some pistols!" There was some artillery not too far ahead so they called the tanks to go and try to knock it out. And they moved up, I don't know how far. It's hard to tell now, 100, 200, 300 feet and BOOM, their tank got hit by an 88-millimeter. And that destroyed their tank and killed them all. So we didn't get them their pistols. So later on we did pick up some pistols, and we gave them to a tank crew in memory of our commitment to them.[8]

Infantryman Murray Leff, also with Combat Team Three, recounts in great detail:

> We attacked in the morning and came across this large field with no buildings in the immediate vicinity, all were in the distance. When we got closer, I don't know why, but we hit the dirt. I saw this fellow, Kibbler, who was a rifle-shooting enthusiast as a civilian I see he's got his rifle pointed. He's in the prone position. We all were. He's pointing his

rifle and I didn't know why he would do that. And then without me expecting it, he fires. And I said, "What the hell are you shooting at!" He says, "There's a Kraut out there and I think I got him." I looked and didn't see anything. The next thing I can remember, we attacked into the city, it was a village at the time, and we came down the main street taking one building after the other. These were dwellings, mostly single-family homes. No factories. They had barns, not really clear how these people made a living there. We drew fire from the right-hand side. I think Ossenberg is very close to the Rhine River. It might be on the river. It's possible that some of the fire we were getting was from across the river. Anyway, they are firing at us and we don't hang around. We ducked into a house and held there. Then along comes a tank and this fellow pokes his head out the hatch and I see he's black, which I never anticipated and never knew that there were black troops near us. It was a surprise. In any event, I told him that we were drawing fire from the area on the right. When I say right, the right would be where the river was. This fellow has his machine gunner open up. The machine gunner was down below him. They opened up with the .30 caliber and they finished an entire box of ammunition. I know that because before they moved away they threw out the ammunition can and the empty belt and a

As infantryman Murray Leff recalls, "Advancing against small arms fire, we ducked into a house. A tank from the 784th battalion pulled up. I pointed out the direction the fire was coming from and the tank opened up on it." *Courtesy Murray Leff*

8. Eighty-eight Alley

whole bunch of spent cartridges. Here the ground was grounded up, the front yard, the iron fence, along with the ammunition box and spent cartridges.

The next thing we went into the house and this tank moved around to the side. I don't remember what happened after that except that we stayed in this house where we cooked some K-rations in the basement and had a meal. The next thing we did was to continue our attack. We went up some 4 houses and we held there at that point for the night. Our company CP was across the street. My buddy and I had bedded down under a window of this farmhouse that we went into. This was a genuine farmhouse. I say that because I see in the pictures that there is a big farm wagon, the kind that's drawn by a horse. Anyway, we went to sleep and the next thing I know, it is just breaking daylight and this large artillery barrage comes in. It's very intense. There must have been quite a number of big guns, artillery shooting at us. One shell landed maybe 10 feet from the house right under

Murray Leff: "Vernon Kearns and I were sleeping under the window in front of which I am here standing, when the barrage came in. We were showered with plaster and broken glass but were not hurt. I am pointing to the hole made by the shell that caused the damage. It also tore up the wagon wheel and the roof." *Courtesy Murray Leff*

the window we were sleeping under. The picture of me standing in front of the house shows how the shell made a hole in the ground and where it threw shrapnel up at an angle.

It tore away part of the wagon wheel and the shingles on the house and a good portion of the shrapnel came into our window and tore up the window and hit the ceiling. Plaster and glass rained down on us. We just kept our heads down until the firing stopped. We looked around and we were not hurt. We just shook off all that stuff that had fallen on us. What I didn't know was what happened when we were in the house.

When the artillery stopped, I don't know how long after that when I felt brave enough to stick my head out the doorway and that's when I saw this tank that had been hit. It was exploding and burning. I decided that I was going to take a picture of this because it was an unbelievable sight. I just poked my head around the corner where if any exploding shells were to come I would be mostly protected, with one eye looking out from the corner of this house. At that point I took this picture and I went back inside and stayed there. I considered the situation pretty hazardous. The next thing I could remember was the following day. That tank had been burning all that time. That following day had been quiet. We received no more artillery. So I thought it was quiet enough for me to go out and look at things and see what's going on. I have to tell you that not everyone was as curious about the surroundings as I was. They were content to stay where they were. At any rate, I see that tank is still smoldering. I walked up to it and I see 2 holes, 88-millimeter, clean holes. It was from a very high velocity shell. I took a picture of the tank with me in front of it with a self-timer.

Murray Leff: "We moved up a couple of houses and held there overnight. At dawn the next day we received a very intense artillery barrage when the Germans rolled out an 88 millimeter. With it they set the tank afire." *Courtesy Murray Leff*

Top: Murray Leff: "March 10. I took this self-timed photo while the tank was still smoldering. There is one shell hole behind my shoulder and another a few feet in front of me." *Courtesy Murray Leff*. *Bottom:* Murray Leff: "The company CP across the road from our house was hit twice by the 88 millimeter. Kiplinger, who helped me dig my first foxhole, was killed. There were several other casualties. The self-timed photo went off just as I saw the horror inside the doorway. Ray Lux was one of those wounded." *Courtesy Murray Leff*

Murray Leff: "Inside the CP, covered with plaster dust, is a severed leg with shredded trousers hanging from it." *Courtesy Murray Leff*

Shortly thereafter, that afternoon sometime, this chaplain is in the tank taking out the bodies. I was thinking that maybe I can take a picture. This chaplain says to me, "You don't really want a picture of this!" I agreed with him and put the camera away and he continued to do what he was doing. He pulled out a shapeless something that could not be identified as a human being, all black. He put it in a blanket. I turned away. Across the street where our company command post was located, had received a couple of shells. I went there to see what was happening and took pictures of that too. I set the camera up with the self-timer and I aimed at the destruction of the house and as I walked up to it the camera went off.

When I looked inside I saw everything covered in plaster. Two or maybe more shells had come right above the door and through the door and there leaning against a wheelbarrow was a dismembered leg with shredded trousers falling away from the knee. It was standing up and you can see the boot, you can see the leg. It was very unreal.

The following day, this fellow who had shot this German and I didn't know he had shot him but he had claimed he did or at least shot at a German on the way into town. He says he's going to go find this guy that he shot so one other fellow and I go with him to see what he's talking about. Sure enough, when we got back to that area we found the dead German. This German was a scout, scouting us out for the artillery. He probably had just his head above this small rise. This fellow had shot him squarely in the middle of the helmet. When he did that this German had slid down the embankment, out of sight,

8. Eighty-eight Alley

that's why I never saw him. We got there that particular day and this guy who shot him looked through his clothes and at that point I took a picture of that.

Last July when I visited the cemetery at Margraten I found the grave of my buddy Howard Keplinger, who is shown as having been killed on March 9, 1945. I believe it is possible that the 2 men in the burning tank and Keplinger, all might have been killed within minutes of each other by the same 88. They were only 100 to 200 yards from each other at the time.[9]

On March 9, Task Force Murray continued its 3-pronged assault at 0700 hours. Combat Team One punched ahead to the eastern outskirts of Millingen. Combat Team Two began mopping up bypassed resistance in Ossenberg. Combat Team Three continued being pinned down by sporadic enemy fire coming from the eastern side of the Rhine River.

Meanwhile Task Force Byrne continued pushing ahead on the left flank of Task Force Murray trapping the enemy in a vise — the Wesel pocket. The roads and open

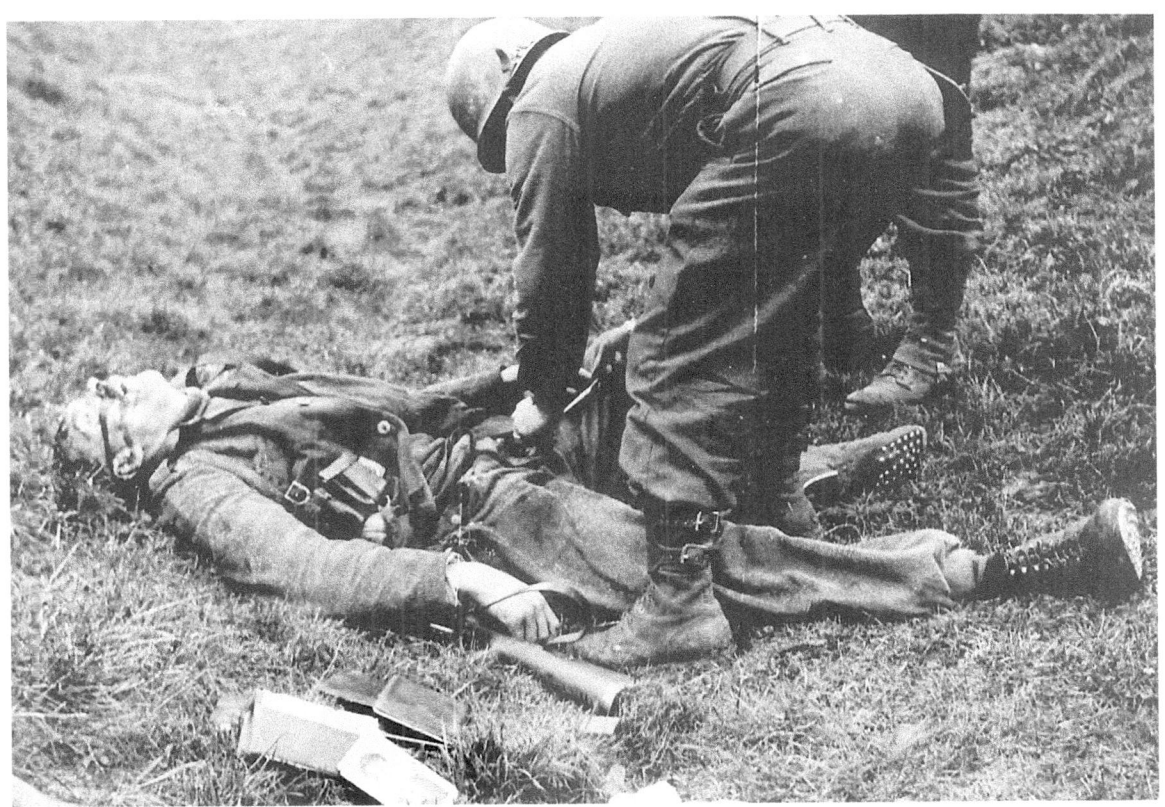

Murry Leff: "March 11. It's now relatively safe to walk around. Kibler leads us to this German he shot in the action on the way into town. Obviously the bullet hole in the helmet explains what happened. Kibler is examining the dead German. A picture of the German as a civilian lies in the foreground. What a waste!" *Courtesy Murray Leff*

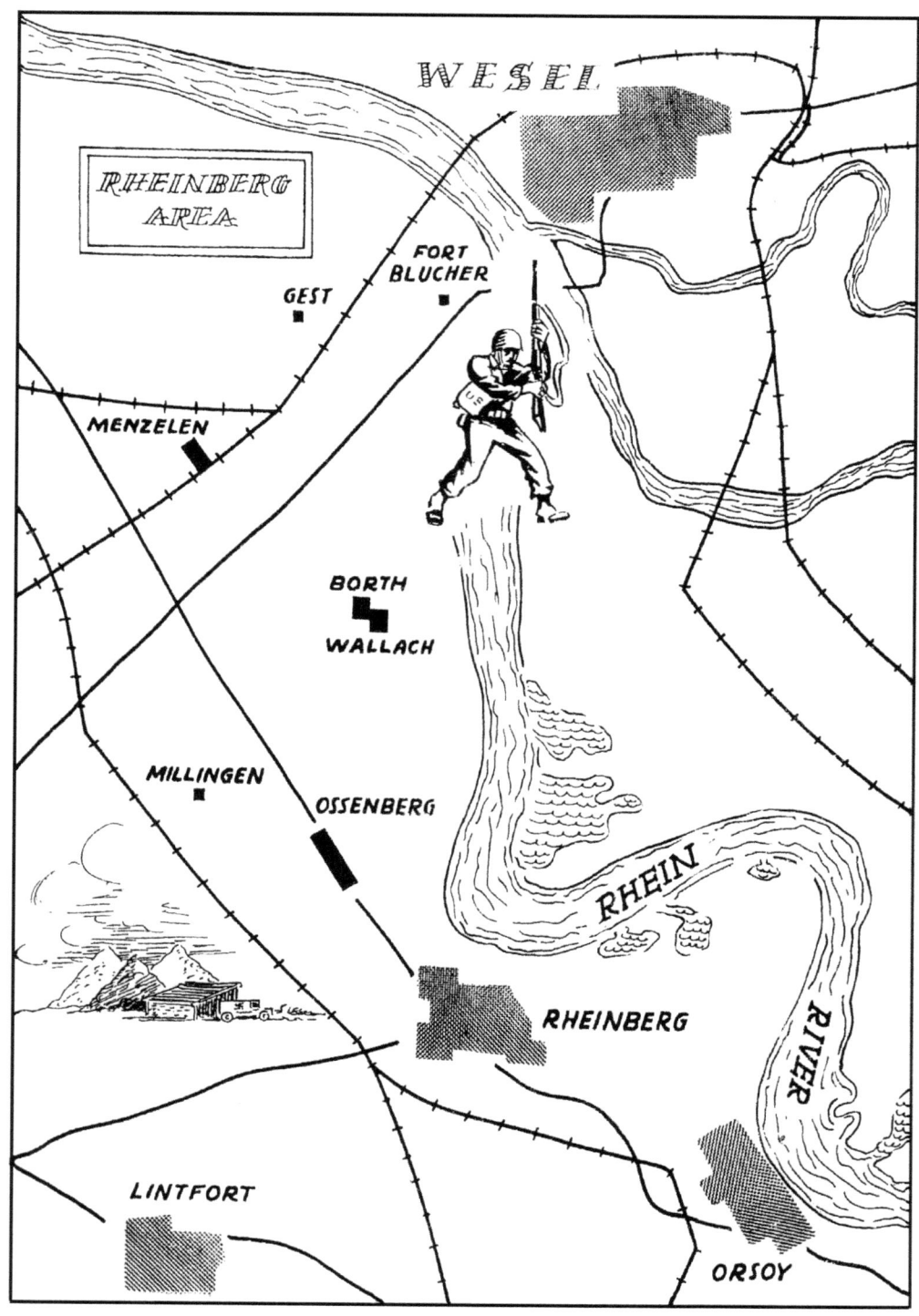

"Valor for Service." 137th Infantry Regiment map, courtesy National Archives and Records Administration.

fields were heavily booby-trapped with anti-tank Teller mines. The tanks provided covering fire as the infantry crawled through the minefields, prodding the earth with bayonets. The tanks then passed single file through the minefields. At times the tanks led the way, exploding smaller anti-personnel mines, while the infantry followed in the tank tracks.

On March 10, Task Force Murray had its boundaries shifted right after the 137th Infantry Regiment broke out of "88 Alley" and pushed forward to the Rhine River. The 134th Infantry Regiment pinched them out and pushed north with Task Force Byrne. The 137th Infantry Regiment then started mopping up bypassed enemy pockets. At 2200 hours, CCB and other elements of the 8th Armored Division detached from the task force. For Task Force Murray and Task Force Byrne, it was mission accomplished. They finally made it to the banks of the Rhine River.

Infantryman Bernard "Jack" Kirsch remembers reaching the banks of the Rhine:

> We were near Ossenberg and we left soon after the fighting quieted down. We were there a number of days when a jeep came up with a colonel and a driver in it. We were right on the banks of the Rhine River. So this colonel crawls up to the top and had some of our officers with him and looked over this river. They crept up a bank to peek over. We asked that driver, "What are you guys doing up here?" "Corps of Engineers! We're going to build a bridge here!" Yeah, you know all about how many rumors we have heard. Well, that's where they built the bridge and that's where we crossed on a pontoon bridge.[10]

9

Crossing the Rhine

March 12, 1945: the 75th Infantry Division pinched out the battle-weary 35th Infantry Division from its zone along the Rhine River front. The entire division displaced to an area southeast of Venlo, Holland, where they conducted refresher training and maintenance. During this period they issued passes to Brussels and Paris, and made time for recreation, movies, and Red Cross club mobiles with special refreshments.

The 784th Tank battalion set up its command post in Tegelen, Holland, where they performed maintenance, trained replacement personnel, and took time for R & R.

Tech-5 James Hamilton, Charlie Company, 784th Tank Battalion points out: "We lost 32 tanks in that section. Man! When I got back my hair had been up through my helmet and it looked like I had a cross on top of my head. We stopped at Liege, Belgium, and all got baths and deloused and they gave us clean uniforms. Then we went to town in Belgium for a weekend. It was sure nice to get a relief and come back for a rest. We got some fresh food and we had steaks and everything."[1]

Corporal James Baldwin, Headquarters Company, 784th Tank Battalion painfully remembers:

> Even though we were segregated there was some interaction. We wouldn't be in combat for more than 10 days I think before they pulled us back and we would stay back for over a week sometimes. So while we were back we got passes to go into town. There we had to fight white America! I will never forget that! We had an experience in some little old Belgian town. When we got there blacks and whites started to fight. They ordered us all to something like a town hall. It was a huge room and a full colonel was in charge. He was trying to tell us that we are all from the same country we should not fight each other. Then one white guy rose up and shouted: "But these are our girls!" That colonel, it will

9. Crossing the Rhine

always stick with me he said "Oh yeah, I understand what you're talking about." I remember I just walked out.

You see, they had their clubs, and, then well, um, that's OK. They went around with all whites and the girls that they dated didn't bother with blacks for the most part, and the girls that the blacks dated didn't bother with the white guys. It was that type of thing, like at home.[2]

The intense fighting had taken such a toll that the 784th required emergency replacement tanker crew members. This tank battalion received no replacements from the Armored Force Replacement Training Center at Fort Knox. The experimental tank battalions (758th, 761st and 784th) were intended to pacify Eleanor Roosevelt and never intended for combat. They received the call to duty only when well-trained separate tank battalions were desperately needed.

The emergency replacements came from a variety of service units. Completely untrained in tanks, these men wanted the opportunity to fight in a combat unit. An initial 2-week training course took place before matriculating them to on-the-job-training while in combat.

The critical losses sustained in Task Force Byrne and Task Force Murray resulted in this dangerous shortage of tank crew members. The M4 Sherman tank normally operated with a crew of 5: The driver; the assistant driver/bow gunner; the loader/assistant gunner; the gunner; and the tank commander.

Corporal James Baldwin on leave from combat duty in Belgium, March 1945. *Courtesy James Baldwin*

As casualties became acute, the assistant driver/bow gunner would be eliminated first. This denied the tank the use of the ball-mounted machine gun, which proved effective against infantry. The loader/assistant gunner was next to go and the tank commander doubled as the loader. This gave the tank a bare minimum, a 3-man crew.

The high productivity of the automotive industry back in the United States sufficiently replaced the Sherman tanks destroyed in combat. The Germans were not so fortunate because most of their production efforts had been lost as a result of the Allied bombings. In many instances the Germans were reduced to horse-drawn weapons.

Sergeant Simmons Washington, Headquarters Company, 784th Tank Battalion recollected:

> I recall places like Rheinberg. From there we pulled back into Tegelen, Holland, to fuel up and get ready for the last big move. I don't remember all of the towns because we moved so fast but in some of the towns we slowed down to get ammunition and things like that. It was cold in Holland. I remember the windmills but we didn't get a chance to see the poppies that grow there but we remember the canals and all of that. From out of Holland we came back and crossed the Rhine into Germany and we made our last move on the route to Berlin! But we never got there.[3]

War correspondent Ted Stanford of the *Pittsburgh Courier* peered across the smoke and fog-covered Rhine with binoculars for his first glimpse at fortified German positions. Although he observed no movement, obviously the enemy was there. Then it suddenly occurred to him that the Germans had been watching him where he knelt, squinting through the fog: "At once I felt tremendously large and conspicuous and for the first time I noticed that at some time a shell had carried away a part of the roof of the building in which I stood. A young sergeant with an easy Southern accent smiled at me understandingly.[4]

The combat engineers had already prepared slit trenches to retreat to when harassed by German artillery and strafing aircraft. They spent most of the daylight hours in these trenches and at night worked under the cover of darkness. They labored as silently as possible, knowing that every sound brought small arms and mortar fire in their direction. The mortar fire was not intended for the 784th tanks but simply an attempt to acquire the range on the combat engineers. Despite the heavy casualties, they completed their mission.

Combat Engineer Robert Martin, 208th Engineer Combat Battalion, U.S. Ninth Army recalls:

> Other engineers were building a road up to the Rhine to get a division through. They had it built up out of rubble, generally bricks and stone. They built it straight. I was at the Rhine River helping to build pontoon bridges and it was a big river. When we built the pontoon bridge, the pontoons were hauled there by truck and then we just kept adding them on. First off all we had to make a bridgehead on the other side and put cables across, something to hold it. Then we put one on the cable and ran it across. No electrical tools

9. Crossing the Rhine

Left to right, Tank Driver Lee Askew, aka, "Jelly Belly"; Bill "Baby Slim" Hart; and Simmons Washington. *Courtesy James Baldwin*

Privates George Cofield (left) and Howard Davis guard a construction site over the Rhine River, built by U.S. Ninth Army Engineers, March 30, 1945. *Courtesy National Archives*

or air-powered tools, it was all hand work. Anytime we could get away from screwing on a nut or a bolt we would use a pin, less work and less time. We kept pushing them out. Then we put treadways over them. You then had a bridge. When it was light enough, you could see the Germans on the other side of the ridge shaking their blankets and whatever. But when it got dark, they would start sending 88s in to try to blow us off the map. This one night I was sitting by a shell hole and they started firing. One 88 sounded like it was coming right at me and it landed right behind me but it never went off. What do you think of that? Isn't that something? The other ones all went off. If it went off, it would have cut my throat or taken my head off easily. So that was another close shave. Anyhow, it was quite a bit of work with everything you put into it but by golly, they went across. I thought that was great to build a bridge in no time and then get a division across the Rhine River. That was amazing!⁵

Combat Engineer Robert Martin went on to say:

I got to see "Whitie" Kolack. His name was Stanley and everybody called him "Whitie" because of his hair — it was real white. I was coming out one evening and I recognized Whitie, who lived up the road from my home. He was driving a jeep and he didn't have his helmet on. I told my driver, "I know that guy." And sure enough, that's who it was. I got to see him later and talked to him. There were about 6 brothers in that family in the

9. Crossing the Rhine

war at the same time. The youngest brother got killed in Germany. We talked about home, the things we did at home to have fun, and the square dances we went to. We didn't really talk much about the war. We talked about things we liked to do, things that brought us home for the minute.[6]

March 23, 1945: Operation Plunder — the Twenty-first Army Group's offensive to cross the last great natural barrier from the West and finally end the war in Europe jumped off. This date was referred to as D-day for the Rhine River crossing. Elements of the Canadian First Army, the British Second Army, and the U.S. Ninth Army crossed the river on a variety of assault boats under the cover of a 66-mile-long smoke screen. They landed and attacked north and south of Wesel on the east bank. The Rhine was the historic defensive line protecting Germany from its enemies since the days of Caesar.

The banks of the Rhine River reminded one of the earlier D-day in Normandy, France (June 6, 1944). Barrage balloons, anti-aircraft batteries, convoys of personnel and supply trucks, and field artillery batteries firing in support of the crossing inundated this flat, beach-like area. An enemy plane strafed and hit a barrage balloon that

Tanks of the 784th escort the infantry along the Rhine plain, March 1945. *Courtesy U.S. Army Military History Institute, Carlisle Barracks, Pennsylvania*

errupted into an enormous ball of fire. Landing craft, equipment of all types, stockpiles of supplies, along with debris littered the beach on both sides. The civilian population had to be evacuated for several miles along the west bank.

On the morning of March 24, 1945, the largest airborne operation in history flew over the Rhine in Operation Varsity. The entire column took 2 hours and 18 minutes to fly over. This great air armada consisted of 226 C-47s and 72 C-46s plus 610 C-47s towing 906 gliders. To the left of this formation, the British 6th Airborne Division employed 42 C-54s, 752 C-47s, and 420 gliders. There were 676 U.S. Army Air Force fighters and 213 Royal Air Force fighters flying escort protection. The sky was full with nearly 4,000 aircraft. The 17th "Thunder from Heaven" Airborne Division Association describes this event:

> It was a sight never before seen. Stretched across the sky as far as one's eye could see was the largest sky armada ever assembled then and now. There were literally thousands of aircraft — gliders, C-47s, C-46s, and fighter cover of all sorts — transporting men, equipment, supplies, and ammunition. Several records were set: first time C-47s double-towed gliders in combat, first and only time troopers jumped the double-door C-46 in combat, and the first time glider combat troops landed on fields not previously secured by paratroops.[7]

As the airborne conveyor belt approached the Rhine, anti-aircraft fire put up a thick blanket of flak that shook and rattled the planes. Shrapnel broke through the wings and the sides hitting paratroopers waiting in line to jump. Axis Sally had previously made continuous announcements over the radio regarding Operation Varsity: "We know you are coming, 17th Airborne Division, you will not need parachutes, you can walk down on the flak."[8]

For the next several minutes each paratrooper preparing to jump did almost the same things. They double-checked their equipment. Many said a brief prayer, made the sign of the cross, and wished their buddies good luck. The jump masters bellowed: "Stand up! Hook up! Check equipment! Stand in the door!" Then the green light flashed all too soon: "GO!!!" The paratroopers shoved each other out into the cold blast. Everyone feared being hit by the flak outside the aircraft and going down in flames with the aircraft. The descent was fast but seemed an eternity because they came under direct fire. Many paratroopers were killed during the descent, some landed in trees, some on rooftops, and some got caught up in power lines. When they looked up they saw flaming planes and crashing gliders. Under fire they fought their way to the assembly areas and consolidated their forces and moved towards their objectives.

Paratrooper Everett Cook recounts:

> The 507th Parachute Infantry Regiment was a part of the 82nd Airborne Division until around February/March 1945 when we were attached to the 17th Airborne Division. We took off our 82nd patches and put on what our sergeants called the "clutch and hook."
> Operation Varsity was going to use the 507th to spearhead the Rhine crossing because

of our combat experience. When we crossed the Rhine I was in one of the first planes and we were the first ones out of the plane. All hell broke loose! When that old jump master said, Get out of here!" I jumped and my main chute opened. Then I let my machine gun down and looked down into that open field — the DZ. It was solid tracers coming from all directions. I got rid of my reserve chute and I slipped over a house and a road with streetcar tracks and came down through a big tree. When my feet hit the ground I popped my release and the tree pulled the chute off of me. Did you ever see a C-47 shooting straight up like a rocket? Well, that's what they did after they dropped us out.

I had my carbine because I couldn't get to my machine gun. The Germans were all around us, everywhere, and we just started shooting. We were not supposed to take prisoners so there were dead all around. Then we moved out and reached our objective by 1400 hours. It was around 1100 hours when we hit the silk. Then we held up for the night and nobody moved and we knew if anything moved it was not one of us. For the rest of the operation I just covered the guys with my .30 caliber machine gun.[9]

The airborne objective was to secure and broaden the bridgehead east of the Rhine and take the high ground overlooking the crossing and also the bridges over the Issel River. They achieved all objectives within 24 hours. The 17th Airborne Division had taken approximately 3,100 prisoners, many of them high-ranking German officers, as they overran and eliminated the German 84th *Infantrie* Division and destroyed at least 13 enemy tanks, 2 self-propelled assault guns, and several artillery batteries that had the beach zeroed in. The British had similar successes.

Operation Varsity was a success despite heavy casualties. The British 6th Airborne Division suffered 1,078 men either killed or wounded with 50 aircraft and 11 gliders shot down. The 17th Airborne Division suffered 159 killed in action, 522 wounded, and 840 missing in action and a large number of aircraft destroyed. Fortunately, 600 of the 840 men reported as missing in action rejoined their outfits.

Infantryman James Graff, Charlie Company, 134th Infantry Regiment comments on the aftermath of the enormous airborne assault:

> The area was littered with all kinds of airborne equipment. All kinds of abandoned ordnance and supplies attached to parachutes was scattered over a huge area. Different color parachutes meant different kinds of supplies, green for medical supplies and red for ammunition. German soldiers and civilians had dumped large amounts into canals and streams. We found one dead paratrooper whose chute had failed to open. He was half buried from the fall, a sad sight. Also there were a good deal of wrecked gliders and several C-47s. We believe the airborne attack was completely unnecessary. It wasted a lot of supplies and resulted in a larger number of casualties than a straight infantry attack and, as the Germans were falling back anyway, it was a wasted effort and wasted lives for just a big show.[10]

March 25, 1945: Brig. General Butler Miltonberger, Assistant Division Commander, 35th Infantry Division ordered the formation of Task Force Miltonberger. His former command, the 134th Infantry Regiment, now commanded by Colonel Alford Boatsman, executed the leading role. Support came from the 161st Field Artillery

Battalion; 127th Field Artillery Battalion; Able Company, 654th Tank Destroyer Battalion; 60th Engineer Combat Battalion; Able Company, 110th Medical Battalion. Able Company, 784th Tank Battalion spearheaded this task force with the objective of crossing the Rhine River; relieving the 315th Infantry Regiment, 79th Division on the line; and seizing intact the bridge crossing the Schwarzer River. This task force would be attached to the 79th Infantry Division for this operation.

March 26, 1945: D-day plus 3 for the Rhine crossing — Able Company, 784th Tank Battalion with Task Force Miltonberger crossed the Rhine River at "Blue Beach" near Rheinberg on "Love Bridge." Sergeant Bill Hughes, Dog Company, 784th Tank Battalion recalls:

> I think it was "A" Company that went over first at night. The rest of the battalion crossed later and met no resistance. We were told the bridge could be dangerous crossing since the Germans were expected to blow it up. However, since other heavier tanks had crossed earlier, my main concern was would it collapse and toss us into the river. How could I survive such a fall and even if I did, what does one do, not knowing how to swim? After crossing the Rhine, several of our tanks joined the forward tank column. I heard over the radio that one got hit and the crew escaped safely. We met periodic small arms and mortar shelling, but moved very rapidly out of harm's way.[11]

Infantryman James Graff adds: "The engineers had completed a big pontoon bridge in less than 24 hours which was quite a feat. Its code name was 'Love.' The Rhine was almost a half-mile wide here. Searchlights lit up the crossing site and we walked across while vehicles, tanks and trucks also were moving across. After the crossing we walked all night and finally got into some buildings and stayed until morning."[12]

After relieving the 315th Infantry Regiment, Task Force Miltonberger pushed forward through a wooded area under sporadic resistance, including considerable 20-millimeter flak guns and a variety of direct-fire artillery. One 784th tank received a direct hit and caught fire. Tech-4 Albert Marshall of Mississippi perished inside the blazing inferno. By 1242 hours the task force had reached its objective and captured the bridge intact. Several hours later the task force was dissolved and control reverted back to the 35th Infantry Division.

Meanwhile, on March 26 and 27, the 137th Infantry Regiment and the remainder of the 784th Tank Battalion crossed the Rhine River south of Mehrum on a pontoon bridge. Staff Sergeant Franklin Garrido, Baker Company, 784th Tank Battalion recalls:

> We crossed the Rhine at night. They were still bombing and machine gunning, sending artillery into the area. We crossed on a pontoon bridge. Being a Southern Californian, I'm not used to seeing wide, deep, swift rivers and it scared the heck out of me. At midnight with no lights I had to lead my tank across this deep, wide, fast-flowing river under fire. I was scared. I was a good swimmer and I kept telling my crew, if the tank goes down or if a shell hits one of the pontoons, just ride with the flow of the current. We made it across the bridge. It was scary.[13]

9. Crossing the Rhine

Tech-5 James Hamilton adds: "We crossed the Rhine on pontoon bridges. As we went across we shot down one plane and it hit the water like a piece of hot iron. The pilot came down in his parachute and we got him too, we captured him."[14]

Infantryman Murray Leff, Easy Company, 137th Infantry Regiment adds:

> We crossed the Rhine River on a pontoon bridge. We were loaded on trucks and there was a long line of trucks waiting to get across the river. Then finally it was our turn. There were these smoke generators and you couldn't see too far because of the smoke. It was intended to hide our position from any German air or forward observers who could direct artillery to the bridge. We drove across and we got out in a town called Duisberg, or something like that, and we spent the day there waiting to attack the next morning. When we moved out, we were attacking this position and took fire from a 20-millimeter automatic cannon. We dived into a drainage ditch on the side of the road. We were all in there waiting for tanks to come up or artillery to take care of the Germans in front."[15]

Tanks of the 784th are among the first armor of the U.S. Ninth Army to go into action on the east bank of the Rhine River, March 28, 1945. *Courtesy U.S. Army Military History Institute, Carlisle Barracks, Pennsylvania*

March 27, 1945: elements of the 137th Infantry Regiment and the remainder of the 784th Tank Battalion relieved elements of the 79th Infantry Division on the right flank of the 134th Infantry Regiment. The 137th advanced east towards the *Autobahn* north of the Rhein-Herne canal. They extended through territory intelligence predicted could be defended by the enemy's 180th and 190th *Infantrie* Divisions and the 116th *Panzer-Grenadier* Division. The resistance showed some signs of disorganization but not a willingness to surrender. The coordinated tank/infantry teams of the 137th knifed into the northern section of the Ruhr industrial area against resistance from *Infantrie* and *Panzerfaust* teams. There was no indication of an enemy withdrawal from this front. Heavy enemy fire checked the 137th's crossing of the *Autobahn*. From there they inched towards the city of Essen with its Krupp Steel Works. The fact that this major assault had only captured 290 enemy soldiers is a clear indication of the enemy's determination to hold this industrial area for the *Reich*.

The 320th Infantry Regiment had crossed the Rhine on March 26 near the Wesel bridgehead. The outfit assembled in the vicinity of Letkampshof on the north side of the Ruhr pocket. Infantry Platoon Leader Royal Offer, King Company, 320th Infantry Regiment recalls: "We went across not too far from the Remagen Bridge. We didn't go over that bridge. The outfit that went over it took the pressure off of us. Later we had pontoon bridges set up and we crossed the Rhine and didn't lose a person. We worried about the Rhine all the way there because we thought it was going to be a bad deal but when we went across, we went across so easily that it was quite a relief to us."[16]

The assault into the heart of the German war machine could be described as "deliberate and careful aggressiveness." The high command was still angst-ridden that the enemy could launch a surprise counterattack out of the Ruhr Valley, similar to the Battle of the Bulge. The Germans were now desperately defending their homeland and many were determined to carry out Hitler's orders to fight to the last man.

During the grim month of March 1945, the 784th Tank Battalion suffered 104 battle casualties and 76 non-battle casualties with 4 missing in action. Included in the battle casualties are 20 men killed in action. These include Private First Class William Beamon, Mississippi, killed in action on March 3, 1945; Tech-5 Whitney Bland, Louisiana, killed in action on March 3, 1945; Corporal Wilson Griswel, Mississippi, killed in action on March 6, 1945; Tech-5 Albert Harte, New York, killed in action on March 4, 1945; Private William Hogue, Mississippi, killed in action on March 4, 1945; Sergeant Benjamin Isabelle, Mississippi, killed in action on March 8, 1945; Sergeant Charles Jefferson, Mississippi, killed in action on March 1, 1945; Sergeant James Laurie, New York, killed in action on March 5, 1945; Private Willmore Mack, New York, killed in action on March 5, 1945; Tech-4 Albert Marshall, Mississippi, killed in action on March 26, 1945; Tech-5 John Tompkins, Pennsylvania, killed in action on March 3, 1945; Tech-4 Arthur Whitbeck, New York, killed in action on March 4, 1945; Private Raymond Womack, Tennessee, killed in action on March 5, 1945. In addition, there are 5 men unaccounted for by the American Battle Monuments Commission. These men could have been shipped home for burial. Finally, of the 4 missing in action, Private Napoleon Black, Illinois, missing in action/non-recoverable and presumed killed on August 29, 1946, and 2nd Lieutenant Alexander Carr, Massachusetts, missing in action/non-recoverable and presumed killed on March 7, 1946, were never recovered. The American Monuments Commission explains these unusual dates: "The date of death of those listed as missing in action or lost at sea or non-recoverable is a presumed date of death established by a military review board and *usually* a date which is a year and day from the date the decedent was placed in missing status."[17]

Infantryman Murray Leff commented on these inconsistent dates:

> My squad leader, Sergeant Rich, was recorded as having been killed on November 10, 1944. I was there when he was actually killed on November 8, 1944. I believe the recording of the date of death depended on the one doing the recording, on how long after the event he made his record, whether he got the information first hand, and the "Fog of War" in which the recording of past events is a distant concern when more immediate problems need to be addressed.[18]

10

The Ruhr Pocket

March 27, 1945: about 6 miles inland from the eastern banks of the Rhine River, in an area of rolling wooded hills and villages, the entire 35th Infantry Division prepared to assault the northern edge of the Ruhr Valley, the "Pittsburgh-like" industrial heart of Germany. Far off in the distance they saw high smokestacks marking locations of manufacturing plants, coal mines, and steel mills. This smoke indicated that the German war factories continued operating, business as usual. Many were just a few city blocks behind the main line of resistance. These factories were well dug in below ground level and untouched by aerial bombings. This well-defended industrial hub of the German war machine is the largest and most efficient industrial complex in Europe. It has an extensive network of streets, railroads, inland waterways, and the *Autobahn* serving it. The Ruhr Valley is bordered on the north by the Lippe River, on the south by the Ruhr River, on the west by the Rhine River, and it extends east to the city of Hamm.

The small villages, dubbed "cow towns," encountered directly east of the Rhine would become a sharp contrast to the industrial area several miles away. The smell of manure permeated the air. Robustly built stone houses with outer walls lined with neatly stacked firewood stood on the narrow winding dirt roads through the villages. The assault left many of the stone houses in smoldering heaps. The once neatly stacked firewood, along with dead enemy soldiers, dead animals, and debris, left the passageways nearly impassable. Instead of the familiar manure smell, now the stench of smoldering and decomposing bodies and carcasses filled the air, a reflection of the bitter fighting.

War had come to the German people with a breathtaking violence. The 784th Tank Battalion found that the destruction meted out to the German villages, towns, cities, and countryside was unbelievably worse than anything they saw in France, Belgium, or Holland. In Holland they traveled through tranquil countryside with long green valleys similar to the foothills of Pennsylvania. In Germany it was entirely different. The air was thick with lifelessness and a feeling of danger. The fields were pock-marked with craters, foxholes, and trenches. They went through town after town of gutted buildings, gaping shell holes, and rubble heaps. Birds did not chirp. There was complete silence with no inhabitants in sight. Entire areas had been leveled — a painful spectacle to behold.

Tech-5 James Hamilton, Charlie Company, 784th Tank Battalion recalls:

> I was assigned to the motor pool. I started doing maintenance because I had mechanics training back in Texas. Once we were going across a field way out there in the country somewhere. A country home is where the CP was. There was a colonel and a general and we were protecting them. While pulling across the field in a half-track, the Germans shot mortars at us. Man! They started ringing up the side the half-track and I'm glad they didn't come inside. Anyway, we got near the barn and that's where we jumped off and headed for the window at the kitchen. That's when we got hit, me and the other fellow. It was shrapnel from the mortars. One hit me in the wrist and the other one in the back of the head because my helmet came off when I jumped through that window.[1]

(Left to right) Trent Worthy, "Radio" Jones, Vernell Roberts and Grosvenor Cooper. Worthy is with the Reconnaissance Platoon and the others are from the Communications Squad. HQ Company, 784th Tank Battalion, Germany, 1945. *Courtesy James Baldwin*

The tank/infantry teams fought from village to village. They encountered roadblocks, anti-tank mines, anti-tank guns, assault guns, plus infantry armed with deadly *Panzerfausts*. The roadblocks consisted of large cobblestones dug up from streets and logs reinforced by heavy steel girders that had been salvaged from bombed-out buildings. The tanks' 75-millimeter cannons blasted away relentlessly at every roadblock and every perceived sign of resistance. Any area that offered resistance became a raging inferno. The wreckage-strewn countryside was dotted with burning villages where SS and other Nazi fanatics fought to their death, prolonging the war past its expected conclusion. Some were gunned down by the tanks or physically run over.

Sergeant Simmons Washington, Headquarters Company, 784th Tank Battalion recalls the coordination between the infantry and the half-track mounted 81-Millimeter Mortar Platoon:

> We got shot at a lot and got strafed by German aircraft. Artillery stayed on our case. Artillery was tough and we had to dodge a lot of it. Close combat, not too much because the infantry took care of that but we were right there with them. We had some close calls but for most of them the infantry was right there. The infantry got hit bad and it was bad to see it happen like that. But that is just the way it was. We all did the best we could and we were fortunate that we didn't lose more people.[2]

The 134th and 137th Infantry Regiments with attached tanks of the 784th Tank Battalion pushed ahead while the 320th Infantry Regiment remained in division reserve.

On the main roads, crowds of ashen-faced refugees stumbled along the thoroughfares leading from the cities. They were tired, un-bathed, and disheveled. They had just survived an ordeal of indescribable horror in the city ruins with barely enough food and water to survive. They were sad to have lost almost everything but glad to still be alive. It became a common sight to see senior citizens, children, and mothers with babies who carried whatever they could. Some pushed wobbly baby carriages or pulled wagons containing their remaining possessions. They had just left their bombed-out apartment buildings to escape the impending invasion. Behind them was a ghostlike scene and huge rolling clouds of smoke. While leaving their cities they encountered charred, mummy-like corpses of people—victims who had decided too late to leave and seek shelter from the air raid. They had passed by burned-out smoldering shells of apartment buildings. Many of the buildings had been completely leveled to the ground while others were still ablaze. The refugees had recently experienced a major dilemma. They had 2 options: barricade themselves in their air-raid shelters and possibly burn and suffocate versus confronting the firestorm infernos that raged on the city streets. This dilemma raced through their minds before and after the first bombs became audible from hundreds of feet above and followed by the ensuing series of deafening explosions and earthquake-like tremors.

At this point the *Wehrmacht* fell into disarray with soldiers capitulating by the thousands. It became obvious that the enemy could no longer launch a major counteroffensive. Some of the disarrayed units offered an extraordinary miscellany of *Luftwaffe* personnel, police, old men, boys, and even special units composed of men with stomach troubles or men with ear ailments. The few newly formed standard-equipped units had received virtually no training and had come straight from the parade field to the battlefield. Small units of *Volksgrenadiers* offered sporadic resistance and made good stands before they tore and ran. Unfortunately, the SS made a deadly exception. They preferred death to surrender and would summarily execute any German soldier or civilian who abandoned his post or tried to surrender.

March 28, 1945: Able and Baker Companies of the 784th Tank Battalion supported the infantry against scattered *Wehrmacht* forces and *Panzerfaust* teams in a wooded area near Neukoln and Kirchhellen. The infantry provided excellent protection to the tanks by keeping the *Panzerfaust* teams out of range as the tanks laid down direct fire on enemy positions. Stiff resistance and poor terrain slowed this advance.

When the tanks rolled past a line of ditches, the doughboys riding on the tanks fired away into each ditch with their M1 rifles. Experience showed that Nazi fanatics would fake death until the tanks were alongside them and then jump up and fire their *Panzerfaust*.

If the road conditions allowed, the tanks and vehicles would speed up when they knew that a *Panzerfaust* was near, as a faster-moving target was difficult to hit. Sergeant Simmons Washington recalls: "We were moving so fast in some of those small towns, it is hard to remember the names because we moved in one day, set up security, and we were gone."[3]

Meanwhile, Able Company 784th Tank Battalion cleared Kirchhellen and Walsumermark with the infantry. They proceeded swiftly until scattered 105-millimeter self-propelled guns firing from the woods slowed their pace. They continued their advance towards Konigshardt when from out of nowhere, *boom*!: Dug-in 20-millimeter flak guns and *Panzerfausts* destroyed the lead tank, leaving the tank column road-bound. This facilitated the retreating enemy to zero in on the roads and intersections, which they did masterfully.

Infantryman James Graff, Charlie Company, 134th Infantry Regiment riding on these tanks recounts:

> Just about sundown as we moved up the street through a residential district, a German knocked out the lead tank with a *panzerfaust* (anti-tank weapon, shoulder fired). As we scattered off the tanks and into the surrounding houses, we were on the receiving end of some vicious machine gun and 20 mm fire. The *panzerfaust* had blown the leg off of one of our machine gunners. Most of the tank crew had been wounded by the 20 mm fire as they abandoned the tank; one man was hit in the elbow. Our medic amputated his arm with a pair of surgical scissors. I went up to cover Young (3rd platoon medic) and assisted in evacuating the wounded. The man with the leg blown off was very lucky. The projectile that hit his leg also knocked out the tank, but the heat of it seared the wound and he did

not bleed to death. As we loaded him on the medical jeep, he asked me if his leg was all right as he didn't have any feeling in it. I told him it would be all right.[4]

After this tank/infantry team regrouped, they launched a counterattack under the cover of darkness that lasted throughout the night. Night fighting in tanks was a nightmare experience. The tanks — not intended to fight at night — bulled their way forward without lights, which would have made them easy targets. Night became a surreal day as detonations flashed in a variety of colors. The crescendo of exploding shells appeared as giant diabolical Christmas trees raining conflagration from their branches. Machine gun tracers crackled and wove designs like electric snakes and hellish fires radiated eerie shadows.

By sunrise, the dug-in flak guns had been destroyed and the advance continued toward the *Autobahn*.

With the loss of the Nazi oil fields in the East and the bombings of their synthetic-oil processing plants, the Germans suffered an acute fuel shortage. Their desperately needed *Panzers* didn't have the fuel to break them out of the tightly squeezed Ruhr pocket and their *Luftwaffe* could not get off the ground and became easy targets.

Infantryman James Graff continues:

By now we had moved into some buildings and been joined by some of our colored tanker friends. One of these tanks was parked at our house and an observer of the heavy mortars (81 mm) was using the second story as an observation post. I went up to have a look. Mortar fire was being directed on a group of Germans digging in along the highway (the *Autobahn*). This was our first sighting of Hitler's superhighway.

I borrowed the observer's binoculars and managed to see some Krauts in the vicinity of an underpass directly to our front. As the mortar crews could not bring their weapons to bear on them, I went downstairs to ask the assistance of the tank crew. They informed me that an officer would have to order them to fire, but I suspected they were afraid of exposing their position or didn't want to have to clean their gun. Lt Neal (our executive officer) happened to come along and I told him of my observation. He ordered them to open fire, which they did with 3 well-placed shots.

Next morning Loos, Landrum and I made a reconnaissance down to the underpass and found a heavy water-cooled machine gun with the bolt jammed by a piece of shrapnel and signs in the dirt where wounded men had been dragged away — 2 parallel marks as if a man had been dragged out by his arms. A pair of boots had been cut down the sides to take off someone's feet and I found a shoe with a sock sticking up out of it. Upon closer examination I found the boot still contained a foot and ankle. His leg had been severed just above the sock. As Bob Landrum was always sending home souvenirs, I threw it to him and said to send that home. We took the damaged machine gun back to show the tankers the results of their marksmanship.[5]

The following day Charlie Company, 134th Infantry Regiment advanced with the tanks of Able Company, 784th Tank Battalion. Infantryman James Graff went on to say:

Moved out the next afternoon riding on tanks. As we approached another large town, the lead tank went into a large bomb crater and a couple of infantrymen riding on it were hurt. The tank recovery vehicle could not pull it out and it had to be abandoned. I believe they did it on purpose so as not to have to lead. As we journeyed through town we came across a German command car that had been ambushed by the third battalion. Three German officers lay dead around the vehicle where they had been cut down trying to escape being made prisoner.[6]

April 1, 1945: as the 784th Tank Battalion celebrated its 2nd anniversary of existence, Able Company spearheaded the 134th Infantry Regiment's assault through villages and towns moving in on Recklinghausen. They came under mortar and artillery fire from concealed hilltop emplacements. As they approached the western edge of town, they saw one enemy tank along with 2 self-propelled assault guns retreat into town. The 134th took heavy casualties breaking into this town, which they seized and held after a brief battle. There they captured a large number of prisoners and 2 hospitals filled with wounded enemy soldiers. They withstood sporadic harassing mortar fire as the townspeople aided rather than hindered their mission. The children went so far as to collect the abandoned enemy weapons for them.

Elements of the 134th Infantry Regiment swung south and engaged in clearing a large coal mine. At 1420 hours the artillery air forward observers picked up on a group of unidentified tanks on an intercepting course with the 134th. Minutes later they determined that they were enemy tanks and brought them under fire by the 161st Field Artillery Battalion that routed this enemy counterattack.

Meanwhile, the 137th Infantry Regiment continued their advance. Infantryman Bernard "Jack" Kirsch, Fox Company, 137th Infantry Regiment, recalls:

After we crossed the Rhine River and we kept pushing ahead and wound up right in the Ruhr — the hub. Essen was where we were. And there was Dortmund and Bochum. We kept moving and we didn't realize it, we had been circling the Germans in the Ruhr pocket. We had them encircled! And we took prisoners. I can't tell you how many — by the thousands. We didn't keep prisoners — we sent them to the rear. Our job was to keep moving. And that was the last of the bitter fighting.[7]

Infantryman Keith Bullock, Headquarters Company (2nd Battalion), 137th Infantry Regiment offers a glimpse of the 784th in the Ruhr Pocket:

Those guys were and are the Tuskegee fellers of the Armored Groups! The 784th was *asked for* to support the 35th Infantry Division in our action into the Ruhr Pocket. One day the 137th, my outfit, was ordered to attack and clear a factory complex. The country was very flat. There was no cover to speak of. I myself and some others got pinned down by heavy rifle fire — when here comes a Sherman tank — and out pops a helmet over a "beautiful" black face and a whole lot of white teeth — grinning like a cheesing cat. He says, "hang on — we'll dig a hole for you." They spun the tank which did make a little cover and as they drove off, he leaned over the turret and he said, "stay put. We'll take 'um out. I love to shoot this gun."[8]

Meanwhile the 320th Infantry Regiment jumped off and crossed the *Autobahn* under a smoke screen provided by the 60th Engineer Combat Battalion. The engineers had also converted a damaged rail bridge into a vehicle bridge. They dubbed this bridge "Remagen Jr." that allowed the 320th to cross the Emscher Canal.

The 320th then battled through a large manufacturing complex. They cleared the Prosper Coalmine and ran into bitter resistance at a fortified slag pile with iron waste littered all around. When the smoke began to clear and the enemy withdrew, they found an estimated 8,000 slave laborers who had been kept underground in mine shafts and basements by armed guards. The 320th advanced towards the northern bank of the Rhein-Herne Canal to consolidate with the 137th Infantry Regiment.

Among the many distressing characteristics of the Holocaust is the issue of the dehumanizing slave labor imposed at German businesses as well as at concentration camps — not to be directly compared. The well-known concentration camps became administrative centers for massive networks of branch camps. The victims often worked 11 to 12-hour daily shifts with little sleep and minimum amounts of nutrition, all in deplorable conditions. The Nazis literally worked them to death.

The biggest culprits were the Nazi-owned enterprises, the munitions and arms manufacturers, and many large German private corporations. Even German divisions of American firms took part in this extreme example of corporate greed.

Sergeant Simmons Washington points out:

> We ran into many slave laborers. There is a difference between the slave laborers and the concentration camp victims. We didn't make it to the concentration camps; they were further up. But we did see the slave labor camps. A lot of them came out when we liberated a town and they told us where the German soldiers had gone and where they were hiding. They had been mainly used for labor. Almost anyone the Germans had something against. But the Jews, they really eliminated them everywhere. That was one of their major campaigns. They spent more time trying to eliminate the Jews than they did fighting the war. And man! They did a job on the Jews.[9]

Infantryman Murray Leff recalls liberating slave laborers in the Ruhr valley:

> On this occasion we were riding on tanks, British tanks I think. They ordered us off the tanks to clear this housing development. So another guy and myself, we go into this basement and we see a bunch of people there all chattering and I make out that they are all slave laborers. They are talking to me in French and I yelled out, "*Vive la France!*" And they nearly tore us apart. It was a very emotional moment as they came out of the basement.
>
> We did run into a lot of slave laborers. There were a lot of Russian slave laborers. At one point they had established a camp on their own or maybe they were directed. There were a couple thousand Russians at this factory. It was a "*Stuhl Fabrik*"—chair factory. I could manage a little German so I got the assignment of trying to get food for them. I roamed around with a driver and one of the Russians. We came to a milk dairy. I ask this fellow for some milk for the people in the camp and factory and he was a dedicated Nazi.

He wasn't going to do anything. So I pointed my carbine at his head and I clicked off the safety. Then everything changed. I got all the milk I wanted. I had no sympathy for the people who had gotten me into this situation. I didn't want to be there. This was all the Nazis' idea.[10]

Infantryman Murray Leff went on to advise about the significance of the "H" on his dog tags:

I was aware that I would not be treated too well because I was Jewish, if I were captured. This was a concern but that concern took its place at the bottom of the list because the ones above it were whether I was going to get killed. Also, my immediate comfort at the time was a concern, it was usually so disagreeable it tended to crowd out all of the other things that were happening.[11]

This area, already overpopulated, began overflowing with displaced persons and recently freed slave laborers who provided useful information. Infantryman Bernard "Jack" Kirsch adds:

We had a lot of contact with the slave laborers, especially when we took an area, usually a town we liberated. They welcomed us and usually there was someone from our outfit who had the nationality that they could converse which was very helpful. They gave us all kinds of tips. They knew everything that was going on because they worked in that area. We had a lot of contact with them. In the larger places, they would be held in camps.[12]

The entire 35th Infantry Division found itself in a densely populated zone, for lack of an exact term, described as "Pittsburgh-like terrain." The steel and coal industry, the manufacturing facilities, the apartment complexes, the overcrowding, all were reminiscent of Pittsburgh. Against enemy resistance, advances through this terrain could be measured in meters per day.

Some areas were nearly impassable for tanks and vehicles. The combat engineers had to be called in to clear the streets and fill shell craters. Combat Engineer Robert Martin, 208th Engineer Combat Battalion recalls:

We cleaned up the streets with the bulldozers by pushing rubble to the side to start with and then later smoothed it out. Then we eventually hauled bricks from piles of rubble to make a road. Anyhow, there was a big ash pile there. They put the ashes on top of the bricks and whatever they hauled in to make a base. The ashes were to smooth it out and then we back bladed it with the dozer to smooth it out more so the vehicles could go by. That was a big job!

Anyhow, while we were helping with this road I heard these P-47 planes coming back and just then our artillery started firing and it evidently hit one of those planes, knocking the guide off. Its motor went wide open and came straight down — full throttle. I thought, "Oh my God! That poor guy didn't have a chance!" The plane hit the ground and blew up and the smoke and flames just came up and then I saw the chute open. That's how close it was for him. That was scary. I heard that he got back to his outfit OK.[13]

In this industrial and residential area, the infantry had the hellish duty of fighting house-to-house. The 784th provided moving cover and protection from sniper fire as the infantry crouched low beside the tanks. The tank crew had limited vision when buttoned up and had to depend on the infantry's hand signals to point out targets. When they reached their objective, the 75-millimeter cannons blasted out walls so the doughboys could gain entrance. They pasted uprooted trees, burning buildings, and twisted streetcar rails. They had to carefully avoid the many cables that the bombs unearthed, which were coiled like angry hissing and sparking snakes ready to unleash their venomous voltage. Grotesquely charred and mangled corpses were scattered around. The cold weather and slight rain chilled to the bone. They had entered a wasteland of massive destruction, of row upon row of burned-out apartment buildings whose empty shells formed ghostly silhouettes against the sky. They had to go around piles of rubble in the middle of the street. Road conditions continued to plague the operations. Snipers from upper-floor windows inflicted heavy casualties on the infantry and any tanker who was unbuttoned. Heavy machine gun fire from cellar windows and from piles of debris skipped off the pavement, attempting to bounce under and into the tanks, until a well-placed 75-millimeter high explosive round silenced them.

The tank/infantry teams encountered a great deal of smoke from burning buildings and from gunfire. In some places it was so thick it became nearly impossible to accurately fire on targets, thus increasing the risk of friendly fire incidents. Making matters worse, a large number of Germans staggered through the smoke waving white rags.

Meanwhile, Baker and Charlie Companies, 784th Tank Battalion, spearheaded the 137th Infantry Regiment's continued assault eastward between the *Autobahn* and the Rhein-Herne Canal into the Ruhr industrial area. During this assault the British provided flame-throwing tanks to add to the already overwhelming firepower. At the end of the day the combat team turned south into a defensive position along the northern bank of the canal and waited for the 320th Infantry Regiment to join them.

The 320th and the 137th Infantry Regiments secured the north side of the Rhein-Herne Canal. They engaged the enemy in a sniper duel. Any movement in town signaled an enemy artillery barrage. At night, burning slag piles lit up the canal area, making undetected movement difficult. Any detection would bring deadly consequences.

Infantryman Murray Leff recalls:

We pulled into this city and there's a canal separating it from the adjoining city. We occupied apartments where we overlooked the canal and we saw the section that still had the enemy there. We had a fairly comfortable combat situation, we were in apartments looking out and we were shooting from where we were. Sleeping inside was so much different than sleeping outside. We were there close to a week. It seemed to me that we had advanced so rapidly that the war must be nearly over. We were here and not moving so this is where we thought we would be until they sorted things out and ended the war. We were celebrating. Well of course, the war was not over and plenty of people got killed after that.[14]

10. The Ruhr Pocket

Infantryman Bernard "Jack" Kirsch adds:

We had some joint activities where we would actually ride on the 784th tanks. When in the Ruhr pocket, they pulled up there and of course we were not moving ahead. We were on the rising edge of a canal. We were there several days and the 784th was right with us. And, I recall we weren't getting hot food, we were getting K-rations all the time. One night they gave us some of their hot food. We had very good relations with the 784th. They were really highly respected.[15]

Infantry Platoon Leader, Royal Offer, King Company, 320th Infantry Regiment recalls:

That is where we did a lot of house-to-house fighting. We lost a lot of men in there. What I remember the most about the Ruhr pocket, a good friend of mine, he was a lieutenant in the 1st platoon. There was a blown-out bridge and he and a couple of guys crawled across it at night. One of them could speak German. Later a German guard challenged them and the guy who spoke German replied, in German of course, "Why can't you just let us have a good time," like they were drunk. The Germans were partying and having a big time and all. Then they looked into the window and saw the whole deal. Then they came back and they got the guard and jumped him to disarm him and brought him back across the bridge. That was somewhere near Essen.[16]

April 4, 1945: the U.S. Ninth Army was officially relieved from British Field Marshal Sir Bernard Montgomery's Twenty-first Army Group and assigned to General Omar Bradley's Twelfth Army Group.

The 134th Infantry Regiment displaced forward to join the rest of the 35th Infantry Division at the Rhein-Herne Canal. Through the early morning fog and rain they saw their first German aircraft since the Rhine River crossing. They also watched artillery catch a group of enemy soldiers in the open with devastating effect.

Infantryman James Graff recounts:

Here in the Ruhr we came across a huge graveyard of our 4-motored B-17s and English night bombers which had been shot down, also hundreds of unexploded bombs. This graveyard represented the cost of the constant bombing of this area. Also near here we came upon several 500 lb bombs buried near the approaches to a bridge. We assumed the Germans had armed them to go off if any vehicles passed over them. Our colored tankers stopped and as we knew nothing about defusing them were forced to halt also. Capt. Jardine (D Company C.O.) was in the area and came up. Although no ordnance officer, he volunteered to disarm them. We cleared out and he began to screw out the fuses. These bombs were not buried very deep. When he had done all he could, he asked a tanker to drive over them. No one would, but a D Company machine gunner volunteered and got in and drove over them. None went off so we then proceeded. This incident shows the faith of a man in his fellow man.[17]

The 35th Infantry Division spread its 3 regiments out along the canal as follows: the 134th in the center, the 137th on the left, and the 320th on the right, all facing south. They continued their aggressive defense with probing reconnaissance patrols.

Sergeant Bill Hughes, Dog Company, 784th Tank Battalion recounts:

Resistance was expected so Company D was employed to support the infantry in mop-up operations at the canal area. Company A operated near the *autobahn* north of the canal. Companies B and C traveled south along the *autobahn* and ran into stiff resistance. Therefore, we were ordered to follow behind them as the Germans scattered around. We picked up a lot of prisoners who surrendered and we marched them back to an MP unit. They had given up their weapons but would be subject to a thorough search. I noticed one German officer was walking sort of funny so I informed the MP Lieutenant. He snatched that guy out of line and made him take off his boots. Sure enough, in the heel of the boot was a hiding place for a small .25-caliber Weiner pistol. The Lieutenant MP said, "So you were going to try and kill one of us? Well now it's my turn!" and threatened to shoot the German. He was only kidding and tossed the gun to me and said it's all yours. I kept it for many years. The German was so shaken that he urinated in his pants. The offensive continued when we went back to join the main tank column. The attack was made toward and across the Rhine-Herne Canal. The Battalion continued to support several infantry regiments in their attacks on Herne and Gelsenkirchen. This must have been during the first week of April 1945.[18]

The *Wehrmacht* employed *Volkssturm* (literally, people's storm), militia to fill gaps in their lines along the canals. The *Volkssturm*, under the control of the Nazi party and not the *Wehrmacht*, consisted of conscripted males in 2 distinct age groups. The first group, ages 15–18, were mostly *Hitler Jugend* (Hitler Youth). The second group, ages 50–65, consisted mainly of disabled veterans and men previously deemed unfit for military duty. Their uniforms consisted only of an armband with the inscription *Deutscher Volkssturm*. The *Wehrmacht* had no uniforms to spare. The officers and noncoms who trained them were highly decorated combat veterans. Several wore eye-patches or carried their arms in slings. Some saluted with their left hand because their right arms were missing. After a brief training and indoctrination program, they took the customary oath to Hitler, and went directly into the final apocalyptic defense of the Third Reich. They fought surprisingly well with their mastery of the user-friendly *Panzerfaust*.

The Allies didn't quite understand why the Germans continued to fight so grimly when they obviously had no chance of winning. After Intelligence interrogated more prisoners they determined that many still believed in Hitler's promise of a new *Wunderwaffen* (secret weapon), and that the years of Nazi indoctrination had convinced them that the German people were invincible. Also, Goebbels' constant radio propaganda convinced many Germans that they would be liquidated, tortured, raped, and enslaved if the Allies won the war.

London and Washington worried about the German atomic bomb project but it made little progress due to Hitler's lack of interest and Himmler's practice of arresting scientists for suspected disloyalty.

April 9, 1945: the 134th and 137th Infantry Regiments jumped off across the

Volkssturm militia receives instruction on firing the *Panzerfaust*. Courtesy Jason Pipes, www.feldgrau.com

Rhein-Herne Canal against sporadic resistance while the 320th Infantry Regiment remained in division reserve. As in the previous water crossings, the 60th Engineer Combat Battalion courageously worked under fire. The combat engineers captured 19 enemy soldiers at this bridge after a fierce fire fight, and 12 other enemy soldiers surrendered quickly when a 784th Tank Battalion tank-bulldozer, commanded by "Pop" Hall, opened fire.

This action by the combat engineers allowed the infantry to secure a bridgehead north of Herne to allow the tanks to cross. Together they broke the enemy's defenses south of the canal. The coordinated tank/infantry assault teams pushed ahead under scattered resistance and made their way to the railroad tracks that ran through Herne. Meanwhile, a group of 20 infantrymen on an island in the canal had to quickly withdraw back across when the enemy started walking artillery towards them.

Infantryman Murray Leff reveals how his unit crossed the Rhein-Herne Canal: "We arrived at this canal in the middle of the night, when we got to it, a buddy and I were sent back to get assault boats to get across the canal. When it came time to do it, we didn't use the boats. We walked along the edge of the canal until we came to some locks, which had been blown apart. They put planks across the top and we walked across to the other side."[19]

Tanks of the 784th Tank Battalion along with elements of the 35th Infantry Division roll into the city of Gelsenkirchen, Germany, April 10, 1945. U.S. Army Signal Corps photo #ETO-HQ-45-31499 (Wilson). *Courtesy National Archives*

After combining forces with the infantry, the 784th Tank Battalion spearheaded through miles of industrial land, taking several suburban towns along the way. Within 2 days the 137th Infantry Regiment made it to the north bank of the Ruhr River and took up defensive positions. The 134th Infantry Regiment routed the enemy defenders from the city of Gelsenkirchen. Meanwhile, the 320th Infantry Regiment jumped off and fought their way to the outskirts of Dortmund.

Amazingly, some of the citizens came out of their houses and apartments and wandered about the debris, some crying and some just gazing in bewilderment. Others remained cringing in their cellars, fearing for their lives.

Infantryman Murray Leff illustrates an incident in this industrial area:

10. The Ruhr Pocket

After that we attacked some factories. Got into one factory and I along with my partner were looking out a door. There was a high stone wall encircling the factory with an opening where trucks could come in and out. So I'm looking out there and everything is quiet and we had no opposition at that point. And then right in front of me crossing that space where trucks can come in and out, I see this German, I see him in my head right now, with this long overcoat and *Schmeisser* submachine gun. He walked right across that opening. I was startled. I started to pick up my carbine but he was gone. Then in a couple of minutes I hear people running towards me from the outside. It turns out to be a squad leader and platoon sergeant. And just as they came through the door, I heard, "BURRRR-UPT! BURRRR-UPT!" And the platoon sergeant falls. He's half inside and half outside so I pulled him in. He was lying on his back when I looked at his leg and I see his foot has fallen over flat on the ground. He was hit in the bone and in such a way that it wasn't supporting his foot anymore. I got some flexible books to make a splint out of to immobilize it. We waited there for the aid men to arrive, which took a while. He was extremely uncomfortable and we did give him a shot of morphine, which I think helped. Before they took him away, he took off his trench knife. Trench knives were in great demand. I always wanted one because all I had was a bayonet. So he gave me this knife which I still have today.[20]

At this point the enemy started a steady withdrawal southeast, deeper into the heart of the Ruhr pocket, yielding a large number of prisoners to the tank/infantry teams. This indicated the beginning of the complete disintegration of the *Wehrmacht*.

Sergeant Bill Hughes portrays:

The Germans were rapidly withdrawing in the Ruhr towns and villages. We were not in the big cities (Koln, Dusseldorf, Essen, etc.), but in towns and villages in the pocket of the Ruhr Valley. As an example, I remember Companies B and C were attached to the 17th Airborne Division when they attacked a town called Oberhausen. I was at battalion headquarters in Gelsenkirchen monitoring radio traffic and many reports were coming in that the Germans were on the run and surrendering in large numbers. In fact, no one, tankers or infantry, had time to take prisoners. The Germans were told to discard all weapons and march in a column with hands over the back of their heads, staying on the main road until they were picked up. I saw one such column marching into a barbed wire make shift imprisonment area. They were waving and you could see they were relieved to have it over with.[21]

The enemy attempted to control the speed of the Allied advance with frequent roadblocks defended by squads equipped with small arms and *Panzerfausts*. This, along with the large amount of debris to clear and prisoners to take, proved effective in delaying the inevitable.

April 10, 1945: Baker and Charlie Companies of the 784th Tank Battalion attached to the hard-hitting paratroopers of the 17th Airborne Division for 2 days. Baker Company supported the 513th Parachute Infantry Regiment and Charlie Company supported the 507th Parachute Infantry Regiment. Together they assaulted the industrial areas of Oberhausen and Mulheim.

Sergeant Simmons Washington recalls: "I remember another division we were attached to, the 17th Airborne Paratroopers. We were not with them very long, maybe for 1 or 2 missions, but those men could fight! I'll tell you that. When we got together, they looked out for the tanks and we looked out for them. We had to, a tank is no good without infantry and infantry is no good without tanks. So we had to work together and that's what we did."[22]

Staff Sergeant Franklin Garrido, Baker Company, 784th Tank Battalion remembers the 17th Airborne Division: "Before we saw a target, they engaged it. They jumped off our tanks hollering Geronimo! They were aggressive!"[23]

Paratrooper Everett Cook, 507th Parachute Infantry Regiment, remembered the 784th Tank Battalion:

> We didn't get to talk to them much. They knew what they were doing. They would fire those big guns and sometimes they fired them when we were too close and it would just about break our eardrums. When they supported a unit like ours, we just followed them. They had the binoculars and would fire on the enemy when we got fired on. They would lay those shells into the woods, hedges, towns, and buildings. That's the way we fought. They were on the ball!
>
> There is another town called Warden that we fought in together. I changed my machine gun from a tripod to a bipod similar to a BAR. I used this machine gun more like a Tommy gun than a heavy machine gun. It doesn't take long to learn these things when you're protecting yourself. The riflemen were the ones who followed behind the tanks. As a machine gunner I moved to certain strategic points and watched for enemy fire. When I saw then I laid in on them. Then this one time a guy up in the turret yelled down at us, "Guys, we aren't hitting any resistance and you can crawl on the tank and ride." When we hit that town he made a real quick turn and half of us fell off. His driver pulled that stick back. He said, "Didn't you see that 88 pointed directly at us!" Then we spread out and moved down there and found the 88 already knocked out. Then we moved into town and saw a large wooden fence with a white flag waving. I had my machine gun at the ready like a Tommy gun. I walked up and looked behind there and saw 17 *Wehrmacht* officers. They hollered —*Bitte! Bitte! Nicht Schiessen!*—begging to surrender. I told them *Kommen sie hier*. I took them out and marched them over to the officer in charge. He asked them, "Where are your weapons?" They pointed to the schoolhouse. When the GIs heard that they took off and went in there and grabbed up their pistols and swords. After that I kind of lost track of the tank. We moved on to Essen and that's where the war ended for us.[24]

Meanwhile, Able Company stumbled into a fierce pocket of resistance in the vicinity of Linden near the Ruhr River. Several well-placed *Panzerfausts* took out 2 tanks. Corporal Eldon Lee perished in the blast.

With the Germans completely encircled and trapped in the industrial ruins of the Ruhr Valley, the main line of resistance caved in. They began surrendering in larger numbers in their last morale-crushing hours of defeat.

Meanwhile, elements of the U.S. First and Ninth Armies dashed towards the Elbe

10. The Ruhr Pocket

River, deep into the heart of Germany. On April 11, the first elements arrived near Magdeburg, only 60 miles from Berlin. Meanwhile, back in the Ruhr Valley, the entire pocket collapsed on April 18. Two *Panzer* armies with 21 divisions, along with a miscellany of stragglers made up of over 350,000 soldiers and 30 generals, capitulated.

War correspondent Ted Stanford of the *Pittsburgh Courier* summed up:

War correspondent Ted Stanford of the *Pittsburgh Courier* interviews 1st Sergeant Morris Harris, March 1945. *Courtesy National Archives*

The battle from the Rhine to the Ruhr was a series of running engagements with stubborn elements of Hitler's badly disorganized armies offering fanatical resistance from numerous well-defended positions. Along the lonely German fields and roads that beckoned to the Ruhr, I had a chance to test the truth or falsity of those stories, and I found that the glowing tales of heroism which had been attributed to these brown warriors were only a small part of a greater truth.[25]

April 12, 1945: the 75th and 79th Infantry Divisions pinched out the 35th Infantry Division. The 320th Infantry Regiment detached from the 35th Infantry Division and attached to the 75th Infantry Division.

The 35th, along with the 84th and 102nd Infantry Divisions, had orders to bypass enemy resistance and expeditiously advance to the Elbe River on a direct line to Berlin. Infantryman Bernard "Jack" Kirsch recalls: "We made a dash after the Ruhr pocket. They put us on trucks. The tanks, I'm sure, were following us but not as fast. We hit the *Autobahn* and headed for the Elbe River. I think it was a very risky endeavor. We didn't encounter much fighting at all. We just kept driving on the *Autobahn* and took no land on either side. We could have gotten cut off at any time."[26]

During this transition the heartrending news arrived that President Roosevelt had died suddenly of a massive cerebral hemorrhage at his cottage in Warm Springs, Georgia. The commander in chief had been posing for a portrait when at 1300 hours on April 11 he said: "I have a terrific headache." At 1315 he fainted and at 1535 he died without having regained consciousness. Vice President Harry Truman took the oath of office at 1908 hours and became the 33rd president of the United States. Coincidentally, Truman served as an officer with the 35th Infantry Division during the First World War.

Combat Engineer Robert Martin recalls: "We felt very bad hearing that news because I think he was a great guy. We didn't really think of him as being crippled because he did ride a wheelchair. When he died it was a big letdown to the country, to the war, and everything. Then Harry Truman took over and he was a different person altogether."[27]

When the news of FDR's demise reached Berlin, Josef Goebbels, Hitler's Minister of Propaganda, became ecstatic. The world's greatest spin doctor immediately called Hitler to congratulate him. Some astrological hocus-pocus assured them that the president's death foretold the turning point of the war. Meanwhile, the U.S. Ninth Army closed in on the Elbe River, about 60 miles from Berlin, while the Soviets closed in from the east, blocking any chance for Hitler and Goebbels to escape.

Infantryman Murray Leff explains:

> I think that any sensible German soldier would have to come to the conclusion that they had lost the war at this point. They were giving up a lot easier than they used to. So we were taking prisoners in large numbers. The next thing we knew, we got on trucks again, and this time we rode all day, going east. We hit one ambush but we saw them before they saw us. They got killed, I suppose, just days before the war was over. We stopped in this

village and at that time we heard that Roosevelt had died. The next day we drove another 75 miles and we ended up on the Elbe River and that was as far as we went.[28]

Infantryman James Graff recalls being transported by the former Red Ball Express:

On the evening of April 13 colored truck drivers and their vehicles moved into our area. We were to move toward the Elbe River in the direction of Berlin. On the morning of the 14th we moved out. I was positioned right behind the cab of the truck so as to have a good field of fire should opposition develop. The Elbe had already been reached while we were still involved in the Ruhr pocket, but the areas behind were still full of the Germans that the armor had bypassed. We moved out and rode 231 miles that day, our longest one-day ride of the war. We headed north-east from Bochum, Germany and arrived just short of the river.[29]

During the dash to the Elbe River, they watched a flow of enemy prisoners meandering along like a river and wondered how much more the Germans could take. A background noise of gunfire and artillery continued intermittently. Air cover alerted the column of any possible dangers ahead. The enemy had changed warfare with their *Panzer*-led motorized columns. Now they were in a headlong capitulation employing horse-drawn carts and wagons. The German soldiers encountered were middle-aged men and youngsters with a sprinkling of regular troops. The enemy began realizing the harsh reality of defeat. They were anxious to surrender, which they did, unless driven by SS or Nazi fanatics.

Knowing that ground was falling into the Allied hands, Hitler ordered the "scorched earth" directive. He wanted all industrial plants, electrical facilities, waterworks, gasworks, food stores, bridges, railway installations, communications centers, waterways, ships, freight cars and all locomotives destroyed. He believed that the German people let him down and future generations should be punished.

The German people were spared this final catastrophe due to the rapid advance of the Allies and heroic efforts of a number of German officials. In direct disobedience to the *Fuhrer*, they dashed about the country to make sure that fanatic Nazis did not execute Hitler's orders.

11

Eyewitness to Genocide

On this expeditious dash to reach the Elbe River, Staff Sergeant Franklin Garrido, Baker Company, 784th Tank Battalion, was about to become an eyewitness to genocide:

One of the last large cities that we captured was the medieval city of Hanover. We entered under a plethora of white sheets, pillow cases, towels, underwear, socks, anything white; signs of surrender. When we reached the edge of town we stopped, reloaded, and prepared to jump off at 0600 the next morning. In the cavalry tradition we fed and groomed our iron steeds before we fed and groomed ourselves. Feeding consisted of re-fueling 300 gallons of petrol. Grooming was greasing and lubricating the bogey wheels and sprockets. Feeding for the tank crews consisted of K and C rations along with instant coffee. At 0600 we were lined up for what we thought would be Berlin; it was only about 100 kilometers away. We took off in a convoy, traveling along at a clip of about 35 to 40 miles-per-hour. The sun was out. It was a beautiful spring morning in Central Germany. The sky was clear, dew was on the ground, and I was lulled into daydreaming about Los Angeles and the California girls. And then I saw this large tall spiral of black greasy smoke ascending into the sky. I alerted my crew and the platoon, telling them to prepare for combat. When we rounded the curve, I saw this compound. There was a large hangar like building surrounded by a wire fence. On the nearest corner, there, what I thought was laundry, clothes hanging on the fence. As we got closer, I saw the clothes, to my horror, were human skeletons, alive! Human skeletons were clinging onto the fence begging us with their eyes to help them. At this point the radio crackled and we heard an urgent message over the air telling the tanks not to run over the bodies.

We hadn't reached the gate yet and the urgent sounding voice said, "Slow down! Don't run over the bodies!" The convoy slowed down from 35 miles-per-hour to 5 miles-per hour. And sure enough, as we came closer to the gates of the camp we had to thread our way through the bodies. When the barn-like structure was set on fire, it was where the inmates were kept and the doors were locked. As the inmates scrambled to escape the fire, they were machine-gunned. Some made it to the road, but they were machine-gunned and their bodies strewn all over the place. We didn't stop. In fact, the same urgent voice, probably an officer said: "Don't stop! There are people in the rear echelon who can help these people. Your job is to continue to pursue the enemy. It was the *SS* that did this and we want to catch them. Don't Stop!"[1]

Sergeant Bill Hughes adds: "Company D was not involved. I do however recall hearing about some camp one of the companies found with starving prisoners. I don't know which one but it could have been Company B. I think we were still working with the 134th Infantry somewhere along the Elbe River picking up stray enemy soldiers who had retreated to the woods."[2]

Back on April 4, 1945, while the 35th, 84th, and 102nd Infantry Divisions were still bogged down in the Ruhr pocket, the SS begin evacuating thousands of slave laborers from camps and subcamps to avoid capture by the rapidly approaching Allies. Many of these inmates labored in top-secret aircraft and missile production factories. The Nazis remained determined not to share the secrets their slave laborers possessed with the Allies.

Many traveled by train in grossly overcrowded boxcars with open tops. Some starved while en route and others were shot when they begged. These hellish trains chugged along as far as possible until American planes took out one locomotive and destroyed rail lines in that direction. Twice the American planes attacked and both times withdrew when the prisoners frantically waved their hands. During this aerial attack many prisoners attempted to break away. The SS guards immediately opened fire, killing many, but a few managed to escape. The trains terminated near Letzlingen, where the prisoners disembarked and were forced-marched in the direction of Gardelegen.

The SS employed the death-march strategy as they forced their prisoners to march away from the approaching Allies. The prisoners too ill or exhausted to keep up were shot immediately. The march lacked provisions for the captives, and they just struggled along and slowly starved to death. The SS took vicious pleasure in testing the nerves of their captives by taking pot shots at them. The prisoners learned to pay scant heed to the shootings, knowing that if they turned around, they too would be shot. On several marches the column ran directly into the approaching Allies, and the SS guards fled. The starving prisoners scattered throughout the villages and countryside in search of food.

Between April 10th and 13th, the remaining prisoners reached Gardelegen, and many received temporary shelter in the stables of the Remonte Cavalry School. Meanwhile the SS guards considered ways to dispose of their human cargo.

The local Nazi officials held an emergency meeting. During this meeting, the

Kreisleiter (local Nazi party leader) of the Gardelegen area, Gerhard Thiele, and his staff; the *SS* guards; *Volksturm* (local civilian militia); *Luftwaffe* (Air Force) and *Fallschirmjager* (Paratrooper) officers; local police; and other concerned officials argued over what to do with the prisoners. Thiele emphasized that they must do everything to prevent what had recently happened in the village of Kakerbeck, 16 kilometers north of Gardelegen, where escaped prisoners looted homes. The distorted stories included the rape of women and children. This constant reminder of Kakerbeck convinced the perpetrators and gave them the rationale and deceptive justification to murder. A decision had to be made fast because the Allies would be there in days.

While the Nazi decision makers contemplated the disposal of their captives, more prisoners from the surrounding area continued marching towards Gardelegen. The SS guards marching these prisoners knew that their human cargo would soon die of starvation.

The *Fallschirmjagers* rounded up some of these prisoners arriving in wagons and took them to the forest west of Estedt. There a small group of civilians from that village dug a large ditch. The *Fallschirmjagers* made prisoners kneel down in it and then shot them in the back of the head. The next wagon to arrive carried 35 prisoners, of which 5 were already dead. They forced this group to dig their own ditch and killed them in the same manner. The next group pleaded that they were prisoners of war and not political prisoners. Needless to say, they perished the same way. This digging and shooting went on all day with a total of 110 murders.

Another group of about 150 prisoners arrived in Gardelegen but continued marching until they reached Javenitz. They spent the night in a barn and the next morning were taken into a forest. The SS left only 2 guards with them who told the prisoners that the Americans would soon be there to liberate them. They started making white flags to greet the Americans with. They felt relieved knowing they finally had a future to look forward to. Then around noon more SS guards appeared and opened fire on the prisoners, killing 35. The captives scattered in all directions. Some couldn't get too far due to their weakened condition. Local men and boys came in to help the SS round them up from the woods. They gathered up about 80 and marched them back to Gardelegen. The rest apparently escaped.

April 13: the SS guards and the *Fallschirmjagers* marched all of the remaining prisoners to a large masonry hangar — the infamous Isenschnibbe barn. They prodded the prisoners through the doors, ordered them to sit down on the gasoline-soaked straw, and secured the doors with heavy rocks. The guards gave the beleaguered prisoners false hope telling them that they will be turned over to the Americans the next day and the only reason they are in the smelly hangar is due to lack of space in the stables.

After it got dark, the scene was complete chaos. The door on the southwest side opened and 2 Germans entered and set the straw on fire and left in a hurry. The prisoners immediately rushed over and frantically put out the flames. Then they pushed all of the straw to the center of the hangar. The Germans reentered and shot flare guns igniting another fire and the prisoners put that fire out too. Finally the Germans started lobbing phosphorus grenades, shooting off *Panzerfausts*, and firing automatic weapons into the frantic masses. During this pandemonium, a group trampled each other as they rushed the opposite door and broke it open. They started pouring out. The *Fallschirmjagers*, with the help of the local *Hitler Jugend*, mowed them down with machine gun fire.

The dead and dying men started piling up around the doors. Some men feigned death and hid under dead bodies. The screams rang out into the dark and could be heard in Gardelegen in between the sporadic gunfire. Dying men screamed, cried, pleaded, prayed. Some sang their national anthems. The ones from France yelled: "*Vive la France!*"

By now the fire blazed out of control as the flames radiated a macabre glow over Gardelegen. The fire filled the hangar with asphyxiating smoke and soot and stench filled the air outside.

Several prisoners escaped death that hellish night. One of the survivors, Eugene Sczwincz from Poland, lay buried under a mass of charred bodies for 3 days:

Concentration camp evacuees who made it out of the burning structure only to be machine gunned down. U.S. Army Signal Corps photograph. *Courtesy Harry S. Truman Library*

I stumbled, and others coming behind me were mowed down. Some of the Germans firing the machine guns were *Luftwaffe* troops. I could see their uniforms. I lay under a pile of dead from Friday until Sunday morning without moving, because on Saturday the Germans came in and asked who needed medical attention. When someone moved and asked for help, the Germans shot them. I got out when the Germans left and the Americans arrived.[3]

April 14: local civilians came out to help the SS dig a ditch to bury the dead. The SS, the local Nazi officials, the *Volkssturm*, and the *Hitler Jugen* worked frantically to hide the evidence while the *Fallschirmjagers* set up an ambush to delay the advancing Americans.

Later that day, somewhere east of Hanover and north of Gardelegen, elements of the 102nd Infantry Division encountered a small but determined battle group of *Fallschirmjagers*. A blanket of intense fire from 20-millimeter flak guns and small arms blocked their advance through the village of Estedt and into Gardelegen. After holding out as long as they could, the *Fallschirmjagers* capitulated and surrendered the prized *Luftwaffe* airfield and parachute training school along with the horse cavalry school. The massive presence of U.S. tanks in the vicinity persuaded the Germans to make a speedy surrender.

The timing of the capitulation and formal surrender caused even more delays. On the outskirts of Gardelegen the perpetrators continued disposing of the evidence while *Kreisleiter* Gerhard Thiele, the main instigator and the one who gave the final order to kill all prisoners, made a successful escape. He disguised himself as a soldier and traveled with false documents to the Western zone of occupation. He lived in West Germany as a fugitive until he passed away in 1994 at the age of 85.

Sunday, April 15: elements of the 102nd Infantry Division, while on their way to inspect the *Luftwaffe* airfield, came across several bullet-ridden bodies in striped prison garments. Then they stumbled upon a large masonry storage hangar. There they found more bullet-ridden bodies scattered about. The stench coming from inside the hangar became sickening. Despite this they still peered inside. They could barely believe their eyes when they saw the hellhole filled with hundreds of charred smoldering bodies.

Walking around the hangar they found several large trenches, some covered over and some partially covered, entombing hundreds of charred remains. When they thought they'd seen it all, they saw heads and hands protruding from under the doors and walls. The hands had fingers worn down to the second knuckle from the desperate digging. They reported this grim discovery up the chain of command.

Soon 102nd Infantry Division representatives rounded up the town leaders and took them to the scene and made them clear a walking path through the hangar from door to door. After clearing several lanes, they had everyone from the area able to walk to pass through the hangar and eyewitness the atrocity. Those that fainted got carried by those that didn't.

The Supreme Commander of the Allied Expeditionary Forces, General Dwight

An atrocity exposed at Gardelegen when the U.S. Ninth Army captured the area before the Germans had time to remove the evidence. U.S. Army Signal Corps photograph. *Courtesy Harry S. Truman Library*

Eisenhower ("Ike"), had plans for a post–Nazi Germany and the rehabilitation of the German people. Part of this plan included having the German citizens see the atrocities committed by their leaders. After Ike had seen the forced labor camp at Ohrdruf days earlier, he gave the order to have as many German citizens as possible to eyewitness the carnage of the liberated concentration camps. In respect to this order, Maj. General Frank Keating, Commanding General of the 102nd Infantry Division, ordered the male citizens of Gardelegen and the surrounding communities to manually prepare a military-style cemetery.

This work detail involved disinterring the bodies from mass graves and interring them in separate graves. Crosses and Stars of David were constructed to mark each individual grave. Survivors were brought to the site to point out the men involved in the atrocity. The survivors kicked and beat the Nazis and called for the American soldiers to shoot them. The Americans had a near riot on their hands as they prevented the former prisoners from lynching the local Nazis they recognized.

April 25: the victims of the Gardelegen mass murder received a military funeral, including a 21-gun salute, in the newly constructed military-style cemetery. Maj. General Keating ordered the entire town to attend and admonished them: "You have lost the respect of the civilized world."[4]

This funeral marked the only time in World War II that concentration camp victims received this type of treatment. One of the reasons to justify this is the fact that some of the victims were Russian prisoners of war and some were resistance fighters who continued fighting after their countries had surrendered.

Of the 1,016 victims, many were political prisoners who wore a red triangle on their prison garments. The fact that their clothing did not completely burn made it possible to see the red triangles. The Jewish victims had a yellow triangle with a red triangle sewn on top, forming a 6-point Star of David. Initially only 186 victims could be identified by nationality. Among those remains were 60 Poles, 52 Russians, 27 Frenchmen, 17 Hungarians, 8 Belgians, 5 Germans, 5 Italians, 4 Czechs, 4 Yugoslavs, 2 Dutchmen, one Mexican and one Spaniard. Many of them were Jews. Years later, more victims were identified when researchers matched the recorded prisoner numbers to captured documents.

At the entrance to the cemetery stands a large sign in the German and English languages immortalizing the victims and charging the citizens of Gardelegen with the perpetual upkeep of the cemetery:

> Here lie 1,016 Allied Prisoners of War who were murdered by their captors. They were buried by citizens of Gardelegen who are charged with responsibility that graves are forever kept as green as the memory of these unfortunates will be kept in the hearts of freedom loving men everywhere. Established under supervision of 102D Infantry Division United States Army. Vandalism will be punished by maximum penalties under laws of military government.[5]

Endorsed: "Frank A. Keating, Major General, USA. Commanding."[6]

Staff Sergeant Franklin Garrido concludes:

Years later I had a librarian at the Holocaust Museum in Los Angeles do some research for me. I told her the only name I could remember about the area was Gardelegen. It was not a concentration camp. It was a temporary holding facility. In this area the Nazis farmed out forced laborers to the various war industry factories. One of the factories was Wolfsburg. Wolfsburg was and still is the home of Volkswagen. After we threaded through the bodies, we continued pursuing the retreating Germans until we reached the Elbe River.[7]

12

Elbe River

April 14, 1945: the 784th Tank Battalion set up its command post in the town of Braunschweig (Brunswick), approximately 50 miles east of Hanover and 60 miles west of the Elbe River. There they came across more recently freed slave laborers. This area is approximately 40 miles southwest of the infamous town of Gardelegen and 30 miles south of Fallersleben, the Volkswagen branch camp used for military production.

Countless recently liberated slave laborers roamed this area in search of food and their way back home. Many were hundreds of miles from home and many had no homes to return to. They shuffled along in tattered clothing with their feet wrapped in rags. Some used horses, wagons, wheelbarrows and even baby carriages. Some carried huge packs on their backs. They waved at the passing American soldiers and made motions to their mouths pleading pitifully in broken English for food, water, even cigarettes. Some didn't get far and died along the road.

The following day the 784th Tank Battalion's command post displaced forward to an area approximately 20 miles north of Magdeburg and 17 miles southeast of Gardelegen. There they set up operations in the village of Blatz along the west bank of the Elbe River.

Scattered individual and small tank groups assisted the infantry in clearing the nearby woods to prevent counterattacks. During this operation they encountered sporadic artillery, mortar, and *Panzerfaust* fire. There they discovered large quantities of abandoned ammunition, equipment, and supplies. They also seized a combined artillery range and ordnance proving ground with several large caliber railroad guns parked on a siding. During this mission, *Panzerfaust* fire knocked out one tank. Private Henry

Sergeant F.M. Loos, assistant squad leader (left), and PFC James Graff (right), both of 3rd Squad, 3rd Platoon, C Co., 134th Infantry, at Zibberk, Germany, April 1945. *Courtesy James Graff*

Unidentified members of the 784th and a young lady at the end of the trail, April 1945. *Courtesy James Baldwin*

Underwood of Ohio perished inside the burning tank on April 18, 1945, the last member of the 784th Tank Battalion to be killed in action.

Sergeant Bill Hughes, Dog Company, 784th Tank Battalion recounts:

Shortly before mid–April, most of the Battalion was on the west side of the Elbe River picking up enemy stragglers and materiel they left behind during retreat. Various companies were assigned to perform specific missions with infantry troops. D Company as I recall was assigned to the 134 Infantry Regiment to clean out an enemy pocket in a wooded area. The enemy was using hit and run tactics. They would come out of the woods and blaze away periodically and then retreat to the woods to hide. You had to seek and find. This was risky because more than likely they would see you first to fire upon. It was not a healthy situation so a decision was made to take the offensive and dash through the wooded area with a wide sweep of infantry and tanks. You could see the enemy getting up from hiding places and running like mad toward the *autobahn*. We were blasting away but our fire was not too effective because of the trees in the woods. It was enough however to keep the enemy on the run. Somebody yelled over the radio. "LOOK OUT! HERE THEY COME AT 2 O'CLOCK!" The Infantry Commander gave the order for all machine guns and small arms to fire in that direction at will. What a barrage and knowing nothing could survive? Sure enough they came. I never saw so many deer in my life in the line of fire. There was a herd of them and most were slaughtered. It was so sad but the deer were over populated because of little hunting activity in Germany during the war. All that fire scared the hell out of the enemy so we pressed on to the autobahn finding hundreds of enemy soldiers sitting, squatting, or standing sharing a cigarette butt (*kipper* in German) with their guns neatly stacked in piles waiting for capture. War is weird. A half hour ago those guys were trying to kill us and now here they were in defeat calling us comrades and asking for food, water, and cigarettes. The infantry called for MPs to come take the prisoners. Some of the guys tossed cigarettes from their rations to the prisoners and medics gave first aid treatment to those who were totally exhausted. I could not help but ask myself, would someone do this for you if being captured? I thought hell no way with all the hatred in Nazi teachings. We were not too far from Berlin so everyone thought there was a chance of our being the first to enter that city. That was not going to be the case because soon afterwards the word came down that the Russians are coming. Sure enough they were coming down the road in droves. What a meet up with singing and dancing all night long, not to mention that homemade vodka the soldiers were drinking. I tasted it with a quick gulp and choked with a burning throat. Gasping, water only made it worst. It took me almost 20 minutes to recover. We were told by the Russian troops that they were chosen to take Berlin. The word came down to us that we were to halt any further drive toward Berlin. What a disappointment?[1]

Staff Sergeant Franklin Garrido, Baker Company, 784th Tank Battalion pointed out: "The Elbe River was approximately 40 or 50 miles from Berlin. I told my crew to get ready for the big one. We are going in to Berlin. But unknown to us the 'Big Three' had already made a decision that the Allies on the west side of the river would halt. That would give the Russians the honor of capturing Berlin, which was all right with us."[2]

Infantryman Bernard "Jack" Kirsch, Fox Company, 137th Infantry Regiment adds:

When we went to the Elbe River, they told us at the time we were 42 miles from Berlin. That was about a month before the war ended. They moved up tanks and everything else up there too at the time. But the fighting had generally subsided. There were still Germans but they were not doing any aggressive action. Our orders were to sit on the Elbe River and make sure we did not cross it. They gave us flares, red and green. We had the red flares. Every once in awhile, we shot up a flare to make sure we didn't clash with the Russians."[3]

Tech-5 James Hamilton, Charlie Company, 784th Tank Battalion adds: "We went up to the Elbe River and we stopped there because we had the Germans trapped. We had them from this side and the Russians had them from the other side. We had them in a pocket. That's where the war started coming to an end. We had some rough times but we did it!"[4]

Infantryman Murray Leff, Easy Company, 137th Infantry Regiment adds: "We were there a little while and the Russians shot off some green flares and that was the signal for us to get out of the way because they were going to come in. So we went back to an area for occupation and spent several months in various occupation duties."[5]

At this point the enemy was generally no longer aggressive. On the road, thousands of German soldiers staggered to the rear, some with and some without guards.

Unidentified members of the 784th celebrate on a trophy Tiger tank, April 1945. *Courtesy James Baldwin*

Soon the prisoner of war cages started to overflow. The captured units represented a motley, disillusioned crew glad that their fighting days were over. They regarded American captivity as a stroke of good fortune.

The 784th Tank Battalion continued aiding the infantry in rounding up prisoners; flushing enemy soldiers out of hiding; mopping up small bands of die-hard Nazis; dismantling the Nazis' power structure; collecting weapons; feeding and controlling thousands of displaced persons; restoring civilization; and helping shattered communities rebuild.

Before departing the Elbe River on April 26 and 27, the 35th Infantry Division, with the 784th Tank Battalion attached, enjoyed the distinction of being the closest of any American unit to Berlin. Staff Sergeant Franklin Garrido recalls: "My company, Company B, was held in reserve. Two companies of the 784th were at the Elbe River when the Russians swept through Berlin. They swept through Berlin with a vengeance, Hitler committed suicide, and the war ended."[6]

April 26, 1945: The 102nd Infantry Division relieved the 35th Infantry Division along the Elbe River.

13

Occupation

April 26, 1945: The 784th Tank Battalion traveled approximately 75 miles west with the 35th Infantry Division to the Hanover area. They had followed signs marked as the "Santa Fe Trail." The 784th located their command post in the town of Immensen and set up outposts in Arpke, Hanelerwald, and Dolgen. They secured, governed, and occupied this small sector of northern Germany. There they rounded up straggling German soldiers and contended with the remaining die-hard Nazis; screened Nazi officials; cared for displaced persons; and enforced civilian curfews. Sporadic firefights were reminders that fanatical Nazis were carrying the war past its conclusion.

April 30, 1945: Adolf Hitler committed suicide with his new bride Eva Braun in his underground command bunker as Berlin burned above. The *Fuhrer*, age 56, died 12 years and 3 months after he established the Third Reich. The day before his suicide, Hitler appointed Grand Admiral Karl Dönitz, Germany's Naval Commander-in-Chief, as his successor. Göring had fled to Berchtesgaden and Himmler attempted to negotiate a separate peace.

During the following day, German radio played gloomy music interrupted by *"Achtung!"* warnings that an important announcement would follow. A 3-minute silence preceded the announcement and a phantom voice of a German resister broke in on the airwaves: "This is a day of rejoicing for the German people!" The announcement finally came: "It is announced that our *Fuhrer*, Adolf Hitler, this afternoon at his command post in the Reichs Chancellery, fighting till his last breath against Bolshevism, fell for Germany." Hitler's successor personally read a proclamation while the phantom voice interrupted each reference he made to the *Fuhrer's* heroic death: "Nonsense! He was one of the world's greatest criminals!" Grand Admiral Dönitz demanded discipline and obedience to him as Hitler's successor. He went on to say: "My first task is to save the German people from annihilation by the advancing Bolshevist enemy. The military struggle will continue only with this aim. Inasmuch and as long as the attainment of this aim is being hindered by the British and Americans, we shall have to fight against them."[1]

There was an obvious cover-up of the cowardly way in which the *Fuhrer*, for whom so many Germans had given their lives voluntarily and otherwise, escaped accountability by committing suicide.

With this news, waves of suicides, desertions, and executions swept through the German ranks. Hitler met his maker 3 days after his Axis partner in crime, Benito Mussolini. He had modeled his empire on Mussolini's Fascist hierarchy. Together, the 2 dictators forced the Western world into the grimmest war it has ever known.

Sergeant Bill Hughes, Dog Company, 784th Tank Battalion remembers:

It was late April when we heard Berlin was entered by Russian troops and Hitler was thought to have fled or died. We also learned that Mussolini, the Italian dictator was captured and shot several days earlier. This was confirmed in a short-wave length broadcast from England on a radio we had captured. Several days later, it was also announced on German radio. We all were happy that it was over and wondered how soon we would go back to the States."[2]

There was utter pandemonium as thousands of regular German soldiers poured into city streets in the American and British zones. They came on trucks, cars, motorcycles, bicycles, and on foot. Some had deserted, while others had become separated from their units in the chaos caused by the total disintegration of the *Wehrmacht* chain of command. They appeared to be relieved to have escaped the fate of so many of their comrades, who had become eleventh-hour casualties of a war already lost.

During the month of April 1945, the 784th Tank Battalion reported 15 battle casualties and 48 non-battle casualties. Included in the battle casualties are 2 men killed in action. According to the American Battle Monuments Commission, there are 2 men listed: Corporal Eldon Lee (April 10, 1945) and Private Henry Underwood (April 18, 1945). Both men were from Ohio. Included in the non-battle casualties is one fatality, Corporal Alpheus Hughes of the Reconnaissance Platoon, who perished in a motorcycle accident while on assignment controlling traffic.

On May 2nd, an ME109 aircraft with loaded guns landed near the 784th Tank Battalion's area with its landing gear damaged. The pilot had fled. The following day, 18 enemy soldiers drove into the area and turned themselves in. One of the soldiers, who had changed into civilian clothes, was very arrogant. They immediately turned him over to division interrogators. The next day, 13 more enemy soldiers turned themselves in. Their equipment included a sniper rifle and a pair of binoculars, a cause for consternation. Hours later another group of 13 wounded enemy soldiers turned themselves in. With them came 2 nurses and a civilian woman with a baby. Behind them came 2 trucks carrying 40 enemy soldiers. All were turned over to the division prisoner of war cage.

The Third Reich survived the death of its founder for 7 days, like a dead snake twitching its tail until sunset. Victory in Europe, VE Day, finally arrived. At 0241 hours on May 7, 1945, General Alfred Jodl and Admiral Hans von Friedburg signed the surrender documents in Rheims, France: "We the undersigned, acting by authority of the

Grosvenor Cooper (center) and two unidentified tankers in Paris, 1945. *Courtesy James Baldwin*

13. Occupation

German High Command, hereby surrender unconditionally to the Supreme Commander, Allied Expeditionary Forces and simultaneously to the Soviet High Command all forces on land, sea, and in the air who are at this date under German control." The German High Command had delayed this capitulation to allow more of it population to escape into British or American-held territory. General Eisenhower had to threaten to leave the Germans to the tender mercies of the Soviets to get them to sign.

Finally, at midnight on May 8, the guns in Europe fell silent and a strange but welcomed hush settled over the continent. However, a great part of Europe now lay in ruins, a vast wasteland of death and rubble. With the increase in temperature, the stench of the countless decomposing corpses filled the air.

Sergeant Bill Hughes remembers:

Victory in Europe was achieved on 8 May 1945, when the Germans unconditionally surrendered at Rheims, France. There was much jubilation around the world. The 784th Tank Battalion suffered 140 total casualties from all causes; including 24 killed in action. Needless to say, we all were proud to have been part of an enormous operation to bring the war to a close. The big question on everyone's mind now was when do we go home? The answer was not immediately forth coming. We became part of the forces exercising an occupation role to maintain order.

Soon thereafter it was announced that one could be discharged from the Army if he had accumulated 45 points of service time. One point for each month served within the USA and 2 points for each month

"The buddy on my left is Clyde Combe," recalls Bernard "Jack" Kirsch. "He was from Rochester, New York, and a good soldier and a great person. The photograph was taken in Brussels, Belgium. The 137th Infantry Regiment was relocated from occupation duty in Germany to Brussels to serve as Honor Guard for all the English and American officials and dignitaries that were attending the Potsdam Conference." *Courtesy Bernard "Jack" Kirsch*

served overseas would be creditable. We had hoped that all personnel in the Battalion would be returned to the USA together. In view of the 45-point policy, some of the men left the Battalion for the trip back home because they had enough points. I was short of points.[3]

A few days later an attempt to halt a truck traveling through the area failed. The vehicle came under immediate fire by a 784th governing group of 6 enlisted men and one officer. The vehicle turned over, killing one of its time occupants. The other fled.

A few days later the 784th discovered a well-stocked *Panzer* parts warehouse. As they searched around, they discovered a food storage warehouse that would prove vital to the survival of the people in the area.

Soon it became known that the 35th Infantry Division and their attached 784th Tank battalion were allotted for duty in the war against Japan. Victory in Europe, VE Day, could only be an anticlimax. Celebrations would be tempered, knowing that there was still another war to fight. Sergeant Bill Hughes remembers: "Around this period, a rumor was put out that we were going to be shipped to a port in France where we would board ship and sail straight to the Far East to fight. I did not believe it as well as others but many did."[4]

During this period, as Germany lay in turmoil, with hunger, disease, and social unrest at critical levels, hunger and the lack of shelter became life-or-death concerns in the cities. This was not the case in the farming villages, where they had a generally sustaining supply of food and shelter.

Throughout the war, the Nazis had managed to provide an ample supply of food to the German people. They accomplished this by limiting the occupied nations to near starvation diets and shipping most of their food production to Germany. All of that changed with the defeat of Germany. The tables had been turned, and ironically, many Germans died of starvation after surviving the war.

After standing in food lines for grueling hours only to be told that supplies had run out, the Germans became desperate. The inevitable consequence was the spread of the brazenly open black market. Food, clothing, even cigarettes were bartered for luxury items. Cigarettes became the black market's not-so-legal tender. Elements of the German populace became increasingly insolent and resentful towards the occupiers.

May 26, 1945: the 784th displaced from Immensen and located their command post in Harsewinkel the following day. There they supervised the governmental activities of its assigned towns and villages. They granted passes to civilians for travel between adjacent towns, settled minor altercations between German citizens and displaced persons, transported displaced persons to railroad stations for transportation home, and found time to continue training in armored warfare.

On June 3rd, the 784th was on the move again. The tanks proceeded by rail to the station at Hillesheim and road marched the balance of the way. They arrived in Kelberg the following day and set up their command post. There they continued moving displaced persons to collection points and maintaining order. The unit conducted

Best friends Sergeant Jesse Roberts (left) and Corporal James Baldwin at Kelberg, Germany, 1945. *Courtesy Simmons Washington*

(From left) Sergeant Simmons Washington; Staff Sergeant Hills (Mortar Platoon Sgt); Sergeant Spencer; Charles Hester; and Robert Keeley prepare to cook a chicken. *Courtesy Simmons Washington*

around-the-clock security patrols between the towns of Bodenbach, Gelenberg, Rothenbach, Borler and Bongard. Their continuing armored warfare training intensified with new courses that emphasized Japanese tactics of warfare.

Sergeant Bill Hughes recalls:

> We were assigned an area to control which involved setting up check points and road blocks primarily to insure against any build up of resistance from enemy troops still on the loose. Later we moved to Kelberg. A military governor was appointed and we guarded all the surrounding areas around Kelberg. For the first time, we learned something about the German people. We saw how they lived. Very few spoke English and none of us knew German, but we got along well with the population. It was obvious that none had seen black people before so they were very curious about us. The kids would follow us wherever we went hoping for the piece of candy or gum. The men were after us for cigarettes, a treasure as well as coffee and butter. There were many German volunteers to do kitchen work, clean up the area, wash our clothing etc just to be near these basic essentials, hoping for a handout which they got. Each town in our area had an officer and about 6 enlisted men who governed the people. A constant guard and patrol system was set up day and night to make sure the curfew and travel restrictions were enforced. This went on well into June 1945. It was forbidden to fraternize with the German people but very difficult to enforce. It boiled down to not showing any open affection toward the people. Rules and laws are made to be broken. I never saw anyone being punished for breaking the rule, but some were admonished.[5]

Sergeant Simmons Washington adds: "We were in a camp out in the country, a tent city, that's what we called it. There was no fraternization with the enemy. They hadn't lifted the ban yet, so we just played ball, we swam, and we went through our regular training. We went to the firing range getting ready to go to Japan."[6]

Although the war had been over for more than a month, German soldiers in dust-covered uniforms still straggled along the roads heading towards their homes. It was a far cry from the goose-stepping *Wehrmacht* of a few years earlier. Some showed signs of malnutrition and they had to wear their tattered uniforms, their only clothing. Most of these men were either very young, in their teens, or very old, in their 50s and 60s. There was a noticeable absence of men in their prime years. Most had been killed, wounded, or captured long ago.

14

Whatever Happened to the 758th Tank Battalion

The 758th Tank Battalion (Light), the first of the 3 tank battalions to be activated, landed in Italy on November 17, 1944. Assigned to the segregated 92nd Infantry Division in the Fifth Army, they received orders alerting them for front-line duty on December 24th.

Unfortunately, the 758th remained a light tank battalion by the neglect of the segregated Army. The obsolete light tanks could not provide the required range and firepower with their 37-millimeter cannons. Their armor was also too thin. These unwanted tanks were continuously shuffled around to different infantry, tank, and reconnaissance units within the 92nd. Consequently, tactical errors resulted from the battalion's use in combat. Despite this, the tankers performed with distinction.

The 758th was composed of Companies A (Able), B (Baker), and C (Charlie), and each company conducted operations with 17 light tanks. They had Service and Headquarters Companies supporting them. The 37-millimeter cannons of the light tanks were extremely accurate for target practice but could not reach the enemy high up in the mountains of Italy. Headquarters Company had a platoon of 75-millimeter open-turret assault guns that helped make up for this shortcoming but it was too little too late.

The M-4 Sherman medium tanks of the 760th Tank Battalion provided the main armored support to the 92nd Infantry Division. The 758th helped out whenever they could but many times they were in the way.

Early on, the 758th supported the 370th Infantry Regiment's advance up Italy's

14. Whatever Happened to the 758th Tank Battalion

eastern coast. They encountered fierce enemy resistance as they pushed forward on the heavily mined roads. Three light tanks fell into deep craters in the bed of a canal during a crossing and drowned out. Sergeant Jefferson Hightower will never forget this incident:

> In my memory it was February 12, 1945, and the Germans were retreating to the north and the 92nd Infantry Division wasn't able to break through. There was a canal that went down to the Mediterranean Sea. 758th, A Company, First Platoon, which I was a part of, was given the job of crossing that canal and picking up the infantry and making an advance up the coast. I was in tank number 3, Lieutenant McLain was in tank number one. When he hit the canal he turned over and all of them jumped out into the cold water and made it back to the beach. Tank number 2 tried to pass him and they turned over too. I'm in tank number 3 and I'm sure he is going to tell me to turn around and go back. He is lying there in the sand on the beach cursing and waving me to go across. My driver, who was very good, went around those 2 tanks and kept his foot on the gas long enough to keep water from sucking up into the engine and we made it across. Tank number 4 turned over and tank number 5, commanded by Sergeant Seymour Miller of New York, made it across. As soon as we make it across some officer from the 92nd told us to go back: "We can't go any further right now and all you guys do is draw fire." He was right. We were drawing fire. We drew fire from those big naval 12- and 14-inch guns. We stayed around and did a little bit of firing and then the officer insisted that we go back because he had infantry out there and he didn't want their positions given away. We made it back across that canal by taking the same route. I will never forget that because the shells were coming so close to us that I could see fire coming out of the tail ends. They came right at us and we had to maneuver through them. If they caught you right — you were gone!¹

On April 5, 1945, elements of the 758th Tank Battalion supported the 370th Infantry Regiment for its final offensive action in Italy. They advanced north to take the mountain town of Massa. Stiff enemy resistance and mountainous terrain slowed the pace. After several weeks of fighting, the regiment reached its objective.

It was during this assault in the predawn darkness of April 5 that 1st Lieutenant Vernon Baker, a platoon leader in Company C, 370th Infantry Regiment, 92nd Division, led his 25-man platoon up Hill X under intermittent artillery and mortar fire. The objective was the Aghinolfi Castle near Viareggio, which the Germans had fortified into a mountain stronghold.

This was during the Germans' last desperate stand in Italy, and the fighting was fierce. Baker kept his men moving forward, always mindful of his OSC training: "Keep going! Keep the men going! Set the example! Complete the mission!" The rest was reflex.

Baker's platoon advanced to about 250 yards from the castle when he noticed a telescope pointing out of a bunker at the edge of the hill. He low-crawled to the opening, stuck his M-1 Garand into the slit, and fired off his entire clip. He looked inside and saw 2 dead German soldiers; one was still sitting slumped in his seat.

Baker then stumbled upon a well-concealed machine gun nest and liquidated 2 more German soldiers. He went back to report on the situation to his company commander, Captain John Runyon, who, like all of Baker's superior officers, was white. Then a German soldier appeared from out of nowhere and tossed a "potato masher" hand grenade that bounced off Runyon's helmet. Luckily for Baker and Runyon it failed to explode. Baker shot and killed the German soldier as he fled.

By this time Baker's platoon was being ripped apart by small arms and mortars coming from a bunker and several dugouts. He went into the canyon alone and found the hidden bunker entrance and blasted it open with a grenade. He dropped 2 German soldiers who emerged after the explosion and 2 more as he dashed inside with his weapon ablaze.

Realizing that reinforcements were not going to show up, Captain Runyon ordered a withdrawal. Baker volunteered to draw enemy fire upon himself to effect the evacuation of his surviving men. Only 7 of his original 25 men survived the battle. Together they liquidated 26 German soldiers and destroyed 6 machine gun-nests, 2 observation posts, and 4 dugouts, and silenced the bunker.

Runyon told Baker that he was going to get reinforcements. The reinforcements never came and Baker never saw Runyon again. Fifty years later Baker was stunned to find out that Runyon had been put in for the Medal of Honor by the racist leadership of the 92nd Infantry Division. Probably nowhere in the segregated U.S. Army were prejudice and stereotyping more prevalent than in the 92nd Infantry Division, where racism at the highest levels and a lack of leadership totally demoralized the men. This division was best described as a "recipe for failure." Regardless, Baker received the Distinguished Service Cross for his actions on April 5, 1945.

From another direction, the 758th Assault Gun Platoon provided support to the famous 100th Infantry Battalion of the 442nd Regimental Combat Team (Nisei) in its push up Mount Belvedere near Seravezza. Orville Shirey, author of *Americans: The Story of the 442d Combat Team*, describes the firepower: "The 100th Battalion had attacked to the north at 0500, April 5, behind a tremendous demonstration of power by artillery. The 599th and the 329th Field Artillery Battalions, Company B of the 84th Chemical Battalion (4.2 mortar), and the Assault Gun Platoon of the 758th Tank Battalion had all let fly a ten-minute concentration on the enemy position."

In the ensuing assault, Orville Shirey describes one of the many instances of heroism by the 442nd Regimental Combat Team:

> Private First Class Sadao S. Munemori, as assistant squad leader of Company A, also contributed immeasurably to the success of the attack. When his unit was pinned down by the enemy's grazing fire and his squad leader was wounded, command of the squad devolved on him. He made frontal, one-man attacks through direct fire and knocked out 2 machine guns with grenades. Withdrawing under murderous fire and showers of grenades from other enemy emplacements, he had nearly reached a shell crater occupied by 2 of his men when an unexploded grenade bounced from his helmet and rolled toward his helpless comrades. He rose into the withering fire, dived on the grenade, and smothered the blast

with his own body. By his swift, supremely heroic action, Private First Class Munemori saved 2 of his men at the cost of his life and did much to clear the path for his company's advance. PFC Munemori was posthumously awarded the Medal of Honor.

A member of the 758th Tank Battalion recalls the attack through the mountains:

> Our biggest problem with the little Japanese-Americans was keeping up with them; they moved like greased lightning. Instead of following the paths which tanks have to do, they went across the mountains like crazy. We worked out a system. As they took out across the mountains, we wound our way along until we received a signal from them. Then we would lay down a barrage as a diversion. Jerry would be concerned about us and the Nisei would move in swiftly from the rear and mop up. I do mean mop up; they turned those Germans every way but loose.[2]

As the Fifth Army increased its pressure, the German lines caved in. On April 24, elements of the 758th Tank Battalion entered La Spezia Naval Base and took up defensive positions. The Gothic Line had been pierced and the division's objective was reached.

The 758th Tank Battalion held and defended its positions and assisted in mopping up bypassed pockets of resistance as the war came to an end. Then, on September 25, 1945, the battalion deactivated in Italy.

On June 14, 1946, the 758th Tank Battalion reactivated at Fort Knox, Kentucky, and became a part of the Armored Force School. In 1943, the battalion moved to Fort Bragg, North Carolina, and became part of the 82nd Airborne Division.

In November 1949, the 758th Tank Battalion was re-designated the 64th Heavy Tank Battalion and assigned to the 2nd Armored Division at Fort Hood, Texas. In July 1950, the battalion received orders for deployment to Korea and was assigned to the 3rd Infantry Division. They trained in Japan with the new M-48 tank, the best armored and armed vehicle in the Far East.

In November 1950, the 64th Heavy Tank Battalion performed an assault landing on Wonsan, North Korea, where it relieved elements of the 1st Marine Division, the "Frozen Chosen," and held the main line of resistance. Together they withdrew under the onslaught of a massive Chinese intervention. They assisted in the evacuation of U.S. Marines and Korean civilians by holding the final line of resistance behind which 105,000 troops, 100,000 civilians, and 17,500 vehicles were evacuated in the largest beachhead evacuation in U.S. military history.

In early 1951, the battalion joined Task Force Bartlett to clear a path for the 25th Infantry Division. They inflicted heavy enemy casualties and accomplished the mission in 5 days, giving the Allies a needed boost to their confidence.

In March the battalion participated in Operation Tomahawk. They raced north with the 3rd Infantry Division and linked up with the 2nd and 4th Ranger Companies and the 187th Airborne Regimental Combat Team, the "RAKKASANS," who had parachuted behind enemy lines. Together they caught the enemy in a crushing vise and continued pushing north. On March 29, the battalion was among the first American units to cross the 38th parallel in the current Eighth Army advance.

In late April 1951, the Chinese launched another major offensive, this one a 2-army attack against the United Nations' front, that pushed the Allies south. The 64th Heavy Tank Battalion covered the 3rd Infantry Division's withdrawal to the Seoul area, where the line of resistance stabilized at the 38th Parallel.

From May 1951 to July 1953, the battalion held and defended positions around the 38th Parallel while it underwent a historic change with the integration of white soldiers into its ranks. This came as a result of Executive Order 9981, signed by President Harry Truman on July 26, 1948: "... It is essential that there be maintained in the Armed Forces of the United States the highest standards of democracy with equal treatment and opportunity for all in our country's defense."

In its final action of the Korean War, the battalion repelled an enemy penetration into the South Korean lines. In the fierce fighting that ensued, Company A drove into an enemy regimental assembly area, where they fought at point-blank range. Finally, they had to call artillery on themselves. When the smoke cleared, 300 enemy soldiers lay dead. For this action, Company A received the Distinguished Unit Citation.

In November 1954, the 64th Heavy Tank Battalion departed Korea with a Distinguished Unit Citation and 2 Korean Presidential Unit Citations.

In April 1958, the battalion was again deactivated. Then in June 1963, the 64th Armored Regiment with 3 battalions was activated. In May 1966, a 4th battalion was activated and assigned to the 3rd Infantry Division in Wurzburg, Germany. In August 1983, the 4/64th Armored moved to Fort Stewart, Georgia, and joined the 24th Infantry Division.

In August 1990, the 4/64th Armored was alerted for duty in the Persian Gulf. They deployed in August to Saudi Arabia, where they joined Operation Desert Shield and trained with the new M1-A1 Abrams Tank.

In January 1991, the start of Operation Desert Storm, the 4/64th Armored jumped off and began routing the Iraqis from Kuwait. In February they began cross-border operations into Iraq and spearheaded in a sandstorm with less than 100-meter visibility. They destroyed dug-in elements of Iraq's 26th Republican Guard Commando Brigade and cut lines of communications to Baghdad.

In March, the 4/64th Armored moved back to Saudi Arabia and prepared for redeployment to the United States. On March 23, 1991, they arrived at Fort Stewart to a hero's welcome.

15

Whatever Happened to the 761st Tank Battalion

April 1, 1942: the War Department activated the 761st Tank Battalion (light) at Camp Claiborne, Louisiana, with an authorized strength of 36 officers and 593 enlisted men. On September 15, 1943, the 761st Battalion moved to Camp Hood, Texas, for advanced training; there they changed from light to medium tanks.

On July 6, 1944, one of the 761st's black officers, 2nd Lieutenant Jackie Robinson, was riding a civilian bus from Camp Hood to the nearby town of Belton. He refused to move to the back of the bus when told to do so by the driver. Court-martial charges ensued but could not proceed because the battalion commander, Lt. Colonel Paul Bates, would not consent to the charges. The top brass at Camp Hood then transferred Robinson to the 758th Tank Battalion, whose commander immediately signed the court-martial consent.

The lieutenant's trial opened on August 2 and lasted for 17 days, during which time the 761st departed Camp Hood. They had charged Robinson with violating the 63rd and 64th Articles of War. The first charge specified, "Lieutenant Robinson behaved with disrespect toward Captain Gerald M. Bear, Corps Military Police, by contemptuously bowing to him and giving several sloppy salutes while repeating, O'kay Sir, O'kay Sir, in an insolent, impertinent and rude manner." The second charge stipulated, "Lieutenant Robinson having received a lawful command by Captain Bear to remain in a receiving room at the MP station disobeyed such order." Robinson was eventually acquitted, and he was not charged for his actions on the bus. Three years later, Robinson was riding buses in the major leagues after breaking baseball's color barrier.

In October 1944, after 2 years of intense armored training, the 761st Tank Battalion landed in France. The tankers received a welcome from the Third Army commander, Lt. General George Patton, Jr., who had observed the 761st conducting training maneuvers in the States:

> Men, you're the first Negro tankers to ever fight in the American Army. I would never have asked for you if you weren't good. I have nothing but the best in my Army. I don't care what color you are as long as you go up there and kill those Kraut sons of bitches. Everyone has their eyes on you and is expecting great things from you. Most of all, your race is looking forward to you. Don't let them down and damn you! Don't let me down![1]

On November 8, 1944, the 761st became the first African American armored unit to enter combat, smashing into the French towns of Moyenvic and Vic-sur-Seille. During the attack, Staff Sergeant Ruben Rivers, in Able Company's lead tank, encountered a roadblock that held up the advance. With utter disregard for his personal safety, he courageously climbed out of his tank under direct enemy fire, attached a cable to the roadblock and removed it. His prompt action prevented a serious delay in the offensive and was instrumental in the success of the attack.

On November 9, Charlie Company ran into a hellish anti-tank ditch near Morville. The crack 11th *Panzer* Division began to knock out tanks one by one down the line. The tankers crawled through the freezing muddy waters of the ditch under pelting rain and snow while hot shell fragments fell all around them. When German artillery began to walk a line toward the ditch, the tankers' situation looked hopeless.

After exiting his burning tank, 1st Sergeant Samuel Turley organized a dismounted combat team. When the team found itself pinned down by a counterattack and unable to return fire, Turley ordered his men to retreat. He climbed from cover and provided covering fire that allowed them to escape. His fire was so accurate that the enemy gunners had to flee their positions.

War Correspondent Trezzvant Anderson described Turley's devotion to duty:

> Standing behind the ditch, straight up, with a machine gun and an ammo belt around his neck, Turley was spraying the enemy with machine-gun shots as fast as they could come out of the muzzle of the red-hot barrel. He stood there covering for his men, and then fell, cut through the middle by German machine-gun bullets that ripped through his body as he stood there firing the M.G. to the last. That's how Turley went down and as his body crumpled to the earth, his fingers still gripped that trigger.... But we made it![2]

On November 10, Sergeant Warren G.H. Crecy fought through enemy positions to aid his men when his tank got hit. He immediately took command of another vehicle, armed with only a .30-caliber machine gun, and liquidated the enemy position that had destroyed his tank. Still under heavy fire, he helped eliminate the enemy forward observers whose direction of artillery fire had the American infantry pinned down.

The next day, Crecy's tank bogged down in the mud. He dismounted and fearlessly faced anti-tank, artillery and machine-gun fire as he extricated his tank. While freeing his tank, he saw that the accompanying infantry was pinned down and that the enemy had begun a counterattack. Crecy climbed up on the rear of his immobilized tank and held off the Germans with the tank's exposed anti-aircraft machine gun while the foot soldiers disengaged and withdrew. Later that day, he again exposed himself to enemy fire as he wiped out several machine-gun nests and an anti-tank position with only his machine gun. The more fire he drew, the harder he fought. After the battle, it was said that Crecy had to be pried away from his machine gun.

War Correspondent Trezzvant Anderson reported:

> To look at Warren G.H. Crecy (the G.H. stands for Gamaliel Harding) you'd never think that here was a "killer," who had slain more of the enemy than any man in the 761st. He extracted a toll of lives from the enemy that would have formed the composition of 3 or 4 companies, with his machine guns alone. And yet, he is such a quiet, easy-going, meek-looking fellow, that you'd think that the fuzz which a youngster tries to cultivate for a mustache would never grow on his baby-skinned chin. And that he'd never use a word stronger than "damn." But here was a youth who went so primitively savage on the battlefield that his only thought was to "kill, kill, kill," and he poured his rain of death pellets into German bodies with so much reckless abandon and joy that he was the nemesis of all the foes of the 761st. And other men craved to ride with Crecy and share the reckless thrill of killing the hated enemy that had killed their comrades. And he is now living on borrowed time. By all human equations Warren G.H. Crecy should have been dead long ago, and should have had the Congressional Medal of Honor, at least![3]

Crecy was indeed nominated for the Medal of Honor, for possibly the second time, when Lt. Colonel Philip W. Latimer, USAR-Ret, and Chief Warrant Officer Christopher P. Navarre, USA-Ret, submitted a recommendation through the office of Senator Barbara Boxer (D-Ca) in 1999. The Military Awards Branch denied this recommendation. According to Captain Ivan Harrison (Commanding Officer HQ Co), Crecy, along with Rivers and Turley, were put in for the Medal of Honor. They all received the Silver Star, their glass ceiling.[4]

The 761st pushed on. It was rough during that period with the rain, mud, and cold driving sleet, and the crack enemy troops bitterly contested every inch of terrain. The 761st smashed through the French towns of Obreck, Dedeline and Chateau Voue, with Rivers leading the way for Able Company.

Rivers, a tank platoon sergeant, became adept at liquidating the enemy with his .50-caliber machine gun. The dashing young fighter from Oklahoma was soon a legend in the battalion. His platoon leader, 2nd Lieutenant Robert Hammond, Jr., radioed, "Don't go into that town, Sergeant, it's too hot in there." Rivers respectfully replied, "I'm sorry, sir, I'm already through that town!"[5]

On the way to Guebling, France, on November 16, 1944, Rivers' tank ran over a Teller anti-tank mine. The explosion blew off the right track, the volute springs and the undercarriage, hurling the tank sideways. When the medical team arrived, they found Rivers behind his tank holding one leg, which was ripped to the bone. There was a hole in his leg where part of his knee had been, and bone protruded through his trousers. The medics cleansed and dressed the wound and attempted to inject Rivers with morphine, but he refused. He wanted to remain alert. The medics informed Rivers' commanding officer, Captain David Williams II, that Rivers should be evacuated immediately. Rivers refused. Pulling himself to his feet, he pushed past the commanding officer and took over the second tank. At that moment a hail of enemy fire came in. Captain Williams gave orders to disperse and take cover.

The 761st was to cross a river into Guebling, after combat engineers completed a bridge. The Germans tried desperately to stop the construction, but Able Company, 761st Tank Battalion held them off. The bridge was completed on the afternoon of November 17. Rivers led the way across, and the Black Panthers took up positions in and around Guebling. On the way into town, Rivers, despite his wounds, engaged 2 German tanks. Still in great pain, he took them on, and with the help of his platoon, forced them to withdraw.

Before dawn on November 18, Captain Williams and the medical team visited each tank. When they reached Rivers, it was obvious that he was in extreme pain. They reexamined Rivers' leg and found it to be infected. The medical team said that he must be evacuated immediately or the leg would have to be amputated. Rivers still insisted that he would not abandon his men. Throughout the day, both sides held and defended their positions.

At dawn on November 19, Able Company, along with elements of the 26th Infantry Division, began an assault on the village of Bougaltroff. When Able Company emerged from cover, all hell broke loose as the morning air outside Guebling lit up with tracers from enemy guns. Rivers spotted an anti-tank gun and directed a concentrated barrage on to it.

Rivers continued to fire until several tracers were seen going into his turret. "From a comparatively close range of 200 yards, the Germans threw in 2 H.E. [high explosive] shots that scored," Anderson wrote. "The first shot hit near the front of the tank, and penetrated with ricocheting fragments confined inside its steel walls. The second scored inside the tank. The first shot had blown Rivers' brains out against the back of the tank, and the second went into his head, emerging from the rear, and the intrepid leader, the fearless, daring fighter was no more."[6]

The platoon leader, 2nd Lieutenant Robert Hammond, Jr., also died heroically that morning. He took the machine gun out of his disabled tank and covered the escape of crewmen from other disabled tanks when he got shot down.

Captain David J. Williams tells the aftermath:

> A runner came and said, "Colonel Lyons from the infantry just lost his eye and a leg, you're in charge!" I told the runner to get the grunts back and hide in the cellars. They have too much for us. Another bundle of joy, the infantry said, "They are coming around behind us." I said, "Once you're in the houses, let them attack." I had the cannon company from the infantry there. War is strange. Suddenly there was a lull, silence. The

medics started checking the tanks. My job was to identify my dead. In my company we had a rule to go after the wounded because tank wounds are terrible, they're vehicular. If they get out of that tank, there is a leg off....

Then along comes Lt. Colonel Hunt, who took Bates' place. He is standing in a half-track looking immaculate and he says: "Williams, you had quite a battle here." I said, "Yes Sir!" Then the TD Captain said, "Listen, this company stayed in there." I didn't have much of a company left and there was infantry all over the place. The infantry takes terrible casualties. I said, "I want to put Sergeant Rivers in for the Congressional Medal of Honor." He said, "What did he do? He got the Silver Star already." I said, "Sir, that was for November 8. He's up in that tank there." He said, "Well, put it in writing." He didn't show any interest.... It was subtly told to me not to put anything in over the Silver Star. We called it the battalion commander's good conduct medal; I even got one. Once they saw 761st with "N" behind it, Silver Star. I didn't deserve any more.[7]

Ruben Rivers did not have to die on that cold, dreary November morning in France. Three days earlier, he had received what GIs called a "million-dollar wound." He could have gone home a war hero with his Silver Star and Purple Heart, knowing that his comrades respected him as an outstanding soldier and comrade. But he stayed — and he died. His Medal of Honor would become a "dream deferred."

The 761st pushed on. From December 31, 1944, to February 2, 1945, the 761st took part in the American counteroffensive of the Battle of the Bulge. In a major battle at Tillet, Belgium, the 761st operated for 2 continuous days against German *Panzer* and infantry units, who withdrew in the face of the 761st attack. The operations involving the 761st in the Bulge split the enemy lines at 3 points — the Houffalize-Bastogne road, the St. Vith-Bastogne highway, and the St. Vith-Trier road — preventing the resupply of German forces encircling American troops at Bastogne.

Later, as the armored spearhead for the 103rd Infantry Division, the 761st took part in assaults that resulted in the breach of the Siegfried Line. From March 20 to 23, 1945, operating far in advance of friendly artillery and in the face of German resistance, elements of the 761st attacked and destroyed many defensive positions along the Siegfried Line. The 761st captured 7 German towns, more than 400 vehicles, 80 heavy weapons, 200 horses and thousands of small arms. During that 3-day period, the battalion inflicted more than a thousand casualties on the German army. It was later determined that the 761st had fought against elements of 14 German divisions.

The 761st was among the first American units to link up with Soviet forces in Austria. On May 5, 1945, the 761st reached Steyr, Austria, on the Enns River, where they met the Soviets.

Through 6 months of battle, without relief, the 761st Tank Battalion served as a separate battalion with the 26th, 71st, 79th, 87th, 95th and 103rd Infantry Divisions and the 17th Airborne Division. Assigned at various times to the Third, Seventh and Ninth armies, the "Black Panthers" fought major engagements in 6 European countries and participated in 4 major Allied campaigns. During that time, the unit inflicted an exorbitant number of casualties on the German army and captured, destroyed or aided in the liberation of more than 30 towns, several concentration camps, 4 airfields, 3 ammunition supply dumps, 461 wheeled vehicles, 34 tanks, 113 large guns, and thousands of individual and crew-served weapons. This was accomplished in spite of extremely adverse weather conditions, difficult terrain not suited to armor, heavily fortified enemy positions, extreme shortages of replacement personnel, an overall casualty rate approaching 50 percent and the loss of 71 tanks.

The quest for the Presidential Unit Citation began on July 25, 1945, when the 761st Tank Battalion submitted to General Eisenhower's Headquarters, United States Forces Europe, over the signature of Captain Ivan Harrison, a recommendation that it be awarded the Distinguished Unit Citation. Also known as the Presidential Unit Citation, it is the highest honor that can be bestowed upon a military unit.

Ivan Harrison remembers:

Everyone else was doing it for themselves but no one was doing it for us. Frankly, I just love those men, like father to son. I was much older than them. I made Jimmy Lightfoot my adjutant when I was acting battalion commander. His father was a professor at Howard University and Jimmy Lightfoot became a lawyer when he was about 22 years old. He and I got together and he wrote most of this draft and we sent it in. We sent it in through the commander of a regiment to the Commanding General U.S. Forces European Theater. Bates was on leave then in Holland and I was acting battalion commander. Bates would have signed it if he was there, he would have.[8]

The recommendation consisted of a 4-page narration, 4 exhibits, a report of damage to the enemy, remarks by Undersecretary of War Robert L. Patterson, and a Chart of Path of Origin. The exhibits were letters of commendation from the commanding general of the XII Corps along with the commanding generals of the 26th, 103rd, and 71st Infantry Divisions.

The recommendation stated: "This unit had distinguished itself by extraordinary heroism in battle and has exhibited great gallantry, determination, and esprit-de-corps in operations against the enemy, overcoming such hazardous conditions as adverse weather, mountainous terrain, and heavily fortified enemy positions."[9]

General Eisenhower's office sent the recommendation to Third Army Headquarters for an evaluation. The reply, dated August 18, 1945, stated: "1. Not favorably considered. 2. After a careful study of the 761st Tank Battalion described in basic communication, it is considered that the action, while commendable, was not sufficiently outstanding to meet the requirements of a unit citation as set forth in Section IV, Circular 33, War Department, dated 22 December 1943." The letter was signed; "For the Commanding General; RW Hartman, Lt. Col. Assistant Adjutant General."[10]

After having fought and died in Northern France, the Ardennes, the Rhineland, and Central Europe, the "Black Panthers" asked nothing, but hoped that their sacrifices would not go unnoticed by history. Trezzvant Anderson, the war correspondent attached to the 761st, noted:

15. Whatever Happened to the 761st Tank Battalion

The going was not always smooth, and the tempo was not always pleasant to the Negroes, for the fact remained that they were Negroes, and there were occasions when they were brutally reminded of that fact, after the battle had ended. The problem of race, which had *not existed* on the field of battle, raised its ugly head after the din of battle had subsided, and it hurt, it really hurt! To think that while the enemy shells were falling, and death was a matter of moments, yeah, seconds, and every man was a brother when safety could save a life, that all that could be so easily forgotten after the risks and perils of the battlefield had vanished. But it was a ghastly truth, and it *hurt* to the very core! But these grim warriors, who had faced the enemy's "finest troops," took it with quiet solicitude, and realized in their hearts, that they were men of quality, men of character and of caliber! That had been proved in the crucible or war, where one mistake is the last mistake.[11]

On February 12, 1946, the final decision from General Eisenhower's office regarding the Distinguished Unit Citation came down to the commander of the 761st Tank Battalion: "1. Disapproved. 2. While the operations of the 761st Tank Battalion were commendable, it is not felt that they meet the requirements for a Distinguished Unit Citation." It was signed: "By Command of General McNarney: LS Ostrander, Brigadier General, USA, Adjutant General."[12]

Able Company's Walter Lewis, after hearing the bad news, stated: "This was an unfortunate occurrence and something must be done to rectify it. It does not reflect the democratic principles on which the country is founded. I will not be at rest until the day of adjustment for this fiasco comes."[13]

During 1947 and 1948 a formal board took into consideration the compiled facts of this case and concluded with disapproval. After that time numerous requests for consideration were denied as no new evidence was uncovered that could substantially affect the initial denial of the citation.

In 1967, Congressman Frank Annunzio, from Illinois, introduced a bill to Congress. A member of his district brought this to his attention. The bill would enable the president of the United States to award the Presidential Unit Citation to the 761st Tank Battalion.

In 1977, Congressman Annunzio brought this to the attention of his colleague, Congressman John Conyers of Michigan. Congressman Conyers sent a letter to the Secretary of the Army, Clifford Alexander. This resulted in the reopening of this case to see if, after 32 years of continuous correspondence, the 761st Tank Battalion and Allied Veterans Association could be assured that their case had been given every opportunity for fair and just consideration. Times had changed.

Finally, on January 11, 1978, the Secretary of Defense, Harold Brown, sent a memorandum to the president of the United States proposing the award of the Presidential Unit Citation. A handwritten correspondence on the memorandum was returned: "Presume that in comparison with other tank battalions the 761st exhibited extraordinary heroism. Therefore, am signing. J.C."[14]

January 24, 1978: "By virtue of the authority vested in me as President of the United States and as Commander in Chief of the Armed Forces of the United States, I have today awarded the Presidential Unit Citation (Army) for Extraordinary Heroism to the 761st Tank Battalion, United States Army."[15] Signed, "Jimmy Carter."

In 1997, 53 years after giving his life on the battlefield, Staff Sergeant Ruben Rivers was posthumously awarded the Medal of Honor, a "dream no longer deferred."

The motto of the 761st Tank Battalion has always been "Come Out Fighting." In World War II, that is exactly what they did.

16

Deactivation

Now back to the 784th Tank Battalion. A final formation with the 35th Infantry Division was carried out on July 1, 1945. A special dedication ceremony took place at the stadium at Koblenz, Germany. The American Army of occupation had originally built this stadium following the First World War. The Nazis later used it for propaganda rallies and sporting events. It received major damage during the Second World War that had been repaired in time for this rededication. The Americans renamed it "Santa Fe" stadium in honor of the 35th Infantry Division.

Along with the rededication, a parade, and unit review took place and unit citation streamers and badges were affixed to the colors of the following units of the 134th Infantry Regiment: 1st Battalion, Charlie Company, and the 2nd Platoon of Dog Company. Colors were also affixed to the 1st Battalion of the 320th Infantry Regiment. Charlie Company, 134th Infantry Regiment, of which Infantryman James Graff was a member, received a majority of the unit citations of the entire 35th Infantry Division.

The 784th Tank Battalion sat directly east of the north gate near the 134th Infantry Regiment. Following the ceremony, a baseball game took place. Infantryman James Graff provides the details: "We saw a baseball game that afternoon. The 35th Division played the 106th Division. We won 5 to 3. Murray Dickson who was a member of the 35th pitched and he later played with the St. Louis Cardinals and the Pittsburgh Pirates."[1]

Ceremoniously the 784th Tank Battalion parted ways with the 35th Infantry Division: "Until we form again."

Tech-5 James Hamilton, Charlie Company, 784th Tank Battalion recounts: "After that we all came back to France to the embarkation camp. They told us we had to come home for 30 days and after that we had to go to Japan. But before we could leave they dropped the atomic bomb."²

Infantryman Murray Leff, Easy Company, 137th Infantry Regiment adds: "They sent us right next door to a little village near Le Havre. They had Camp Lucky Strike where we waited to board a ship to go home. At that point they dropped the atom bomb. All of the logistical plans to take us back home and then to Japan were still in effect. We were going to go home for our 30-day leave and then go on and attack Japan."³

Sergeant Bill Hughes, Dog Company, 784th Tank Battalion remained in Europe:

In early July I heard about a program the Army endorsed by contracting with several universities and other schools. It was approved and I applied for studies at Manchester University, England. The course of study was a semester of English. All costs were paid by the Army. Additionally, you received your regular pay plus a monthly allowance. You wore only civilian clothes and were free to go or do whatever you want before and after class hours. My course was Monday, Wednesday, & Friday, 1–3 PM. This gave me much time to explore Manchester and other parts of England. I really felt like being free of the military environment. I applied again for another semester but the quota was already filled. I then applied for Wharton Technical College, England to study telecommunications and was accepted. When I returned after 6 months they sent me to Brussels, Belgium as the 784th had returned to the States. Duty was just about nil. You had to sign in every morning and check the roster for any duty assignment. The food was excellent and much of my time was touring Brussels by day and at night I found a great jazz club called the Blue Note where I spent many hours listening to some of Belgium's best jazz artists. Duty time finally caught up with me. I was given a jeep, driver, and an armed guard with a mounted .30 caliber machine gun. We all carried side arms. We delivered bags of cash from the Finance Office in Brussels to units in the area. It went without incident. The orders were to shoot to warn of any hostile attempts and if necessary shoot to disable but avoid killing anybody. This was in January 1946. In anticipation that I would soon be eligible for discharge, I wrote to the civil service commission advising I was furloughed into the military and had the reemployment rights. They agreed and asked me to serve overseas which I accepted. My discharge date was established for 20 March and my date back into government service was 21 March 1946, at Frankfurt, Germany. This was really the beginning of an occupation period I witnessed in Germany but this time as a civilian for many years to come. This was the beginning of an overseas career that was continuous in Europe.⁴

The 784th Tank Battalion departed Europe on the SS *Argentina* on Christmas Eve, 1945. The effect of going home with the war finally over was stunning. Some of the men stood speechless, some prayed, and some broke out in tears. They sailed from Le Havre, France and landed in New York in time for the New Year's celebration.

They took up quarters at Camp Kilmer, New Jersey, and prepared to disengage from military service. This was 3 months behind the 35th Infantry Division that had

16. Deactivation

deactivated on December 7, 1945. Finally on April 26, 1946, the 784th Tank Battalion deactivated. By the grace of God, the men had become civilians again.

Tech-5 James Hamilton recounts: "We came home, back to the United States and we landed in New York Harbor past the Statue of Liberty. That was on New Year's Day 1946. From there we went to the camp there in New Jersey and then they transferred us to our different destinations where we lived."[5]

Meanwhile, back in Germany, the International Military Tribunal tried Hitler's remaining intimate collaborators in Nuremberg. A year earlier, while in British captivity, Himmler had ingested a vial of potassium cyanide and was dead within 12 minutes despite frantic efforts to pump his stomach and administer emetics. The trial opened with shabby-looking defendants nervously fidgeting in the dock, feigning amnesia, no longer the arrogant, pompous leaders of the past. Some were acquitted and some sentenced to prison. All others were sentenced to death by hanging.

At 11 minutes past 0100 hours on October 16, 1946, Ribbentrop mounted the gallows first. He dropped through the trap door and gasped as he dangled for over 20 minutes before dying. Following him at intervals were Keitel, Klatenbrunner, Rosenberg, Frank, Frick Streicher, Seyss-Inquart, Sauckel, and Jodl. Göring, in the same manner as Himmler, cheated the gallows by taking potassium cyanide just 2 hours before his date with the hangman. It is believed that one of his guards provided it to him. Hitler's chain of command had passed into history. However, many other Nazis escaped prosecution. Some fled the country and concealed their identities. Due to the passionate efforts of Simon Wiesenthal, many of these Nazis were brought to justice. The Nuremberg Trials stood as a symbolic expression of the world's outrage over the atrocities of the Third Reich.

Civilian James Hamilton (C/784th) returned to his beloved Baltimore, where he found it almost as he left it. The nightclubs up and down Pennsylvania Avenue still jumped. Clubs like the Avenue Café, the Casina, the Gambis, the Comedy Club, and many others. James recalls:

> I got a job driving cars for Park Circle Motor Company. I took them down to a dealer in Durham, North Carolina. I had a tow bar — one car on the back and I drove the other. While unbuckling them someone yelled, "Come out from under that car!" I said, "Wait until I'm finished!" Then I heard, "Who are you talking to, boy? Do you know where you're at?" I slid from underneath and there was this great big white cop. He said, "You don't know where you at. Do you boy?" Then the dealer came out and said, "Hey! Joe, leave him alone, he's working for me!" "Well you better teach him some damned manners!" I drove back and I told Warfield at the dealer, "I'm not taking anymore cars down there."
>
> Then I went to work for the government down at Middle River depot. We handled signal equipment for the government. When we went to lunch they had separate places. Several weeks later we went to lunch and one of our boys sat down on one of their benches and they didn't like that. So we all gathered together and sat down with him. Not long after that President Truman passed an executive order that allowed us to go anywhere, eat anywhere.
>
> Then around 1952 they said they were going to move the depot to Tobyhanna, Pennsylvania. My wife was a school teacher and she told me we can't go up there and you have to

find a job down here. So then I found a job at the ship yard in the rigging department. We had a crane that pulled 20ton wheels, drive shafts, and turbine engines from ships. Sometimes they had to burn a hole in the ship's hull to remove the objects. At that ship yard when I had to use the restroom it had a sign saying "white." And the "colored" restroom was all the way around to the other side. But the foreigners who just got off their ship could go in them but we couldn't. So the Union got together and said we were going to walk off the job if our members can't use any restroom they want. So they changed that. And that was great!

One of the guys that I worked with at the depot told me that they are hiring back. When I got home there was a letter. It said to come back to work for the federal government. I said this is great and gave 2 weeks notice. Someone asked why I'm leaving and I said, "Man! I've got to go! I'm going back with the government where I get annual leave, sick leave, and more pay." Soon after they contracted the place out where we were working and sent us all up to the Social Security Administration where I came out in 1985.[6]

James retired with over 30 years of federal government service in 1985. He resides in Baltimore, where he enjoys watching sports and rooting for his hometown Orioles and Ravens. He gave up golf a few years ago. Now he enjoys quality time with family and friends.

Civilian Franklin Garrido (B/784th) returned to Los Angeles, where he became a postal clerk. He attended Otis Art Institute, where he produced several paintings, some of which were exhibited in the Los Angeles County Museum of Art. Franklin continued his passion for art through painting, sculpting, pottery making, and photography. He never sold his labors of love. He gave them away. He later went into business for himself and opened up a service station. Later he began a 25-year career as a Los Angeles County Marshal. Before retiring he returned to school and earned a bachelor's degree in English from California State University. During retirement he spent a short time teaching ESL (English as a Second Language). Then he kept busy by volunteering his services to his church and serving as a docent for the Los Angeles County Afro-American Museum. As captain of his local block club he was instrumental in having speed bumps placed on his local community street. As a member of the 761st Tank Battalion & Allied Veterans Association — the 784th did not have an association — he was a key player behind the awarding of the Medal of Honor to Ruben Rivers.

Franklin's family describes him: "Frank's connection with God was clear throughout his life by his unyielding generosity and dedication to service — a testament to his Catholic upbringing. His life was filled with his love for family, friends and colleagues, service to his community, and country and an artistic expression that was unmistakably God-given."[7]

Franklin passed away after a long illness at the age of 82 on April 16, 2005. He is truly missed and we thank him for doing his part to build a world more tolerant, compassionate, and dignified than the one he was born into. This book is dedicated to his memory — and may God embrace his soul.

James Hamilton, along with his son-in-law Ray Jones, proudly pins Colonel rank on his daughter, Lynne Hamilton-Jones. The ceremony took place June 30, 2006.

Civilian L.Z. Anderson (761st/784th) found himself caught up in the Civil Rights struggle shortly after returning home:

> I went back to Oklahoma and stayed for a few months. I went back to the job I left, working at a tailor shop for $6.50 a week. My sister was in San Francisco and that gave me an excuse to go out there. It seemed everybody was going to California in 1946. I started working for the San Francisco Municipal Railway in 2 weeks, which made it easy for me to stay. I got my job through civil service. They had just started hiring blacks when I arrived. I worked with them up until 1977 and it was one of the better paying jobs. Driving a bus is nerve wracking, the turnover is great, but it paid well.
>
> It is hard to get a person out of a civil service job. You don't just jump up and fire a man because you don't like him. You have to go through channels. But they would always bring us up on charges. You never did anything right with them. I got along fine though. I was only suspended 2 times in the 31 years I worked there. But I was in to see the boss a lot.
>
> I bought a house in San Francisco in 1956 with no problems. There were fine schools

(Left to right) Franklin Garrido, the author, General Celes King III and L.Z. Anderson at the Celes King Bail Bonds Agency, Los Angeles, 1997.

in that neighborhood. About a year after we got in there they jumped up and rezoned the school system. That's how they eliminated blacks from the better schools in San Francisco. That was in the Ingleside area. That just goes to show that they didn't want the blacks in the better schools. That's when most of the blacks got sent up at Hunter's Point.

Around 1958 I started going on quite few demonstrations against job and housing discrimination. We used to walk up and down Van Ness Avenue where all the hotels were. We did a lot of footwork. We went into those grocery stores, filled up the baskets, pushed them up to the counter, and walked off and left them. We went up to the point of going to jail. We couldn't go to jail because we had jobs to go to the next morning. We would take off and run. The others could go to jail because they didn't have jobs. We went to the churches and asked to take up a collection for the demonstrators, to bail them out of jail. We got a lot done but we caught hell doing it. Terry Francois led many of these demonstrations. He was a leader in the NAACP. Later he was appointed the first black supervisor in the city.

There was this guy who owned a chain of stores and restaurants. His name was Dobbs. He needed to hire blacks in his stores but he was a little slow in doing that. So finally we got in touch with his wife. She told me, "Mr. Anderson, you get the girls and I'll get them hired." So we lined these girls up for her. But when it got back to him he came looking for me to tell me that his wife didn't run his business. But she told me she was going to hire them and she would have. Later that little guy ran for mayor but he didn't make it on account that he didn't want to hire blacks in his stores.

We had a neighborhood group, a men's club of about 20 faithful men called the Pilgrim Community Fellowship. It started out in a church but it was not a church group. If you can get that many men together, you can get a lot done. We told the mayor that when there is something involving our community, "don't run to them preachers and doctors they call our leaders, come to us!" Our group used to go down to City Hall to meet with Mayor Shelley. When he had big meetings he called our group to let us sit in on the hearings. He took aggressive steps to improve the city. He was a good man.

When I applied for my house here in Pacifica in 1964 they didn't want to sell to us. My friend came out here and they told him they didn't have any vacancies and turned him down. So he went to one of his white friends, a teacher in the San Francisco school system. He told her what they told him and she came out and they told her they had plenty of vacancies. She complained and soon they called him and told him it was a mistake. He told me about the model house that I wanted and that it was back on the market. So that's how we got out here. No problems after that except we had this one old gal who came down the hill one day half drunk and ran over my yard. She got out and told me that the whites out here didn't want me there. We had quite a few of them, what do you call them — oh, Rednecks![8]

Since retirement in 1977, L.Z. has been active in the 761st Tank Battalion & Allied Veterans Association. He resides in Pacifica, California, with his wife.

Civilian Bill Hughes (D/784th) stayed in Germany after the war where he observed the US Army desegregate. In 1948 President Harry Truman issued Executive Order 9981 to end segregation in the military and to uphold the standards of democracy. The army dragged its feet on this executive order for 2 years. Finally in 1950, America was completely embarrassed in front of the entire world for sending a segregated army to represented freedom and democracy in the fight against communism in the Korean War. As a result, America immediately began integrating its armed forces. Bill recalls:

I started working as a civilian over here in 1946 and had to fight discrimination on the job until 1950. We had nice apartments but they were segregated until 1950. The military was completely segregated. One exception was the officer's club. All civil service employees could attend those clubs. There were numerous nasty incidents and fights at times between blacks and whites. One thing was certain. You had to be prepared to rumble. As you know I was in Europe during the civil rights movement. I kept abreast of what was going on in the States. Over here we had meetings regarding the movement attended primarily by black participants. There was a sprinkling of whites that attended but most were reluctant to speak out one way or another and were tight lipped on the subject. Most of the foreign nationals I talked with on the subject were very sympathetic to the cause. Most could not understand the horrors of slavery, the hatred, discrimination, and segregation that Blacks faced in a so-called democratic society. The movement did lead the way to many changes that have taken place in America.[9]

Bill retired from the federal government on December 31, 1985, as Deputy Chief, Defense Communications Agency/Commercial Communications Office, Europe. He

Bill Hughes (right) with his son Gary, Brunswick, Maryland, December 2004. *Courtesy Bill Hughes*

travels annually to the States to visit family members and friends in Virginia, Maryland, and Indiana. He resides in Heidelberg, Germany, with his wife.

Civilian Simmons Washington (HQ/784th) returned to a happy reunion in Mississippi, where his wife Elizabeth awaited with their daughter Sandra. He was overjoyed with this reunion and especially seeing his 14-month-old daughter for the first time. Simmons worked for the Meridian Housing Authority for 17 years as the project manager. He recalls:

> Segregation was the way of life in this part of the country. As long as a minority stayed in "his or here place" there was not any major problems. After World War II changes began to take place. The right to vote caused many problems. Northern volunteers, black and white, mostly students came south and these young people were very courageous and deserve much credit.
>
> A lot of violent acts started — the church burnings, bombings, and lynching. Threats were made to blacks and the whites who sympathized with the cause. In the early 1960s there was the murder of the 3 civil rights workers in Philadelphia, Mississippi. One of these workers, James Chaney, was a classmate of my daughter at Saint Joseph's Catholic School. We were always worried that her school would be burned or bombed. All the teachers and priest were white. Fortunately the school and our church survived.

All of these things came about after I returned from the army. Then integration caused more problems. The children had to meet at a local housing project to be escorted to school by local police.[10]

In 1967 Simmons moved his family to Los Angeles and worked for McDonnell Douglas Aircraft, Hughes Helicopter, and Boeing Aircraft in their graphics department. He retired from Boeing in 1987 and moved his family back home to Mississippi: "We were gone for 20 years so when we returned things were different. The relationships between the races had greatly improved."[11] Simmons resides with his wife in Meridian, Mississippi.

Civilian Ernest Mikus (C/784th) returned to his home in New Jersey. His son Wayne describes:

After recuperating from being wounded he was assigned to a POW camp in Germany guarding German prisoners as the war was almost over. Ended on his birthday, May 8th. Assigned to an MP battalion involved with railroad security from June 1945 to July 1946 in the area of Wurzburg. Briefly assigned to Nuremberg for some of the trial. Then came back to New Jersey, Camp Kilmer and out of the service. Went back to Rutgers University in New Brunswick, New Jersey and finished the last year of his college getting a degree in journalism. Sold insurance for a brief period with an uncle. Then started as a salesman for the RJ Reynolds Tobacco Company, worked his way up to be a divisional sales manager until his death of cancer in August 1970. His whole life after service was in New Jersey. His main hobby was model railroading, a love of trains, and the usual upkeep of a house. Met my mother and were married in 1949, I came along in 1951 and my brother in 1954. They were happily married until he died.[12]

Civilian James Baldwin (HQ/784th) returned home to North Carolina:

I never got a chance to use my scholarship because when I came out of the army, I had the GI Bill. I heard a lot about Howard University. In September of 1946, I enrolled there, received my BA and masters degrees in social work. At Howard University I joined the Kappa Alpha Psi fraternity. I was very active in the fraternity as dean of pledges. My first professional job was as a counselor at the DC Department of Corrections, Lorton Reformatory. There I had a caseload of about 78 felons. At that time, the early 50s, they didn't have too many inmates convicted of drugs. They were there mostly for robberies, assaults, and murders. Our job was to try to rehabilitate them. We had some success, but most of them returned as repeaters. I went from that job to a probation officer at the DC Court of General Sessions where I moved up the ladder to a supervisor's position. My next job was director of the Citizens Information Services, a counseling and referral agency. In 1970, Walter Washington became the mayor of Washington, DC, the first black mayor. He appointed me to head up one of his departments, the DC Office of Human Rights. I stayed there for approximately 10 years. I retired from that position. During Mayor Washington's tenure, I got leave to pursue my doctorate's degree. The mayor was very understanding and made this all possible. I graduated from Nova University in Fort Lauderdale, Florida with a PhD in Public Administration. My dissertation was on a familiar subject, the adjustment of inmates coming out of Lorton Reformatory. In 1980, I formed Baldwin

& Associates, Inc where we specialized in the investigation of EEO complaints of discrimination. Presently, I am in semi-retirement. I've been married since 1948. I married my high school classmate, Ann McLaughlin. From that union we had 3 children, 5 grandchildren, and 2 great grandchildren. My oldest daughter passed away in 2001. The remainder of the family still resided in the Washington Metropolitan Area. Recently Ann and I celebrated our 57th wedding anniversary. Our daughters came by and picked us up and said your 57th wedding anniversary is Monday. So the family went out for dinner and we had a lot of fun. We're a close-knit family. My son-in-law is a great guy and we enjoy sports together, we go to Redskins and Wizards games. A good family, I've been blessed.[13]

Civilian Donald Carman (C/784th) was still recovering from his critical wounds when he began his civilian life. His son, Mark Carman, ESQ, describes:

My father received a medical retirement from the military as a Major in approximately 1947. After returning to the states he was in and out of army hospitals until his retirement. He married Charlene "Charlie" Flewharty in 1945. Appropriate that the commander of Company Charlie would marry Charlie. He and Charlie met while the 784th was stationed at Camp Hood. After leaving the military he opened up a small Mission Orange soft drink bottling company with his father in Wichita, Kansas. He operated that plant until he sold it in 1966. He went on to own and operate soft drink bottling companies in Wichita Falls, Texas; Jackson, Mississippi; and Columbus, Georgia. He retired from the soft drink business in 1985 and passed away in 1995 at the age of 78.

My father did not like to talk about the war and I learned quite a bit more about my father's combat experiences in WWII from his life long friend, Tom Redditt, the Maintenance Officer with Company C. My father didn't refer to the men as being black or white but simply as his men, troopers, or tankers. My father had no tolerance for the use of racial slurs but I never thought to ask him if that arose from his service in the 784th. It was just understood that such language or conduct was unacceptable under any circumstances and it never occurred to me to question it. The same is true when we were living in Jackson, Mississippi and the Supreme Court ordered the schools to integrate. While most of my white friends went off to private schools, my father said that was inappropriate and I went to the public school which was comprised of 80% black students.

You got to remember that my dad was raised in Nebraska and Illinois and he was shocked by some things he saw in the South. He was always a Yankee who married a southern girl from Texas. It is interesting that he ended up living so much of his life in the South. He did love the fishing down there. Tom gave the eulogy at my father's funeral and a large part of it was a recap of the 784th in combat. I wish I had a tape of it. Tom's wife, Eleanor, felt like he went on too long about it, but it was clearly very important to Tom to tell that story one last time with Captain Carman. I don't think it is possible to understand the bonding that occurs when men share the experience of war together. My Dad had a military funeral and it was in Columbus, GA in August and it was unbelievably hot. The color guard consisted of black and white soldiers from Fort Benning and they were suffering in their full uniforms in the heat. I went over to speak with them afterwards and told them how much I appreciated them being there and how my Dad would have been happy and honored to have an integrated color guard for his last military event. I explained how he had been drafted as a private and retired a Major after being injured in combat leading a company of black tankers. I think they were so hot and tired that they just wanted to get out of the sun, but I wanted them to know.[14]

Civilian Thomas Redditt returned home to El Paso, Texas where he had a Chevrolet waiting in the garage for him. Soon he moved to Colorado where the air is much cleaner for his asthma condition. There he went into business for himself as a manufacturer's sales representative. Tom sold kitchen equipment, pots, pans, and anything he could get to sell. He earned 30 dollars his first month and from there his business grew and kept growing. Now it has offices in Denver, Salt Lake City, Phoenix, Tucson, and Albuquerque. His son, Thomas Redditt, Jr., describes:

> After the war Dad was assigned to occupation duty in Germany. He returned home in July 1945 to Fort Sam Houston, Texas. There he mustered out on July 4, 1945. Upon discharge, he was promoted to major. He came to Denver, Colorado and went to work selling restaurant equipment in 1949. He started his own business, Tom Redditt Sales Agency. The business grew and his son and now his grandson run the business. He talked about the war many times and kept up with many of his fellow soldiers. He was in partnership with Don Carman in the bottling business for many years. It was a life-long friendship. In all the times of talking about the men in his unit, he never made a distinction. Just said they were the troops he served and fought with.[15]

Tom resides with his wife in Colorado.

Civilian Celes King III (Tuskegee Airman) returned to Los Angeles, where he continued his education. He had the following degrees conferred upon him: LLB from Pacific Coast University, MBA from Pepperdine University, and MA (urban planning) from Pepperdine University. He and his father established Celes King Bail Bond Service. Soon they opened an office on Santa Barbara Boulevard across from the police station. This is where his concern for justice and civil rights grew. He became a civil rights champion in one of our nation's most racially divided and politically corrupt cities — Los Angeles — where police brutality flourished with impunity. There he sadly witnessed 2 deadly race riot/rebellions. Following the Watts uprising of 1965 several investigations pointed out the causes as high unemployment, poor schools, police brutality, and inferior living conditions. The government practically ignored these findings. This coupled with record high unemployment, record high crime, and an abundance of crack cocaine festered for years. Several years later, according to a series of groundbreaking reports by the San Jose *Mercury News* it was revealed that for the better part of the 1980s, a San Francisco Bay Area drug ring, comprised of U.S. Central Intelligence Agency and U.S. Drug Enforcement Agency agents and informants, "allegedly" sold tons of crack cocaine to the Crips and Bloods street gangs of Los Angeles. "Allegedly" the drug profits were funneled to the Nicaraguan Democratic Force, anti–Communists commonly called the Contras. At any rate, all hell was breaking out in Los Angeles. In 1992, Celes had to again sadly witness another riot/rebellion — this time one of the deadliest insurrections in U.S. history.

The following is a partial list of his community achievements: National President, Professional Bail Agents of the USA; California State Chair for the Congress of Racial Equality (CORE); President of the Los Angeles City Human Relations Commission; Co-founder of the Los Angeles Brotherhood Crusade; Co-founder of the Los Angeles Rumor Control established during the Watts riots; Century Freeway Affirmative Action Committee; Brigadier General in the California State Military Reserve; Assistant Professor at California State University Los Angeles; advisor to the California State Senate; sponsor of the Martin Luther King Holiday Commission and street name change from Santa Barbara to Martin Luther King Jr. Blvd; Chairperson of the Martin Luther King Day parade; and the recipient of numerous awards.

Celes served as the state chairperson of CORE — California, from 1989 until 2003 where he led an effort to protect individual and group civil rights. CORE — California frequently joined with the NAACP, Urban League, and other civil rights organizations in press conferences and hearings. Celes quickly acquired an impeccable record of aggressive civil rights leadership and he was honored in Los Angeles for 50 years of civil rights leadership.

Celes always encouraged everyone to strive for their highest potential through honesty, education, and hard work and he set an example first. Celes monetarily supported community programs and individuals to help them reach their highest potential.

On April 12, 2003, Celes King III passed away in Los Angeles at the age of 79, leaving his legacy behind.

Civilian Murray Leff (E/137th) returned to New York following the war:

On returning from WWII I went back to college, graduated in 1947 and began working in advertising. In 1960 I formed my own advertising agency, which I still operate. I was married in 1949 resulting in 2 children and 4 grandchildren. Presently I am Publicity Chairman of the 35th Infantry Division Association. Their annual reunion is always an emotional experience. In 2004 we went back to Europe to receive enthusiastic receptions from the cities the 35th had liberated. Their gratitude is now part of their culture. Even their grandchildren regarded us as heroes. I'm still involved with photography and am in the process of having many of my war pictures published in a book I wrote."[16]

Civilian Royal Offer (K/320th), recipient of the Silver Star, Bronze Star Medal, Purple Heart, and Battlefield Commissioned, joined the U.S. Postal Service after the war. After work he actively pursued his interests of golf and tennis. Before the war he placed in the state tennis finals for Nebraska. He retired as a member of management from the postal service after 35 years. From there he took up several part-time jobs. Several years ago he lost his wife Clarice after 58 years of marriage: "She was the best, I'll tell you. It was very hard adjusting to life without her."[17] Royal is a member of the 35th Infantry Division Association and occasionally attends annual reunions. He plays golf almost daily.

Civilian Keith Bullock (HQ/2–137th) describes coming home:

When I first got out of the service, I jumped up and down and shouted, "Made it, by God." Seriously, I worked several small jobs until the battle rattles wore off. Tried school on GI Bill; received poor counseling for the wrong courses (interested in Forestry); there were equally stiff discipline rules at school as in the army for far fewer reasons; and I had a bad attitude at that time. First long term job was for Kellogg Forest, a branch of Michigan State University for 7 years. Then I got a job with Upjohn Pharmaceuticals in Kalamazoo, Michigan for 32 years. I retired in 1986 as Head of Fine Chemical Warehouse.

My reconnection with the 35th Division waited until the 1980s when I learned there was an Association. I complained about the lack of activity of the 137th Regiment. The answer I got from those present was, "You don't like the cook, son, you the cook." At the first 137th Regiment gathering, 17 attended. Though the start was small, I met and married Marge who gathered data into a roster, which grew to 1,800 names. I was appointed a vice president of the 35th Division. My year as president (private rises to general) was in 1998. I was gratified to see 350 old comrades show up for reunion in Harrisburg, PA. *I have one large regret*: about 5 years ago, when the big thing was to receive a Thank You Certificate from the French government, the ceremony was held in Grand Rapids, Michigan. At that time I saw an African American vet in a wheelchair, like I am, and on his jacket was a tanker emblem. I did not approach him. I should have. He might well have been the one responsible for saving my butt and letting me come home.[18] Keith currently resides with his wife Marge in Delton, Michigan, where they are both very active in the 35th Infantry Division Association.

Civilian Bernard "Jack" Kirsch (F/137th) returned home to Ohio following the war. In 1946 he enrolled at the University of Dayton, where he graduated with a Bachelor of Science degree in civil engineering. He landed a position with the county engineer. After 8 years, he was appointed the public works director for the city of Hamilton, Ohio. After 18 years as public works director, he was appointed city manager of Hamilton and retired 8 years later.

Jack was married for 46 years before losing his wife. He has 5 children and 8 grandchildren. He currently volunteers with organizations that provide services to the needy of his community and on civic committees. His hobbies are golf, genealogy, and dancing. Jack is a life member of the 35th Infantry Division Association and an active member of the Veterans of Foreign Wars. He returned to Europe with the 35th Infantry Division Association in 1998 and followed their combat route:

The trips to Europe were very interesting and exciting. It is very emotional to visit an American Military Cemetery and stand amid the thousands of white crosses. I recognized only one battle location and that was Rhineberg and its suburb of Ossenberg. This is where we had a fierce battle, which you are acquainted with. Most of the other locations have changed substantially and are unrecognizable. Also, being in the Infantry, we were moving most of the time and did not stay in one place more than a few days. Also, being a private, I did not have access to maps so most of the time we did not even know where we were at."[19]

Civilian John Walsh (Cannon/320th) returned to his home in Brooklyn, New York, following the war. John recalls:

> After leaving the army, I attended law school for 2 semesters but dropped out to accept a commission in the Navy in December 1946. I met my wife, Geneva, who was a chief petty officer in the WAVES and we married in November 1947. We have 4 children, 3 daughters and a son. We have 5 grandchildren. After leaving the Navy in 1949, I got into management consulting, specializing in work with not-for-profit institutions. My work took me all over the United States and occasionally out of the country, until I retired in the 1980s. Presently I spend much of my time in various volunteer activities, including teaching basic computer skills to seniors and serving as guide at our local aquarium.[20]

John is currently the president of the 35th Infantry Division Association. He is also an officer with the Western Connecticut Military Officers Association, Inc. He resides in Norwalk, Connecticut, with his wife.

Civilian James Graff (C/134th) returned to his family farm in Middletown, Illinois, after the war. He remains active in the 35th Infantry Division Association. In 1977 he published a "must read" book on his World War II experiences entitled *Reflections of a Combat Infantryman: A Soldier's Story of C. Co. 134th Inf. 35th Div.* Published by the Museum of the Kansas National Guard, it is available online. His book and personal letters to me were instrumental to this book. He wrote:

> Young man, you have done a great job in writing the history of the 784th Tank Battalion. I think that their story has been delayed too long. You know that as a segregated army most rural whites like me had never had much of a chance to commingle with black people. World War II really put an end to it all and it had to be made official and President Truman did that.
>
> My wife Alice and I were able to motor to Washington last year and attend the dedication of the World War II Memorial. On December 10–20 along with 200 plus Veterans and dependents we went to the 60th Anniversary of the Battle of the Bulge. We had 10 very memorable days. At a reception at the US Embassy in Luxembourg City, we met the King of Belgium and the Grand Duke of Luxembourg — a very memorable night vigil on December 16, 2004 the 60th anniversary of the start of the battle. We members of the 134th, there were 8 of us — 3 Veterans, 2 war orphans, plus one spouse, a Vet and daughter. One Vet came up from Italy where he now lives. In Bastogne it snowed and made it that much more realistic. Our night vigil was in a town liberated by my company on January 24–26, 1945. We lost 12 men killed in action in and around there. They are now memorialized in a memorial plaque 2' by 3' with an American flag and Luxembourg flag and an eternal electric light. We dedicated this 7-ton stone monument back on April 1, 1995. We saw every memorial in Luxembourg and eastern Belgium. The Ardennes campaign as you know from my book was a sad one for us in C Company. A total of 199 casualties including over 30 men killed in action, a turn over of over 100 percent. It was a trip of a lifetime.
>
> On August 14, 2005, Alice and I leave for a 12 day cruise on the Queen Mary II, almost 60 years after our return from World War II on the Queen Mary I on September 5–10, 1945.

You know I was 18 when drafted, spent 23 months in service and out before I was 21. I will celebrate my 80th birthday August 20, and Alice and I will celebrate or 57th Wedding Anniversary on September 12, 2005. Joe, you've done a good job and a job that needed telling. Good luck and God bless you and yours. Please keep in touch. If I can be of further help, please feel free to contact me. Your friend, Jim Graff.[21]

Civilian Orval Faubus (Staff/320th) returned to his home way up in the Ozark Mountains in Arkansas. He went back into politics and reestablished connections with the Arkansas Democratic Party, and particularly with progressive Governor Sid McMath. Soon Faubus became the State Highway Commissioner. A life of controversy and misunderstanding would follow.

In 1954 Faubus ran successfully for governor as a liberal promising to increase spending on schools and roads. In the first months of his administration he desegregated state buses and public transportation. He also probed the prospect of introducing multi-racial schools in his state, making him popular with African Americans. All of this brought political attacks from the right wing that went as far as accusing Faubus of being a communist. This rhetoric shook him up and made him extremely sensitive to attacks from the right. This caused Faubus to reconsider his political position for the upcoming election and led him to fight the 1954 *Brown v. Board of Education* decision by the U.S. Supreme Court that separate schools were unequal and therefore unconstitutional.

In 1957, in a political move to remain governor, Faubus brought out the Arkansas National Guard to stop the 9 African American students from attending Little Rock Central High School. This fueled a showdown with President Dwight Eisenhower (Ike), who tried to persuade Governor Faubus to obey the ruling. Ike went on the air to the American public regarding this crisis: "At a time when we face grave situations abroad because of the hatred that communism bears towards a system of government based on human rights, it would be difficult to exaggerate the harm that is being done to the prestige and influence and indeed to the safety of our nation and the world. Our enemies are gloating over this incident and using it everywhere to misrepresent our whole nation."[22]

After 18 days, Ike finally federalized the Arkansas National Guard, removing them from the control of their state governor, and ordered them to return to their barracks. Ike then sent in elements of the 101st Airborne Division to enforce the court order. The white population became furious and spoke out in harsh rhetoric. Faubus took full political advantage of the mass hysteria and called the 101st Airborne Division an "army of occupation."[23]

The now-popular Governor Faubus easily won reelection following this incident and would serve a total of 6 terms. Ironically and despite all of the controversy, Faubus won the majority of the African American vote. He saw to it that blacks could vote, while in the rest of the South blacks were violently discouraged from voting. He carried the black precincts in the farm counties where the wealthy farm owners paid their sharecroppers' poll taxes and hauled them to the polls. In the urban precincts, the black preachers did the same after receiving large sums of money from Faubus operatives.

Years later, in a 1994 *New York Times* interview, Faubus explained his rationale at Little Rock: "It's true in politics as it is in life that survival is the first law." Then he added: "One of my black friends came in during 1957 and said 'Governor, if you hadn't done something, you'd have been a goner.' Voted out."[24]

In 1969 Faubus divorced his wife of 40 years, regarded as a gracious and dignified first lady, for a younger woman, and his popularity dropped. Faubus unsuccessfully ran for governor in 1970, 1974, and 1978. His social standing and financial position deteriorated. He was forced to sell his house and take a job as a bank teller in Huntsville, Arkansas. Faubus died broke in 1994.

Civilian Robert Martin (B/208th) returned to his wife and family in the Irishtown section of Dunbar, Pennsylvania. He resumed his job at the Pennsylvania Wire Glass Plant, became an assistant foreman, then a foreman at the Fruehauf Tanker Trailer Plant before retiring in 1998. Robert joined Post 146 of the American Legion in his hometown upon returning from overseas. He served as post commander in 1952 and again in 1954. He recalls:

> When I first came back I joined the American Legion and I bought a uniform because I was interested in it. I still have the uniform today and I've worn the same uniform for 59 years at the Memorial Day parade. I had 3 good reasons for being in the Memorial Day Parade. One was for respect for the flag; the men that died so that I'd live; and for the men and the women of tomorrow. So that's what has been behind my ego all these years.[25]

His local newspapers recognized him on several occasions for his patriotism.

Robert had served in 3 separate armies during World War II: "I trained under the Second Army. When I went overseas I was put into the First Army and when the Ninth Army started they put me in the Ninth Army. That's why I have 3 patches in my frame. I feel comfortable having them there because I served under all 3 armies."[26]

Robert currently resides with his family in Dunbar, Pennsylvania, where he remains active in the American Legion and the Irishtown Sportsman's Club. He is also active in Irishtown historical research and interpretation.

Civilian Wayne Martin (160th) retuned to his home in Dunbar, Pennsylvania. Wayne recalls:

> I was discharged from the Army in January 1946 and started my civilian life anew. I opened a small coalmine and produced 20 to 50 tons of coal a day. I sold the coal to the coke industry. I employed 3 to 6 men to mine the coal. The coke oven industry slowed down in 1952 and I took a job as a trainman on the Western Maryland Railroad, I worked there until 1982 when I retired. I still kept the mine working until the early 1960s. In the latter part of 1946 I met Lena Littesio of Dunbar and she was the most wonderful person I ever knew! So I married her. We had 2 children, a boy and a girl. The boy named Marvin was almost 16 years of age; he got the flu one day and died the next. It was the worst

tragedy that ever happened in our lives. We never really got over it. We have our daughter Regina who married Richard Hart and they are wonderful. They built their home near the Irishtown Pavilion and they have 2 wonderful children. Lena my wife has been in the Cherry Tree Nursing Home in Uniontown for almost 4 years with "old-timers-disease." She seems comfortable but she doesn't seem to know anyone. I go up and feed her breakfast everyday and Regina feeds her supper every day. She cannot help herself in any way. I stay at home here in Dunbar and I spend some time in the mountains every day walking and enjoying the scenery and that is about the story of my post war life."[27]

Civilian Everett Cook (82nd/17th) returned to his home in Ohio following the war:

I got discharged in January 1946. I ran around a little bit before I went back on the railroad. I worked there until February and got laid off. Then I went to the packinghouse and started boning beef for 75 cents an hour. I was only making 62 cents on the railroad. I worked cutting meat and boning beef for 55 years and then I retired. I had gotten married in 1948 and we had a boy and 3 girls. In 1971 some kid hit my wife with a car and killed her. We had been married about 23 years. I raised my son and 3 daughters. I had no hobbies because I was too busy raising a family. Now I have about 15, 16 grandchildren. I'm a paid-up member of the 17th Airborne Division Association and look forward to reading their "Thunder from Heaven.' I also read the Battle of the Bulge and the 82nd Airborne Division periodicals.[28]

In December 2004, Bill Hughes visited Brunswick, Maryland, to see the Stuart light tank displayed there as a World War II memorial and also to commemorate the 60th anniversary of the Battle of the Bulge.

Earlier that week he reunited with one of his 784th "Brothers in Arms," James Hamilton, after nearly 60 years. The last time they had seen each other was in Kelburg, Germany, at the end of the war.

Bill contacted James from across the Atlantic via the Internet. James' daughter, Lynne Hamilton-Jones, had been trying to find members of the 784th for 4 years. These 2 gentlemen had never seen any members of their unit since the war's end.

This long-awaited reunion took place at the L'Enfant Plaza in Washington, DC. Supported by their daughters and James' nephew and family, they got reacquainted, shared memories of the war, and remembered their fallen comrades. Soon the conversation shifted to their families and the wonderful lives they've led since. After lunch they strolled over to the World War II Memorial on the National Mall, both visiting it for the first time. Once there they peered into the camera together for posterity.

Bill arrived safely home to Germany after a "super flight" of only 6 hours and 40 minutes due to a great tail wind: "Greetings to All, I arrived back in Germany and had a pleasant trip. Thanks for bringing us together in DC. The joy of James and I meeting after some 60 years was evident from the photos. I am happy that it was possible with all of you present as family support members. I sure enjoyed my visit and was very happy to meet up with you and the James Hamilton family."[29]

In conclusion, John F. Kennedy once said: "In the long history of the world, only

(Left to right) Lynne Hamilton-Jones, James Hamilton, Bill Hughes and Natalie Hughes. *Courtesy Bill Hughes*

a few generations have been granted the role of defending freedom in its hour of maximum danger." Tom Brokaw described them as the "Greatest Generation." Thus, in telling the story of World War II, we honor those who fought and died during our nation's hour of "maximum danger."

The focus of this book is to remind America of the courage and sacrifice made by all Americans, and in this case, by African Americans who seemed to be left out of history. They fought under the "Double-V" that called for victory abroad against the forces of global domination, and they also faced an additional and unique enemy. They had to fight for the right to fight! Currently, there is little secret about the way African Americans lived and were mistreated throughout World War II and how they defended a way of life that excluded them from full partnership.

You are witnessing a generation of veterans coming to an end. Of the approximately 16 million who served in World War II, there are fewer than 4 million still alive. The very youngest are in their late 70s. It is estimated that they are passing away at a rate of 1,000 per day. I've listened to their stories over my 50 years, starting with my father—may God embrace his soul. Listen and document their rare stories and pass them along or when this generation ends, their stories will go with them.

This written history has rerecorded the archival documents and photographs of the 784th Tank Battalion, but more importantly, the recollected feelings of the African

16. Deactivation

American tankers and the white American soldiers who endured the deadliest manhood sacrament together, the crucible of war.

To future researchers, historians, and writers, I hope this book will serve as a very small part of a wide database. The veterans have spoken for themselves!

I wish to extend to the men of the 784th Tank Battalion and to the World War II Generation my appreciation and a heartfelt farewell. God bless you!

Bill Hughes will have the final word:

Little did I realize when Chapter Five was unfolding that I would soon learn the whereabouts of Corporal Curley who died in January 1945. It bothered me for years. The author of this book sent me a list of men from the 784th Tank Battalion buried at the American Cemetery Margraten, the Netherlands. The first name on the list was Curley J. Ausmer from the State of Mississippi. The full name left no doubts that this was my fallen comrade who served with me in Company D. Additionally, there were the names of 16 other men from the 784th buried there and 2 others listed as missing in action. I knew I had to go to that cemetery to pay my respects. I drove from my residence in Germany to the cemetery on a beautiful day, the 1st of July 2005. I found the small charming hotel where I had made reservations earlier and immediately drove a short distance to the cemetery. I was very impressed with the wide entrance gate, long driveway to the main administration building, with beautiful trees, plants and flowers on both sides and well-kept lawns. I met the chief, guidance services and discussed my plans to visit each gravesite of the men buried there from the 784th Tank Battalion and to take photos of each site. Since it was close to closing time, we reached agreement that I would return the next day at 9:00 AM to start photographing the gravesites and grounds.

The next day 2 July was not the best of weather as it was threatening to rain. Nevertheless, the appointment was kept. The chief, guidance services had prepared a printout from his data file showing the exact location of each site, maps, brochures, and information about the cemetery. All the tombstones were white marble imported from Italy. The inscriptions on the stones were also white which would not stand out very well in a photo. He therefore told me he would have one of the workers to go ahead of me to fill in the inscriptions with special sand. This proved to be very helpful in highlighting the inscription in the photos.

I went to Private Curley J. Ausmer's grave first. I can't express the relief that came over me after wondering and not knowing what happened to his remains for some 60 years. I had a flash back of seeing his body riddled with .30 caliber bullets as he was reloading the company commander's jeep mounted machine gun. It was a horrific sight that you just don't forget. I placed a small American flag in the sod of grass, stepped back several paces and prayed. Suddenly, I realized I was not alone as several men approached me from behind. The older man apologized for disturbing me and asked if I knew the soldier buried there. I told him we served together and how he was killed when a bomb fragment from our own planes set off a full box of ammunition as he was loading the machine gun. The younger man in his early thirties began to sob. I said, "Son, don't cry. It's over and he is in good hands." We shook hands and introduced ourselves. They departed with the father's arm around his son still sobbing.

I proceeded to each gravesite and planted the little American flag in the sod and took a

Bill Hughes at Margraten American Cemetery, the Netherlands. *Courtesy Bill Hughes*

photo. I said a silent prayer at each site and wondered what their lives would have been like had they lived. I also wondered if their relatives had visited the cemetery or were they forgotten. It was my understanding that the next of kin was always contacted and gave permission for burial overseas. The grounds around the cemetery were maintained in a very efficient manner. While I was taking photos of the grounds, a car stopped and a man asked if I was Bill Hughes? I said yes where did you get the name? He explained that he had been in touch with Mr. Joe Wilson for sometime and heard I would be visiting the cemetery. He introduced himself as Mr. Pierre Ackermans so we sat down and had a good chat. He was very interesting and advised me that each man buried at the cemetery had adoptive parents in the Netherlands who bring visitors and attend ceremonies held annually. I found this was very thoughtful and asked him if he could find the adoptive parents of Private Curley J. Ausmer. He subsequently sent me the address of the adoptive parents who furnished him the address of Private Ausmer's wife. I wrote to her but the letter was returned as not deliverable as addressed.

Upon leaving the cemetery, a certain peace of mind came over me. I felt very good that I had made the journey to pay my respects to my Fallen Comrades. I found relief in knowing that Curley was buried in a very solemn and decent way amidst his Comrades who had also died for a very noble cause. I wondered if mankind would remember the sacrifice these men made. I for one shall never forget.[30]

Afterword
by First Sergeant Joseph E. Wilson, Sr., USA (Ret.)

Joseph E. Wilson, Sr., died before completion of this book. This afterword is condensed from the afterword of Joe Wilson, Jr.'s, *The 761st "Black Panther" Tank Battalion in World War II* (McFarland, 1999).

The United States Army has come a long way since its inception in 1775, making it the nation's senior service. Drifting on a memory, I recall being inside an American tank called the General Sherman. We, as tankers, knew it as the M-4A1, and a later model, the M-4A3-E8. Those of you who have never experienced combat in a Sherman tank, listen to this: The interior is painted a cold, non-color white, but what gets your attention immediately is the frigid atmosphere. It's cold, cold as a winter night on the Lincoln Sea. I think this is what my son had in mind with the working title to this book: *Wrapped in Cold Steel*.

Later in the war 2 new tanks were issued to us: the M-24 light tank, the Chaffee; and the M-26 medium tank, the General Pershing. These 2 new tanks introduced welcomed improvements, but the single improvement that pleased us all was that they had heaters.

Sergeant Joseph E. Wilson

Afterword by First Sergeant Joseph E. Wilson, Sr., USA (Ret.)

Before coming to the 761st I was member of the 2nd Gun Section, Battery C, 686th Field Artillery Battalion, and had not yet developed into a mature, job-sophisticated cannoneer. There were times when my mouth was agape as I watched older black artillerymen perform their duties with an unimaginable sophistication in handling this 155-millimeter howitzer. This medium artillery piece threw a 95-pound explosive shell 9 miles, and when it hit, white American infantrymen would jump and shout: "Fickle Charlie is adjusting!" Fickle was the code name for the 686th Field Artillery Battalion, and Charlie stood for Battery C, and its 4 guns. My section chief was a heavyset black man who answered to the name of Joe Willie, and when he told me to jump, my only response was: "How high, Sarge?" When I first heard this name, I assumed it was a sobriquet, but later I learned that he was so mean, his friends were afraid to give him a nickname. Joe Willie was his real name. He was from Oklahoma.

These were African American soldiers who did their utmost to accomplish their mission. They were dedicated and loyal despite the rigors imposed by white supremacy and segregation, which were more pronounced in those days. Today "Jim Crow" has taken on a subtlety designed to perpetuate its existence.

Looking back in history, we find many whites who swore that the races must be kept apart. Look at the late, great General George Smith Patton, Jr., who often said that the Negro soldier couldn't think fast enough to fight in armor. How ridiculous, especially for an educated man in a high leadership position. However, this deep-seated nescience was canceled prior to his untimely death in Room 101, 130th Station Hospital in Heidelberg, Germany, in 1945. There were other generals who held the Negro back until they too were compelled to revise their thinking. What a waste of time and humanity.

Many of the generals were educated at the United States Military Academy at West Point, New York, an institution where racism was practiced as a matter of routine. I agonized over the treatment black cadets received at this institution. When I read of the abuse meted out to Cadet Henry O. Flipper, graduating class of 1877, my pain was similar but could never equal his. Later, other cadets suffered the same fate. There was Charles Young and others but the one who stands out in my lifetime is Lt. General (Retired) Benjamin O. Davis, Jr., U.S. Air Force, Class of 1936. Cadet Davis, like black cadets before him, was given the silent treatment—no one spoke to him for 4 years. On Sundays, Cadet Davis was forced to go to each dinner table and ask permission to be seated. During the week he ate at a separate table using disposable plates and utensils. What inhumane treatment.

Despite living through this painful period, blacks had to fight for the right to fight, and we fought without the accolades bestowed upon others, even though deserving such recognition. During World War II, not one African American was awarded the nation's highest medal for bravery, even though commanders submitted the proper and necessary recommendations.

World War II, the war that saved humanity from the greatest menace imaginable,

Afterword by First Sergeant Joseph E. Wilson, Sr., USA (Ret.)

found black America fully involved in our national effort. The 686th Field Artillery Battalion landed at Southampton, England, on a foggy morning in October 1944. From there we embarked on trains and disembarked at Pontypool, Wales. Here we occupied Quonset huts on the polo grounds. During the day and often at night, we made ready for combat. Our off-duty hours were spent doing the same thing, but there was time for socializing with the citizens of Pontypool. In fraternizing, we were astounded to learn of some of the beliefs of these British subjects, such as: "Do you colored blokes have tails?"

What has the foregoing to do with the 784th Tank Battalion? Well, there were many other black fighting units that were ignored and are absent from recorded history. Why? Because they were manned by African Americans. There was the 92nd Infantry Division in Italy; the 93rd Infantry Division in Bougainville, South Pacific; there was the 349th Field Artillery Battalion, a sister battalion to the 686th; there were the 969th and the 999th Field Artillery Battalions; the 614th, the 679th Tank Destroyer Battalions; there were the 758th and the 761st Tank Battalions; and there were the volunteer infantry replacements. There were all kinds of Negro (as we were called then) combat units in the war: engineers, transportation units, quartermasters. I could go on and on, but I am especially proud of the 99th Pursuit Squadron, commanded by Lt. Colonel Benjamin O. Davis, Jr. His father, B.O. Davis, Sr., was the first black to attain the rank of brigadier general in the U.S. Army. The 99th Pursuit Squadron became the 332nd Fighter Group when it added other squadrons, and their claim to fame is that they never lost a bomber to enemy fighters while escorting American heavy bombers.

I'm glad to have had the privilege of telling my story, which gives vent to the pent-up emotions that have weighed heavily on my mind and shoulders all these years. I am elated to see that, in accomplishing this rare literary task, you have helped all who peruse these words to face the future with a greater understanding of what really happened.

Chapter Notes

1. The Double "V" Campaign

1. Department of Defense, 50th Anniversary of World War II Publication (1991–1995), referencing a letter dated November 17, 1942.
2. Potter, Lou, Bill Miles, and Nina Rosenblum, *Liberators: Fighting on Two Fronts in World War II* (Orlando, FL: Harcourt Brace Jovanovich, 1992).
3. Quoted in the program for the 1977 Reunion of the 761st Tank Battalion & Allied Veterans Association.
4. Wilson, Dale, *A Recipe for Failure* (1993).
5. Reynolds, Clark, *America at War: The Homefront 1941–1945* (New York: Smithmark Publishers, 1990).
6. King, Celes III, interview, January 1995.
7. Potter, Miles, and Rosenblum, *Liberators*.
8. Hughes, William, letters (email) to the author, 2004–2005.
9. Garrido, Franklin, interview, September 14, 1994.
10. Hamilton, James, telephone interview, January 28, 2005.
11. Washington, Simmons, telephone interview, April 27, 2005.
12. Baldwin, James, letter to the author, October 11, 2005.
13. Anderson, L.Z., interview, September 23, 1994.

2. Camp Claiborne

1. Simpson, William, *A Tale Untold: The Alexandria, Louisiana Lee Street Riot* (1994).
2. *Ibid.*
3. Washington, Simmons, telephone interview, April 27, 2005.
4. Hughes, William, letters (email) to the author, 2004–2005.
5. Garrido, Franklin, interview, September 14, 1994.
6. Anderson, L.Z., interview, September 23, 1994.
7. *Ibid.*
8. Baldwin, James, letter to the author, October 11, 2005.
9. Garrido, interview.
10. Hughes, letters.

3. Camp Hood

1. Washington, Simmons, telephone interview, April 27, 2005.
2. *Ibid.*
3. *Ibid.*
4. Hughes, William, letters (email) to the author, 2004–2005.
5. Hamilton, James, telephone interview, January 28, 2005.
6. *Ibid.*

7. Hughes, letters.
8. Baldwin, James, letter to the author, October 11, 2005.
9. Hughes, letters.
10. *Ibid.*
11. Washington, interview.
12. Washington, Elizabeth, letter to the author, May 15, 2005.

4. Destination ETO

1. Hughes, William, letters (email) to the author, 2004–2005.
2. *Ibid.*
3. Baldwin, James, letter to the author, October 11, 2005.
4. Hamilton, James, telephone interview, January 28, 2005.
5. Washington, Simmons, telephone interview, April 27, 2005.
6. Hughes, letters.
7. Garrido, Franklin, interview, September 14, 1994.
8. Hughes, letters.
9. Hamilton, interview.
10. Jensen, Marvin G., *Strike Swiftly! The 70th Tank Battalion from North Africa to Normandy to Germany* (Novato, CA: Presidio Press, 1997).

5. Baptism of Fire

1. Hughes, William, letters (email) to the author, 2004–2005.
2. Hamilton, James, telephone interview, January 28, 2005.
3. Hughes, letters.
4. Washington, Simmons, telephone interview, April 27, 2005.
5. Hamilton, interview.
6. Washington, interview.
7. Hughes, letters.
8. *Ibid.*
9. *Ibid.*
10. Baldwin, James, letter to the author, October 11, 2005.
11. Garrido, Franklin, interview in Los Angeles, CA, September 14, 1994.
12. 35th Infantry Division Staff, Report after Action, 1945.
13. Washington, interview.
14. Leff, Murray, telephone interview, May 19, 2005.
15. *Ibid.*

6. The Raging Roer River

1. Martin, Robert, interview, July 16, 2005.
2. Graff, James G., *Reflections of a Combat Infantryman: A Soldier's Story of C. Co. 134th Inf. 35th Div.* (http://skyways.lib.ks.us).
3. Martin, interview.
4. Leff, Murray, telephone interview, May 19, 2005.
5. *Ibid.*
6. Graff, *Reflections.*
7. Martin, interview.
8. Kirsch, Bernard "Jack," telephone interview, December 13, 2004.
9. 137th Infantry Regiment, Report after Action, 1945.
10. Faubus, Orval Eugene, *In This Faraway Land: A Personal Journal of Infantry Combat in World War II* (Conway, AR: River Road Press, 1971).
11. Walsh, John, letter (email) to the author, July 14, 2005.

7. Task Force Byrne

1. Walsh, John, letter (email) to the author, July 14, 2005.
2. Offer, Royal, telephone interview, May 2, 2005.
3. Hamilton, James, telephone interview, January 28, 2005.
4. Faubus, *Faraway Land.*
5. Offer, interview.
6. 134th Infantry Regiment, Report after Action, 1945.
7. Graff, *Reflections.*
8. Hughes, William, letters (email) to the author, 2004–2005.
9. Hamilton, interview.
10. Offer, interview.
11. Graff, *Reflections.*
12. Hughes, letters.
13. Offer, interview.
14. Jensen, *Strike Swiftly!*
15. Motley, Mary P., *The Invisible Soldiers* (Detroit: Wayne State University Press, 1975).
16. Graff, *Reflections.*
17. Gallagher, Wes, "Negro Tank Battalion Fights Miniature 'Bastogne' All Alone," *Los Angeles Times*, April 1945.
18. Hughes, letters.
19. Redditt, Thomas. Telephone Interview. July 20, 2006.
20. 320th Infantry Regiment, Report after Action, 1945.

21. Gallagher, "Negro Tank Battalion."
22. 134th Infantry Regiment, Report after Action, 1945.
23. Hughes, letters.
24. Washington, Simmons, telephone interview, April 27, 2005.
25. Faubus, *Faraway Land*.
26. Washington, interview.
27. Garrido, Franklin, interview in Los Angeles, CA, September 14, 1994.
28. *Ibid*.
29. Hamilton, James Interview.
30. Faubus, *Faraway Land*.
31. Mikus, Wayne, letter (email) to the author, March 14, 2005.
32. Faubus, *Faraway Land*.
33. Carman, Mark. Personal affects of Major Donald Carman, USA-RET-DEC.
34. Redditt, Thomas. Interview.
35. Hughes, letters.
36. Faubus, *Faraway Land*.
37. Martin, Wayne, *60th Field Hospital Memoirs* (date unknown).
38. Carman, Mark. Personal affects of Major Donald Carman, USA-RET-DEC.
39. Walsh, letter.
40. 320th Infantry Regiment, Report after Action, 1945.
41. Lee, Ulysses, *The Employment of Negro Troops* (Washington, DC: Center of Military History, U.S. Army, 1966).
42. Gallagher, "Negro Tank Battalion."

8. Eighty-eight Alley

1. *The Stars & Stripes*, Lone Sentry, "Tornado! The Story of the 8th Armored Division" (World War II GI Stories Booklet, http://www.lonesentry.com).
2. 137th Infantry Regiment, After Action Reports, March 1945.
3. Kirsch, Bernard "Jack," telephone interview, December 13, 2004.
4. Garrido, Franklin, interview in Los Angeles, CA, September 14, 1994.
5. Leff, Murray, telephone interview, January 27, 2005.
6. Kirsch, interview.
7. Leff, interview.
8. Kirsch, interview.
9. Leff, interview.
10. Kirsch, interview.

9. Crossing the Rhine

1. Hamilton, James, telephone interview, January 28, 2005.
2. Baldwin, James, letter to the author, October 11, 2005.
3. Washington, Simmons, telephone interview, April 27, 2005.
4. Stanford, Ted, *The Pittsburgh Courier*, April 28, 1945.
5. Martin, Robert, interview, July 16, 2005.
6. *Ibid*.
7. Pay, Donald Raymond, *Thunder From Heaven: Story of the 17th Airborne Division* (Nashville: Turner Publishing, 1987).
8. Hashway, Thomas (513th PIR), "Varsity" (E-history: http://thedropzone.org).
9. Cook, Everett, telephone interview, October 25, 2005.
10. Graff, *Reflections*.
11. Hughes, William, letters (email) to the author, 2004–2005.
12. Graff, *Reflections*.
13. Garrido, Franklin, interview in Los Angeles, CA, September 14, 1994.
14. Hamilton, interview.
15. Leff, Murray, letter to the author, January 27, 2005.
16. Offer, Royal, telephone interview, May 2, 2005.
17. American Battle Monuments Commission, e-mail to the author.
18. Leff, interview.

10. The Ruhr Pocket

1. Hamilton, James, telephone interview, May 25, 2005.
2. Washington, Simmons, telephone interview, April 27, 2005.
3. *Ibid*.
4. Graff, *Reflections*.
5. *Ibid*.
6. *Ibid*.
7. Kirsch, Bernard "Jack," telephone interview, December 13, 2004.
8. Bullock, Keith and Marge, e-mail to the author, October 21, 2004.
9. Washington, interview.
10. Leff, Murray, telephone interview, January 27, 2005.
11. *Ibid*.
12. Kirsch, interview.
13. Martin, Robert, interview, July 16, 2005.
14. Leff, interview.

15. Kirsch, interview.
16. Offer, Royal, telephone interview, May 2, 2005.
17. Graff, *Reflections*.
18. Hughes, William, letters (email) to the author, 2004–2005.
19. Leff, interview.
20. *Ibid*.
21. Hughes, letters.
22. Washington, interview.
23. Garrido, Franklin, interview in Los Angeles, CA, September 14, 1994.
24. Cook, Everett, telephone interview, October 25, 2005.
25. Stanford, Ted, *The Pittsburgh Courier*, April 28, 1945.
26. Kirsch, interview.
27. Martin, interview.
28. Leff, interview.
29. Graff, *Reflections*.

11. Eyewitness to Genocide

1. Garrido, Franklin, *A Brief Encounter with The Holocaust That Is Engraved in My Memories Forever — Gardelegen*, 1994.
2. Hughes, William, letters (email) to the author, 2004–2005.
3. Schwartz, Terese, www.holocaustforgotten.com/gardelegen.
4. *Ibid*.
5. www.scrapbookpages.com/gardelegen/massacre.html.
6. *Ibid*.
7. *Ibid*.
8. Garrido, *Brief Encounter*.

12. Elbe River

1. Hughes, William, letters (email) to the author, 2004–2005.
2. Garrido, Franklin, interview in Los Angeles, CA, September 14, 1994.
3. Kirsch, Bernard "Jack," telephone interview, December 13, 2004.
4. Hamilton, James, telephone interview, January 28, 2005.
5. Leff, Murray, telephone interview, January 27, 2005.
6. Garrido, interview.

13. Occupation

1. Shirer, William, *The Rise and Fall of the Third Reich* (New York: Mandarin, 1960).
2. Hughes, William, letters (email) to the author, 2004–2005.
3. *Ibid*.
4. *Ibid*.
5. *Ibid*.
6. Washington, Simmons, telephone interview, April 27, 2005.

14. Whatever Happened to the 758th Tank Battalion

1. Hightower, Jefferson, interview, August 25, 1996.
2. Matheny, Michael, *The History of the 64th Armored*, 761st Tank Battalion & Allied Veterans Association reunion program, 1983.

15. Whatever Happened to the 761st Tank Battalion

1. Anderson, Trezzvant, *Come Out Fighting: The Epic Tale of the 761st Tank Battalion, 1942–1945* (Salzburger Druckerei und verlag, 1945).
2. *Ibid*.
3. *Ibid*.
4. Harrison, Sr., Ivan, interview in Killeen, TX, August 23, 1994.
5. Anderson, *Come Out Fighting*.
6. *Ibid*.
7. Williams II, David J., MOH Conference. Los Angeles, CA, February 27, 1994.
8. Harrison, interview.
9. Jimmy Carter Presidential Library. NARA.
10. *Ibid*.
11. Anderson, *Come Out Fighting*.
12. Jimmy Carter Presidential Library. NARA.
13. Potter, Miles, and Rosenblum. *Liberators*.
14. Jimmy Carter Presidential Library. NARA.
15. *Ibid*.

16. Deactivation

1. Graff, *Reflections of a Combat Infantryman. A Soldier's Story of C. Co. 134th Inf. 35th Div.* <http://skyways.lib.ks.us>.
2. Hamilton, James, telephone interview, January 28, 2005.
3. Leff, Murray, telephone interview, January 27, 2005.

4. Hughes, William, letters (email) to the author, 2004–2005.
5. Hamilton, James, telephone interview, January 28, 2005.
6. Hamilton, James, telephone interview, July 10, 2006.
7. Obituary of Franklin Garrido, April 16, 2005.
8. Anderson, LZ, telephone interview, July 24, 2006.
9. Hughes, William, letters (email) to the author, 2004–2006.
10. Washington, Simmons, letter to the author, July 5, 2006.
11. Washington, Simmons, letter to the author, July 5, 2006.
12. Mikus, Wayne, letter (email) to the author, August 8, 2005.
13. Baldwin, James, letter to the author, October 11, 2005.
14. Carman, Mark, letters (email) to the author, July 2006.
15. Redditt Jr., Thomas, letter (email) to the author, July 21, 2006.
16. Leff, Murray, letter to the author, July 7, 2005.
17. Offer, Royal, telephone interview, June 20, 2005.
18. Bullock, Keith and Marge, email to the author, June 29, 2004.
19. Kirsch, Bernard "Jack," letter (email) to the author, July 1, 2005.
20. Walsh, John, letter (email) to the author, August 8, 2005.
21. Graff, James, letter to the author, August 1, 2005.
22. http://spartacus.schoolnet.co.uk.
23. http://spartacus.schoolnet.co.uk.
24. http://spartacus.schoolnet.co.uk.
25. Martin, Robert, interview, July 16, 2005.
26. Martin, Robert, interview, July 16, 2005.
27. Martin, Wayne, letter to the author, August 9, 2005.
28. Cook, Everett, telephone interview, October 25, 2005.
29. Hughes, William, letters (email) to the author, 2004–2006.
30. Hughes, William, letters (email) to the author, 2004–2006.

Bibliography

35th Infantry Division. Report after Action, 1945.

134th Infantry Regiment. Report after Action, 1945.

137th Infantry Regiment. Report after Action, 1945.

320th Infantry Regiment. Report after Action, 1945.

784th Tank Battalion, Report after Action, 1945.

Abdul-Jabbar, Kareem, and Anthony Walton. *Brothers in Arms: The Epic Story of the 761st Tank Battalion, World War II's Forgotten Heroes.* New York: Broadway Books, 2004.

American Battle Monuments Commission. Email to the author.

Anderson, L.Z. Interview. September 23, 1994.

Anderson, L.Z. Telephone interview. July 24, 2006.

Anderson, Rich. *The United States Army in World War II.* Militaryhistoryonline.com.

Anderson, Trezzvant. *Come Out Fighting: The Epic Tale of the 761st Tank Battalion, 1942–1945.* Salzburger Druckerei und verlag, 1945.

Baldwin, James. Letter to the author, October 11, 2005.

Baron, Richard, Abe Baum, and Richard Goldhurst. *RAID! The Untold Story of Patton's Secret Mission.* New York: Dell Publishing, 1981.

Bullock, Keith and Marge (35th ID Assoc). Letters (emails) to the author, 2005.

Carman, Mark. Letters (email) to the author. July 2006.

Colley, David P. *The Road to Victory: The Untold Story of World War II's Red Ball Express.* New York: Warner Books, 2000.

Cook, Everett. Telephone interview. October 25, 2005.

Cooper, Belton Y. *Death Traps: The Survival of an American Armored Division in World War II.* Novato, CA: Presidio Press, 1998.

Department of Defense. 50th Anniversary of World War II Publication, 1991–1995.

Faubus, Orval Eugene. *In This Faraway Land: A Personal Journal of Infantry Combat in World War II.* Conway, AR: River Road Press, 1971.

Fleischer, Wolfgang. *Panzerfaust and Other German Infantry Anti-Tank Weapons.* Atglen, PA: Schiffer Military/Aviation History, 1994.

Gallagher, Wes. "Negro Tank Battalion Fights

Miniature 'Bastogne' All Alone." *Los Angeles Times,* April 1945.

Garrido, Franklin S. *A Brief Encounter with the Holocaust That Is Engraved in My Memories Forever—Gardelegen.* 1994.

Garrido, Franklin S. Interview in Los Angeles, CA, September 14, 1994.

Graff, James G. *Reflections of a Combat Infantryman: A Soldier's Story of C. Co. 134th Inf. 35th Div.* http://skyways.lib.ks.us

Hamilton, James. Telephone interview, January 28, 2005 and July 10, 2006.

Hartman, Ted J. *Tank Driver: With the 11th Armored from the Battle of the Bulge to VE Day.* Bloomington, IN: Indiana University Press, 2003.

Hashway, Thomas. "Varsity." E-history: http://thedropzone.org.

Hightower, Jefferson. Interview, August 25, 1996.

Ho, Ron. Letter to the author, October 12, 2005.

http://en.wikipedia.org: Orval Faubus.

http://fact-index.com: Arthur Seyss-Inquart.

http://miniatures.de/htmlpzgr/shelltypen.html : *Panzergranate Geschossarten.*

http://www.spartacus.schoolnet.co.uk: Orval Faubus.

Hughes, William "Bill." Letters and emails to the author, 2004–2005.

Irwin, John P. *Another River, Another Town: A Teenage Tank Gunner Comes of Age in Combat—1945.* New York: Random House, 2002.

Jensen, Marvin G. *Strike Swiftly! The 70th Tank Battalion from North Africa to Normandy to Germany.* Novato, CA: Presidio Press, 1997.

Kirsch, Bernard "Jack." Telephone interview, December 13, 2004.

Lee, Ulysses. *The Employment of Negro Troops.* Washington, DC: Center of Military History, U.S. Army, 1966.

Leff, Murray. Telephone interview, January 27, 2005.

Martin, Robert. Interview. July 16, 2005.

Martin, Wayne. *60th Field Hospital Memoirs.* n.d.

Massaquoi, Hans J. *Destined to Witness: Growing Up Black in Nazi Germany.* New York: Perennial, 1999.

Matheny, Michael. *The History of the 64th Armored.* 761st Tank Battalion & Allied Veterans Association reunion program, 1983.

Mikus, Wayne. Letters and emails to the author, 2005.

Motley, Mary P. *The Invisible Soldiers.* Detroit: Wayne State University Press, 1975.

Offer, Royal A. Telephone interview, May 2, 2005.

Pay, Donald Raymond. *Thunder from Heaven: Story of the 17th Airborne Division.* Nashville: Turner Publishing, 1987.

Pipes, Jason. www.feldgrau.com.

Potter, Lou, Bill Miles, and Nina Rosenblum. *Liberators: Fighting on Two Fronts in World War II.* Orlando, FL: Harcourt, Brace, Jovanovich, 1992.

Redditt, Thomas, Jr. Letter (email) to the author. July 21, 2006.

Redditt, Thomas, Sr. Telephone interview. July 20, 2006.

Reynolds, Clark *America at War: The Homefront 1941–1945.* New York: Smithmark Publishers, 1990.

Sasser, Charles W. *Patton's Panthers: The African-American 761st Tank Battalion in World War II.* New York: Pocket Books, 2005.

Schwartz, Terese. www.holocaustforgotten.com.

Shirer, William L. *The Rise and Fall of the Third Reich.* New York: Mandarin, 1960.

Shirey, Orville C. *The Story of the 442d Combat Team.* Washington, D.C.: Infantry Journal Press, 1946.

Simpson, William. *A Tale Untold: The Alexandria, Louisiana Lee Street Riot.* 1994.

Stanford, Ted. *The Pittsburgh Courier.* April 28, 1945.

Stanton, Shelby L. *World War II Order of Battle.* New York: Galahad Books, 1984.

The Brunswick Citizen. *Veteran Visits Local Tank Memorial.* December 2004.

The Stars & Stripes. Lone Sentry. "Tornado! The Story of the 8th Armored Division." www.lonesentry.com.

Walsh, John F. Letters and emails to the author, 2005.

Warner, Jan. Letter to the author, August 15, 2005.

Washington, Simmons S. Telephone interview, April 27, 2005.

Washington, Simmons. Letter to the author. July 5, 2006.

Wikiverse A World Of Knowledge. *The Netherlands in World War II.*

Wilson, Dale. *A Recipe for Failure.* 1993.

Wilson, Joe Jr. *The 761st "Black Panther" Tank Battalion in World War II.* Jefferson, NC: McFarland & Company, 1999.

Wistrich, Robert. *Who's Who in Nazi Germany.* New York: Bonanza, 1982.

www.707tkbn.org *The Siegfried Line.*

www.combatfan.com. *Panzerfaust Anti-Tank Weapon.*

www.legionmagazine.com. *The Rhine Crossing.*

www.rense.com. *The WWII Dresden Holocaust– A Single Column of Flame.*

www.rollintl.com. *The Rhine River.*

www.thefreedictionary.com. *Volkssturm.*

Yeide, Harry. *Steel Victory: The Heroic Story of America's Independent Tank Battalions at War in Europe.* Novato, CA: Presidio Press, 2003.

Index

2nd Armored Division 11
4th Service Command 17
5th Tank Group 17, 24
8th Armored Division 61, 87, 88, 89, 101
10th Armored Division 17
17th Airborne Division 108, 109, 127, 128
17th Airborne Division Association 183
29th Infantry Division 75
32nd Military Police Company 20
35th Cavalry Reconnaissance Troop 50, 65
35th Infantry Division 48, 50, 53, 55, 56, 58, 61, 75, 78, 89, 93, 102, 109, 110, 114, 119, 121, 123, 126, 130, 133, 145, 146, 150, 167, 168
35th Infantry Division Association 178, 179, 180
36th Tank Battalion 87, 88, 93
49th Armored Infantry Battalion 87, 93
53rd Engineer Combat Battalion 93
60th Engineer Combat Battalion 62, 92, 110, 120, 125
60th Field Hospital 82, 83
70th Tank Battalion 11
75th Infantry Division 102, 130
79th Infantry Division 110, 112, 130

80th Engineer Combat Battalion 93
82nd Airborne Division 108, 183
84th *Infantrie* Division 109
84th Infantry Division 60, 75, 130, 133
92nd Infantry Division 9
93rd Infantry Division 9
101st Airborne Division 50, 181
102nd Infantry Division 75, 130, 133, 136, 138, 145
104th Cavalry Reconnaissance Troop 4, 43, 45
104th Infantry Division 3, 42, 43, 44, 45, 48
106th Infantry Division 167
110th Medical Battalion 62, 110
116th Panzer Grenadier Division 112
127th Field Artillery Battalion 110
134th Infantry Regiment 50, 54, 59, 60, 61, 63, 65, 71, 86, 101, 109, 116, 117, 119, 123, 124, 126, 141, 143, 167
137th Infantry Regiment 50, 51, 56, 60, 63, 71, 87, 88, 89, 90, 92, 93, 100, 101, 110, 111, 112, 116, 119, 120, 122, 123, 124, 126, 168
161st Field Artillery Battalion 59, 109, 119
180th *Infantrie* Division 112
190th *Infantrie* Division 112
191st General Hospital 84

208th Engineer Combat Battalion 54, 104, 121
216th Field Artillery Battalion 62
275th Field Artillery Battalion 62
315th Infantry Regiment 110
320th Infantry Regiment 50, 58, 60, 61, 62, 63, 41, 77, 78, 84, 112, 116, 120, 122, 123, 125, 126, 130, 167
350th Field Artillery Regiment 20
367th Infantry Regiment 9, 20
371st Infantry Regiment 9
507th Parachute Infantry Regiment 108, 127, 128
513th Parachute Infantry Regiment 127
555th Parachute Infantry Battalion 11
654th Tank Destroyer Battalion 62, 92, 93, 110
669th Tank Destroyer Battalion 35
679th Tank Destroyer Battalion 35
758th Tank Battalion 12, 17, 154, 155, 156, 157, 158
761st Tank Battalion 2, 17, 21, 28, 159, 160, 161, 162, 163, 164, 165, 166
761st Tank Battalion & Allied Veterans Association 170

Index

809th Tank Destroyer Battalion 93
827th Tank Destroyer Battalion 35

Aachen, Germany 43, 44
Aberdeen Proving Ground, Maryland 12
Able Company 26, 48, 50, 59, 60, 62, 63, 65, 68, 71, 86, 87, 92, 110, 117, 118, 119, 128
Ackermans, Pierre 186
Adams, Dave 78
Adams, Willy 13
Afrika Korps 5
Alabama State Teachers College, Montgomery 15
Alexander, Joe 61
Alexandria, Louisiana 17, 19, 21, 22
Alfred, Sgt. 70
Alpsray, Germany 80, 85
American Battle Monuments Commission 47, 112, 113, 147
American Legion 182
Amesbury, England 39
Anderson, L.Z. 16, 17, 22, 30, 171, 172, 173
AP (Armor Piercing) 31
Arbeitseinsatz (labor draft) 66
Arkansas National Guard 181
Armored Force Basic Trainees 16
Armored Force Liaison Office 12
Armored Force Replacement Training Center 17, 103
Army Enlisted Reserve Corps 15
Arpke, Germany 146
Assault Gun Platoon 27
Atlantic Wall 66
Atomic Bomb 168
Ausmer, Curley 44, 185
Austin, Texas 29
Autobahn 112, 114, 118, 120, 122, 130
Avenue Café 169
Axis Sally 3, 108

B-17 Bombers 3, 123
B-24 Bombers 3
Baade, Paul 50, 61
Babi Yar 5
Baker Company 26, 48, 50, 60, 77, 78, 90, 117, 127, 128, 132, 133, 133
Baldwin, James 15, 22, 31, 37, 47, 102, 103, 151, 175
Baldwin & Associates 175, 176
Baltimore, Maryland 13
Baptism of Fire 41
BAR (Browning Automatic Rifle) 128
Basie, Count 12, 13

Bastogne, Belgium 50, 74
Bastrop, Texas 29
Baton Rouge, Louisiana 21
Battalion Avenue 25
Battle of the Bulge 43, 45, 47, 51, 112; 60th Anniversary of 180, 183
Bauern, Germany 80
Beamon, William 112
Berchtesgaden, Germany 146
Bergenlen, Germany 86
Berlin, Germany 129, 130, 143, 144, 145, 146
Bethune, Mary McLeod 9
Big Three 143
Birgelen, Germany 60
Black, Napoleon 113
Bland, Whitney 112
Blatz, Germany 140
Blitzkrieg 11, 62, 66
Blue Beach 110
Blue Note jazz club 168
Boatsman, Alfred 109
Bochum, Germany 119
Bodenbach, Germany 153
Bongard, Germany 153
Borler, Germany 153
Bradley, Omar 123
Braun, Eva 146
Braunschweig (Brunswick), Germany 140
British Royal Air Force 33, 56, 108
British Second Army 53, 107
British 6th Airborne Division 108, 109
Brokaw, Tom 184
Brown, Donald 34, 36
Brown v. Board of Education 181
Brunswick, Maryland 174, 183
Brussels, Belgium 149
Buderich, Germany 93
Bullock, Keith 70, 119, 179
Burant, Gustave 33, 36, 72
Burns, Charlie 13
Butler, Albert M. 93
Buzz-bombs 55, 56
Byrne, Bernard 61, 62, 86

C-46 aircraft 108
C-47 aircraft 57, 108, 109
California State Military Reserve 178
California State University Los Angeles 178
Cameron, Alex 54
Camp Beauregard, Louisiana 19
Camp Claiborne, Louisiana 13, 17, 19, 21, 22, 23, 25, 28
Camp Hood, Texas 15, 22, 24, 27, 28, 29, 30, 33, 34, 35
Camp Kilmer, New Jersey 168

Camp Livingston, Louisiana 19
Camp Lucky Strike 168
Camp Shanks, New York 35, 36
Camp Swift, Texas 29, 31, 32, 33
Canadian First Army 53, 61, 107
carbon monoxide 32
Cardiff, Wales 36
Carman, Charlie 34, 84, 176
Carman, Donald 34, 36, 79, 81, 82, 84, 176
Carman, Mark Esq. 176
Carr, Alexander 79, 80, 82, 83, 113
Carver Vocational School 15
Casina 169
Central Avenue 25
Chaney, James 174
Charlie Company 26, 48, 50, 63, 74, 78, 79, 80, 81, 82, 102, 115, 127
Cheeves, Gilbert X. 12, 13
Clear Creek, Texas 29
Club Astoria 15
Coffey, Henry 67, 73
Cofield, George 106
Cologne, Germany 61
Combat Comand B (CCB) 87, 89, 101
Combe, Clyde 149
Comedy Club 169
Cook, Everett 108, 128, 183
Cooke, Brenda & Pamela 39
Cooke, Owen & Gwen 38
Cooper, Grosvenor 115, 148
CORE 9, 178
Cox, Conley 57
Crawford, David E. 79, 81, 83
Crispus Attucks High School 12
Croix de Guerre 9

D-Day 33, 107
Dabner, Hubert 29
Dalia, George C. 17, 29, 42, 77
Daniels, George 29, 37
Daniels, George B/Gen. 12
Davis, Benjamin O Sr. 10, 11
Davis, Howard 106
death-march 133
DeQuier, Maurice 21
Dickson, Murray 167
Dobbins, Freddie 29
Dog Company 26, 28, 38, 41, 42, 43, 44, 45, 49, 50, 67, 73, 110, 124, 133, 143, 147, 185
Dolgen, Germany 146
Donitz, Karl 146
Dortmund, Germany 119, 126
Double V 9, 64, 184
Doveren, Germany 59
Dresden, Germany 57
Drupt, Germany 62, 75
Dunbar, Pennsylvania 182

202

Index

Duren, Germany 44
Durham, North Carolina 169
Dutch Resistance Fighters 64

Edmondson Avenue 15
88-millimeter gun 41, 51, 86, 89, 93, 96, 97, 106, 128
81-millimeter mortar 27, 43, 46, 47, 49, 116, 118
Einsatzgruppen 5
Eisenhower, Dwight D. 138, 149, 181
Elbe River 57, 128, 130, 131, 132, 139, 140, 142, 143, 144, 145
Ellington, Duke 12, 13
Emerson Avenue 15
Emscher Canal 120
English Channel 40
Eschweiler, Germany 43, 47
Estedt, Germany 134
ETO 35, 40
Evans, G. Sheldon 39
Executive Order 8802 7
Executive Order 9096 8
Executive Order 9981 173

Fallersleben, Germany 140
Fallschirmjagers 79, 134, 135, 136
Faubus, Orval 61, 63, 77, 79, 81, 83, 181, 182
Fayetteville, North Carolina 15
Fayetteville State University 15
February Strike 66
.50 caliber machine gun 33, 67, 72
Fitzgerald, Ella 15
Florida A & M College 17
Footbridge 59
Fort Benning, Georgia 15, 17
Fort Custer, Michigan 12
Fort Eustace, Virginia 15
Fort Knox, Kentucky 11, 13, 16, 17, 22, 28, 33, 103
Fort Meade, Maryland 15
Fort Valley College 17
Fossa Canal 87
Foxx, Redd 13
Frank, Anne 66
Frank, Hans 169
Frankfurt, Germany 168
Friedburg, Hans von 148
Friendly Fire ("shorts") 4, 35
Frink, Albert 92

Gable, Clark 15
Gallagher, Wes 74
Gambis 169
Gardelegen, Germany 133, 134, 135, 136, 137, 138, 139, 140
Garrido, Franklin 13, 22, 39, 48, 78, 90, 110, 128, 133, 139, 143, 145, 170, 172

Geilenkirchen, Germany 48, 50, 79, 83
Geldern, Germany 72, 86
Gelenberg, Germany 153
Gelsenkirchen, Germany 126, 127
Georgetown, Texas 29
Gerderath, Germany 60
Gibson, Truman K. 10
Gladbach, Germany 60
Goebbels, Josef 124, 130
Goering, Hermann 5, 146, 169
Gold Beach 33
Graff, Alice 180, 181
Graff, James 54, 57, 65, 67, 72, 109, 110, 117, 118, 123, 131, 141, 167, 180, 181
Grand Duke of Luxembourg 180
Greatest Generation 184
Griswel, Wilson 80, 112
Gunther, Wiliam 7
Gyrostablizer 31

Hall, Walter "Pop" 49, 68, 75, 77, 125
Hamilton, James 13, 29, 37, 40, 42, 43, 63, 67, 78, 102, 111, 115, 144, 167, 168, 169, 170, 171, 183, 184
Hamilton-Jones, Lynne 171, 183, 184
Hamm, Germany 114
Hampton, Lionel 13
Hanover, Germany 132, 136, 140, 146
Harris, Morris O. 26, 39, 129
Hart, Bill 105
Hart, Regina 183
Hart, Richard 183
Harte, Albert 77, 112
Hastie, William 10
Haus-Heideberg Woods 90
HE (High Explosive) 27, 31
Headquarters Company 26, 27, 42, 43, 46, 47, 49, 50, 104, 115, 116
HEAT (High Explosive Anti Tank) 27
Herne, Germany 125
Hester, Charles 152
Hicks, Ambrose 75, 77
Highway 81 29
Highway 190 29
Hilfarth, Germany 54, 57, 59, 86
Hillesheim, Germany 150
Hillmanshoff, Germany 85
Hills, S/Sgt. 152
Himmler, Heinrich 124, 146, 169
Hiroshima 57
Hitler, Adolf 5, 47, 50, 112, 130, 131, 145, 146, 147
Hitler Jugend 124, 135, 136
HMS *Morton Bay* 37

Hogue, William 77, 112
Holiday, Billie 15
Holmes, Johnny 39
Holocaust Museum 139
Horack, Junior 54
House, Frank 30
House Calling 67
Howard University 175
Huffacre, Sgt 59
Hughes, Alpheus 147
Hughes, Bill 12, 21, 28, 29, 32, 33, 35, 37, 39, 41, 42, 43, 44, 45, 47, 67, 68, 70, 73, 74, 75, 82, 110, 124, 127, 133, 143, 147, 149, 150, 153, 168, 173, 174, 183, 184, 185, 186
Hughes, Gary 174
Hughes, Natalie 184

Immensen, Germany 146
Indianapolis, Indiana 12
Indianola Firing Range 33
International Military Tribunal 169
Isabelle, Benjamin 112
Isenschnibbe Barn 134

Javenitz, Germany 134
Jefferson, Charles 71
Jim Crow 19
Jodl, Alfred 148, 169
Jones, Chester 71
Jones, "Radio" 115
Jones, Ray 171
Julich, Germany 54, 58
Juno Beach 33

Kakerbeck, Germany 134
Kaldenkirchen, Germany 63
Kamperbruck, Germany 78, 79, 80, 85
Kearns, Vernon 95
Keating, Frank 138, 139
Keeley, Robert 152
Keitel, Wilhelm 169
Kelberg, Germany 150, 151, 153
Kelly, Douglas 77
Kemp, Germany 85
Kennedy, John F. 183
Kenon, Stan 13
Kibbler 94, 99
Kiev, Ukraine 5
King, Celes III 10, 172, 177, 178
King of Belgium 180
King's Royal Rifles, British 8th Armored Division 86
Kiplinger, Howard 97
Kirchhellen, Germany 117
Kirk, Andy 12
Kirsch, Bernard "Jack" 60, 89, 91, 93, 101, 119, 121, 123, 130, 144, 179

Index

Kisatchie National Forest 19
Klatenbrunner, Ernst 169
Kleve, Holland 50
Koblenz, Germany 167
Kolack, Stanley 106
Koln, Germany 44
Korean War 173
Krupp Steel Workds 112
Ku Klux Klan 19

LaFayette Avenue 15
LaFourche, James 19
Laurie, James 78, 112
Laurinburg Institute High School 15
Le Harve, France 168
Lee, Eldon 128, 147
Lee Street 20
Leff, Murray 51, 52, 56, 90, 91, 93, 94, 95, 96, 97, 98, 111, 113, 120, 121, 122, 125, 126, 130, 144, 168, 178
Letkampshof, Germany 112
Lewis, Ira 9
Liège, Belgium 102
Lintfort, Germany 79, 87
Lippe River 114
Little Rock, Arkansas 182
Little Rock Central High School 181
Liverpool, England 36, 37, 38
Loos, F.M. 141
Lorton Reformatory 175
Los Angeles Brotherhood Crusade 178
Love Bridge 110
Luftwaffe 117, 118, 134, 136
Lunceford, Jimmie 12
Lux, Ray 97

Maas River 53, 68
Maastricht, Holland 54
Mack, Willmore 78, 112
Maddox, Harold 85
Magdeburg, Germany 129, 140
Maginot Line 56
Magnolia Beach, Texas 33
Manchester University 168
Margraten American Cemetery 99, 185, 186
Mariadorf, Germany 54
Marin, O. Wayne 82, 83, 84, 182
Marshall, Albert 110, 112
Marshall, George C. 11
Martin, Lena L. 182
Martin, Robert 54, 55, 56, 58, 104, 106, 121, 130, 182
Martin Luther King Jr. Blvd. 178
Martin Luther King Jr. Day Parade 178
McCullough Street 29
McLaughlin, Ann 176

McLean, Vernon 89
McMath, Sid 181
McMurray, David 29
McNair, Leslie J. 9, 35
McNutt, John T. 74
ME-109 147
Mehrum, Germany 110
Menzelen, Germany 92
Meridian, Mississippi 175
Meridian Housing Authority 174
Merode, Germany 49, 51
Middle River Depot 169
Mikus, Ernest 80, 81, 175
Military Police 19, 21, 22, 80
Miller, Dorie 7, 8
Miller, Henrietta 8
Millingen, Germany 80, 85, 92, 99
Mills Brothers 13
Miltonberger, Butler 109
Mingo, Gerald 14, 15
Montgomery, Bernard 53, 123
Morgan, Earl 60, 61
Mortar Platoon 27, 31
Moton Field 10
Mulheim, Germany 127
Murken, Germany 44
Murray, William 87
Museum of the Kansas National Guard 180
Mussolini, Benito 147

NAACP 9, 20, 172, 178
Nagasaki 57
Nebelwerfer (screaming meemies) 65
Neukoln, Germany 117
Nichols, LeRoy 17
Niederkruchten, Germany 63
Nieukirk, Germany 68
Ninth Air Force 54
Normandy 33, 35, 44, 50, 107
North Atlantic 6
North Avenue 25
North Camp Hood, Texas 26
North Carolina A & T 15, 17
Northern France 50
Nova University 175
Nuremberg, Germany 169
Nuremberg Trials 169

Oberhausen, Germany 127
Offer, Clarice 178
Offer, Royal 63, 64, 65, 67, 68, 70, 112, 123, 178
Omaha Beach 33, 50
105-millimeter assault gun 27, 49, 117
O'Neil, Jack 85
Operation Firefly 11
Operation Grenade 53, 54, 61
Operation Plunder 107

Operation Varsity 108, 109
Ossenberg, Germany 87, 90, 91, 92, 93, 94, 101, 179
Ozark Mountains 181

P-47 aircraft 121
Pacific Coast University 177
Palmore, Vivian G. 86
Panther Tank 27, 40
Panzerfaust 68, 71, 72, 80, 112, 116, 117, 125, 128, 135, 140
Paris, France 11, 148
Park Avenue 25
Park Circle Motor Company 169
Patton, George S., Jr. 9, 12, 90
Pearl Harbor 8
Pennsylvania Avenue 15
Pepperdine University 177
Peterson, Henry 78
Picadilly Circus, New York, NY 36
Pilgrim Community Fellowship 173
Pittsburgh Courier 9, 104, 129
Pontoon Bridge 58, 110, 111, 112
Pontypridd, Southern Wales 37, 38, 39
potassium cyanide 169
Potsdam Conference 149
Powers, John T. 29, 36, 45, 47, 73
Prosper Coalmine 120
Pullen, Pvt 46
PX (Post Exchange) 22

Queen Mary I 180
Queen Mary II 180
Queen of the Netherlands 67

Race Troops 11
Radio Orange 66, 67
Randolph, A. Philip 6, 7, 9
Rangers 33
Rapides Parish 19
Reception Training Center Camp Shelby, Mississippi 22, 23
Recklinghausen, Germany 119
Reconnaissance Platoon 27, 49, 115, 147
Red Ball Express 131
Redditt, Thomas 36, 74, 79, 81, 177
Redditt, Thomas, Jr. 177
Reichs Chancellery 146
Remagen Bridge 112
Remonte Cavalry School 133
Rheims, France 148, 149
Rhein-Herne Canal 112, 122, 123, 125
Rhine River 41, 47, 53, 61, 62, 75, 80, 85, 87, 90, 91, 93, 101,

Index

102, 104, 106, 107, 110, 111, 114, 119, 123, 130; map 100
Ribbentrop, Joachim von 169
Rice's Dinner 13
Ritz Theater 20
Rivers, Ruben 16
Roberts, Jesse 14, 15, 151
Roberts, Vernell 115
Roer River 44, 53, 54, 55, 56, 57, 58, 59, 60, 61, 63, 86
Roer Valley 54, 55, 75
Roermond, Holland 53
Rommel, Erwin 5
Roosevelt, Eleanor 9, 10, 103
Roosevelt, Franklin D. 6, 7, 8, 15, 130
Roseborough, Morgan G. 93
Rosenberg, Alfred 169
Rothenbach, Germany 153
Rouen, France 40
Royal Theater 13, 15
Ruhr Pocket 112, 118, 119, 122, 123, 127, 130, 133
Ruhr River 114, 126, 128, 130
Ruhr Valley 87, 112, 114, 119, 127, 128, 129

Saalhof, Germany 85
Saint Joseph's Catholic School 174
Saint Lô, France 50
San Francisco Municipal Railway 171
San Jose Mercury News 177
Santa Barbara Blvd. 177
Santa Fe Trail 146
Saunders, W.B. 6
Schmeisser submachine gun 127
Schmetshof, Germany 85
Schwammenauel Dam 53
Schwarzer River 110
Scotland County 15
SCR 500 Radio 33
Sczwincz, Eugene 135, 136
Seine River 40
Service Company 26, 48, 49, 50
Sevelen, Germany 70, 71, 72, 73, 74, 78
75-millimeter gun 25, 27, 28, 31, 52, 60, 116, 122
Seyss-Inquart, Arthur 66, 169
Sherman Medium Tank 25, 27, 28, 31, 32, 40, 42, 49, 51, 52, 64, 68, 85, 103, 104, 105, 151
Siegfried Line 50, 51, 56, 61, 63, 66
Simpson, William 53
Sixth Panzer Army 47
67th Street 25
68th Street 25

Slave Laborers 120, 121, 140
Smith, Sgt. 68
Smith, Walter 73
Soissons, France 42, 43
Solow, Arthur 34, 80, 82
Solvay Works 93
South Wales 38
Southern University 17
Spaulding High School 14
Spencer, Sgt. 46, 152
Spring Hope, North Carolina 14
SS 87, 116, 117, 133, 134, 136
SS *Argentina* 168
Stanford, Ted 104, 129
Stanislau, James 59
Straelin, Germany 68, 71
Streicher, Julius 169
Stuart Light Tank 3, 18, 26, 27, 43, 49, 78, 174, 183
Sturmmorser Tiger 89
Sword Beach 33

Tank-bulldozer 68, 74, 75, 125
Task Force Byrne 61, 67, 68, 71, 72, 75, 87, 90, 99, 101; map 69, 76
Task Force Miltonberger 110
Task Force Murray 90, 91, 92, 93, 99, 101
Tegelen, Holland 102, 104
Temple, Texas 34
10-in-1 rations 33, 48
Thiele, Gerhard 134, 136
3rd Street 22
.30 caliber machine gun 27, 31, 44, 63, 72, 95, 109, 185
37-millimeter gun 25, 27, 78
Thompson submachine gun 60, 128
380-millimeter assault rocket 89
Tiger Tank 27, 40, 41, 51, 52, 89, 144
Tobyhanna, Pennsylvania 169
Tompkins, John 112
TOT (Time-on-Target) 58
Tri-system 49
Truman, Harry S. 130, 169, 173
Tuskegee Airman 10, 177
Tuskegee Institute 17
Twelfth Army Group 123
20-millimeter flak gun 110, 111, 117, 136
Twenty-first Army Group 53, 107, 123
25 caliber Weiner pistol 124
280-millimeter railway gun 55

U-boats 6
Underwood, Henry 140, 143, 147
United States Army Air Forces 33

United States First Army 128
United States Ninth Army 50, 53, 57, 58, 61, 63, 104, 107, 111, 123, 128, 137
Urban League 178
USO 22
USS *Liscombe Bay* 8
USS *Rueben James* 6
USS *West Virginia* 7
Utah Beach 33

Van Ness Avenue 172
Van Nortwick, William 39
VE-Day 150
Venlo, Holland 62, 63, 64, 65, 67, 68, 102
Volksgrenadier 50, 51, 117
Volkssturm 124, 125, 134, 136
Volkswagen 139, 140

Waffen SS 67
Wagram, North Carolina 15
Walsh, Geneva 180
Walsh, John 61, 62, 84, 180
Walsumermark, Germany 117
Warden, Germany 128
Warm Springs, Georgia 130
Washington, Elizabeth 34
Washington, Sandra Joyce 34
Washington, Simmons 15, 20, 25, 26, 31, 34, 37, 42, 43, 47, 50, 77, 104, 105, 116, 117, 120, 128, 152, 153, 174, 175
Washington, Walter 175
Wassenberg, Germany 60, 65, 85
Waters, John 45, 70, 73
Watkins, James 79
Watts Riots 177, 178
Wehrmacht 11, 50, 67, 89, 116, 117, 124, 127, 147, 153
Wesel Pocket 85, 87, 99, 107, 112
Western Connecticut Military Officers Association 180
Weymouth, England 39
Wharton Technical College 168
Whitbeck, Arthur 77, 112
Wiesenthal, Simon 169
Williams, Kirby 13
Williams, Sgt. 70
Wingo, Charles 17
Wolfsburg, Germany 139
Womack, Raymond 78, 112
Woodard, R. 30
World War II Memorial 180, 183
Worthy, Trent 115
WP (White Phosphorous) 27
Wright, Harold 59
Wunderwaffen 124
Wurm River 53, 58

205

www.ingramcontent.com/pod-product-compliance
Ingram Content Group UK Ltd.
Pitfield, Milton Keynes, MK11 3LW, UK
UKHW050526150426
5217IPUK00026B/1825